Kant on Sex, Love, and Friendship

Kantstudien-Ergänzungshefte

On behalf of the Kant-Gesellschaft
edited by
Manfred Baum, Bernd Dörflinger,
Heiner F. Klemme and Konstantin Pollok

Volume 222

Kant on Sex, Love, and Friendship

Edited by
Pärttyli Rinne and Martin Brecher

DE GRUYTER

ISBN 978-3-11-129089-8
e-ISBN (PDF) 978-3-11-129113-0
e-ISBN (EPUB) 978-3-11-129142-0
ISSN 0340-6059

Library of Congress Control Number: 2023937756

Bibliographic information published by the Deutsche Nationalbibliothek
The Deutsche Nationalbibliothek lists this publication in the Deutsche Nationalbibliografie;
detailed bibliographic data are available on the internet at http://dnb.dnb.de.

© 2023 Walter de Gruyter GmbH, Berlin/Boston
Printing and binding: CPI books GmbH, Leck

www.degruyter.com

Table of Contents

Abbreviations

Citations of Kant's works refer to the Akademie-Ausgabe:

Kant's gesammelte Schriften, 29 vols., vol. 1–22 ed. by Königlich Preussische Akademie der Wissenschaften, vol. 23 ed. by Deutsche Akademie der Wissenschaften zu Berlin, vols. 24– ed. by Akademie der Wissenschaften zu Göttingen, Berlin: Walter de Gruyter, 1900–.

References use the following format: volume: page number (e. g., 4:429) or volume:page number.line number (e. g., 4:429.10–12). In some cases, section numbers or headings are used in addition or instead.

Unless otherwise noted, authors use translations from

The Cambridge Edition of the Works of Immanuel Kant, ed. by Paul Guyer and Allen W. Wood, Cambridge/New York: Cambridge University Press, 1992–).

Abbreviations used within citations include the following:

AA	Akademie-Ausgabe (Academy edition of Kant's writings)
Anth	*Anthropologie in pragmatischer Hinsicht* (*Anthropology from a Pragmatic Point of View*)
Anth-Friedländer	Anthropologie Friedländer (Friedländer notes of Kant's lectures on anthropology)
Anth-Mrongovius	Anthropologie Mrongovius (Mrongovius notes of Kant's lectures on anthropology)
Br	Briefe (*Correspondence*)
GMS	*Grundlegung zur Metaphysik der Sitten* (*Groundwork of the Metaphysics of Morals*)
KpV	*Kritik der praktischen Vernunft* (*Critique of Practical Reason*)
KrV	*Kritik der reinen Vernunft* (*Critique of Pure Reason*)
KU	*Kritik der Urteilskraft* (*Critique of the Power of Judgment*)
Mo-Collins	Moralphilosophie Collins (Collins notes of Kant's lectures on moral philosophy)
Mo-Kaehler	Moralphilosophie Kaehler (Kaehler notes of Kant's lectures on moral philosophy)
Mo-Mrongovius II	Moralphilosophie Mrongovius II (Mrongovius II notes of Kant's lectures on moral philosophy)
MS	*Metaphysik der Sitten* (*The Metaphysics of Morals*)
MS-Vigilantius	Metaphysik der Sitten Vigilantius (Vigilantius notes of Kant's lectures on metaphysics of morals)
NR-Feyerabend	Naturrecht Feyerabend (Feyerabend notes of Kant's lectures on natural law)
Päd	*Pädagogik* (*Pedagogy*)
PP-Herder	Praktische Philosophie Herder (Herder notes of Kant's lectures on practical philosophy)
PP-Powalski	Praktische Philosophie Powalski (Powalski notes of Kant's lectures on practical philosophy)

https://doi.org/10.1515/9783111291130-001

RGV	*Die Religion innerhalb der Grenzen der bloßen Vernunft* (*Religion within the Boundaries of Mere Reason*)
RL	*Rechtslehre* (*Doctrine of Right*)
TL	*Tugendlehre* (*Doctrine of Virtue*)
VAMS	Vorarbeiten zur *Metaphysik der Sitten* (Preparatory Works on the *Metaphysics of Morals*)
VARL	Vorarbeiten zur *Rechtslehre* (Preparatory Works on the *Doctrine of Right*)

Pärttyli Rinne and Martin Brecher
Introduction

I

For the last 100 years, love and intimate human relations have often been considered topics of little importance for mainstream academic philosophy. A common notion stemming from early 20th century analytic thinkers was that emotions or "emotional ways of relating to the world" were opposed to science and philosophy, the latter of which consisted entirely of the logical analysis of scientific propositions (see Hahn 1930, 96; cf. Sigmund 2017, 142; see also e.g. Carnap 1937, 277–280). Language imbued with emotion was considered neither scientific nor philosophical, and could not express such propositions. In a somewhat similar vein, the 20th century behaviourist school of psychology insisted that talk of feelings such as joy, sorrow, or love should be reduced to descriptions of objectively observable behaviours (see e.g. Watson 1913; Skinner 2005, 160–170). Consequently, most of the discussion around affective human life was deemed elusive, non-serious, misguided or meaningless by many 20th century philosophers. Whereas 18th and 19th century European philosophy (or European philosophy ever since antiquity) had been ripe with theorising and speculation about love in all its forms ranging from sexuality to religious experiences, the 20th century marked a steep decline in love related philosophical research and public discussion.

This mechanic has changed significantly during the last decades. Affective terminology currently abounds in literature and public discourse, and emotion research has become a hot field across disciplines, as can easily be witnessed by observing emotion word frequencies in big natural language data sets such as Google Ngrams, or by generically skimming through publication outputs in fields as divergent as history, political science, economics, psychology, or cognitive neuroscience. This new wave of research on emotions and the intimate sphere of human life can also be seen in the history of philosophy. As topics such as sex, love, and friendship were important for many figures in the history of philosophy, historians of philosophy are now eager to fill the lacunae in research on these topics.

But what does Immanuel Kant and his philosophy have to do with all this? If Kant is known for something in particular, it must be his emphasis on "pure reason", his "coldness" in ethics, and his dislike for feelings in general. It is too farfetched, surely, to argue that the current renaissance in emotion research should have anything to do with Kant's philosophy. Or so one might easily assert. From within the study of Kant, the picture is different, however. In the last couple of de-

https://doi.org/10.1515/9783111291130-002

cades, Kant scholars have directed an increasing amount of attention to Kant's anthropology (his understanding of empirically observable human nature), his discussion of gender relations, his theory of feelings or emotions, and his ethics considered broadly as including the emotive or affective aspects of human life, which the moral agent encounters in herself and in others around her (see e.g. Jauch 1988; Munzel 1999 and 2012; Louden 2000 and 2011; Wilson 2006; Wood 2008; Cohen 2009 and 2014). The intersections of Kant's moral theory and his conceptions of the feelings related to morality have been a particularly lively area of recent debate (see e.g. Baron 1995; Reath 2006; Horn 2008; Baron & Fahmy 2009; Fahmy 2010; Schönecker 2010; Frierson 2014; Guyer 2010; Grenberg 2014 and 2015; Timmermann 2016). Based on the inquiries conducted during the past couple of decades in Kant scholarship, we now know that Kant holds more balanced and nuanced views than traditionally acknowledged – both of the relationship between reason and affective feelings in general and of personal relationships between agents, be they friends or lovers, in particular. The scholarly discussion has moved beyond the common caricature of the emotionless Kant.

The present volume, therefore, does not emerge from a theoretical vacuum, but rather builds on prior research on these issues in the study of Kant. However, previous scholarship has for the most part focused on individual issues. The premise of this volume is that it will be fruitful to think about the issues of sex, love, and friendship in Kant in explicit conjunction with each other. This, we hold, will improve both our understanding of Kant's philosophy and our understanding of these phenomena more generally. So far, there are only a couple of accounts that explicitly strive to connect the notions of sex, love, and friendship together within Kant's philosophy. These include Rae Langton's *Sexual Solipsism* (2009), Pärttyli Rinne's *Kant on Love* (2018), and Helga Varden's *Sex, Love, and Gender – A Kantian Theory* (2020). Langton uses resources drawn from Kant's philosophy to think about friendship as a path away from a sexually solipsistic attitude that objectifies the other (typically and historically women) (see also Denis 2001). Rinne provides a detailed exegetical account of the different aspects of love in Kant's philosophy. Varden develops a new Kantian theory of sex and gender relations, including notably an LGBTQIA perspective. What we aim to provide in this volume are novel points of views onto these areas in the study of Kant. We are confident that the papers in this volume will be a welcome addition to the scholarship, and that they will also provide food for thought for those under the mistaken impression that Kant didn't have anything to say about these kinds of issues.

Before we move on to give an outline of Kant's views on these topics and the scholarship assembled in this volume (sections III and IV of the introduction), in the next section we shall first address some common worries that concern the study of Kant's views on sex, love, and friendship.

II

One common worry regarding scholarship in the history of philosophy in general is that it can be of little to no philosophical importance. Thus, while adding to the growth of historical knowledge is all well and good, we should be able to learn something substantial about sex, love, and friendship from Kant. Through studying Kant's philosophy, the argument goes, one should be able to better participate in contemporary philosophical debates, or construct an "improved" Kantian philosophy, such that the improvements make the philosophy of Kant somehow "applicable" to contemporary life.

Against this, one could argue that improving our understanding of human history or our knowledge of the history of ideas, is valuable even if this understanding does not yield immediate or measurable benefits to our contemporary lives or even to current theorising. Putting ourselves in the shoes of those who came before us may increase our empathetic awareness and our understanding of what it can be to be a human being. To immerse ourselves in the problems of the past, in questions that may no longer be our questions, may yet shed significant light on the problems that we currently face. The study of history (of philosophy) may illuminate parts of the path that got us where we are today, and may help us (as human beings and as philosophers) to obtain a better grasp of who we are, *why* we are who we are, and where our future possibilities may lie. There is value in the discipline of history, even if its insights are not immediately applicable to contemporary problems.

That said, *we do think* that it is possible to learn from Kant on the topics of sex, love, and friendship, and that there is more than one way to understand how this learning might happen. First, by studying Kant on these topics we may clarify misconceptions as to what Kant actually thought about the issues at hand. Kant's philosophy has been the object of constant, vivid debate for well over 200 years, and it should be self-evident that the interpretative discussion ought to be based as closely and accurately as possible on the philosophical positions that Kant actually held. This type of learning is a matter of historical and scholarly justice. In so far as one wishes to say things about Kant's philosophy or ascribe some particular philosophical views to him, one should try to be just. The contemporary philosophical evaluation of historical positions and arguments presupposes their historical study. Second, we may learn about the limitations of Kant's philosophy, or the mistakes he made while he was trying to be "objective" or "rational". By seeing his mistakes, we may learn important lessons about our own prejudices or moral shortcomings, or the kinds of "rationalisations" we may engage in when trying to justify our prejudices to ourselves and to others. Third, by paying attention to what Kant has to say on a given issue, we may indeed arrive at a more refined comprehension of the philosophical topics we are striving to understand. At the very least, if we do not lend an ear, we will never know what we might have learned. A part of the motivation for this volume is to argue that listening is often preferable to drawing caricatures.

Some caricatures, however, are closer to the truth than others, and some pictures that may seem like caricatures, might in fact be accurate representations of the object. In other words, some of the charges commonly launched against Kant's "philosophy of love", understood in a broad sense, may contain more merit than others. Before outlining the contents of our volume and our aimed positive contribution to the philosophical discussions surrounding Kant, sex, love, and friendship, it is worthwhile to address some of these common charges against Kant.

The basic question remains whether Kant has anything important to say about love, sexuality, or affective intimacy. Is it, in particular, not the case that Kant has very "unromantic" views of sex, love, and friendship at odds with our present-day notions?[1] It is well-known that Kant morally rejects sex outside marriage as well as homosexuality and masturbation; and as regards marriage, he seems to think that it is a contract of two parties to use each other's sexual organs. Further, with respect to love outside of sexual relations, Kant appears to reduce love to a form of beneficence and warns friends of disclosing too much to each other. If all this is not unromantic, then what is?

In response, there are several things to consider here. In order to meaningfully discuss the charge that Kant has unromantic views on sex, love, and friendship, we should try to be clear about, first, what we mean by "romantic", second, whether we think that a "romantic" view of sex, love, and friendship is the correct or morally ideal view that everyone should hold about these issues, and, third, what Kant's views of the issues actually are.

First, the notion of something being "romantic" can plausibly be seen as stemming from the philosophies of "romanticism", an intellectual and artistic movement of late 18th and 19th century Europe. In contrast to the earlier empiricist and rationalist schools of thought, romanticism emphasised feeling, imagination, and an ideal of merging or oneness through love, which merging the subject sought in her encounters with a sexual partner or loved one, with humanity, or with the world as a whole. According to intellectual historians of love, it was precisely this pursuit of love and yearning for oneness that was the distinguishing factor of romanticism (Singer 2009, 285 f.). This is of course an oversimplification of romanti-

---

[1] We thank an anonymous referee for bringing up the charge of Kant's views being "unromantic", as well as for the more specific charges explicated in this paragraph.

cism, sketched out here only for the purposes of argument, but nevertheless, if by a "romantic view" we mean something like "a view typical of or exemplified by romanticism", it is very important to note that romanticism (with its "romantic views" of sex, love, and friendship) only came to fruition *after* Kant. There are parts of Kant's philosophy that can be seen as precursors to fully fledged romanticism, such as his discussions of imagination, genius, and love of beauty in the *Critique of Judgment*. On the other hand, much of German romanticism, like that of Schelling, was precisely a *reaction* to Kant's critical philosophy. In other words, if we identify "romantic views" with the views entertained in romanticism, the charge against Kant, according to which his views are "unromantic" is anachronistic – or trivially true.

Second, it is anything but clear that holding such "romantic" views of sex, love, and friendship could be simply or uncritically equated with having the "correct" views of those issues, or that there would be particular philosophical merit in holding "romantic views". For instance, it is not clear that the notion of a loving couple merging spiritually so as to form one single person or identity should in any way be an ethical ideal of loving relationships. Romantic views of love, too, have been criticised and rightly so. As readers of Kant are well aware, even though Kant holds that marriage ideally leads to a benevolent union of two wills, and that friendship is ideally a kind of maximum of mutual love (which are both obviously preromantic if not romantic notions), the critical Kant always emphasises that expressions of love must be conditioned by respect and an acknowledgment of the equal humanity of others (even though Kant does unfortunately hold that a wife deserves less respect from her husband than a husband from his wife). Respecting the equal humanity of others through maintaining distance, or acknowledging the limits between individuals is not something that romanticism is known for – even though such notions of respect may belong to the ethical ideals of loving relationships. From a certain perspective, therefore, Kant's philosophy can serve as a refreshing antidote against unhealthy "romantic" views of love, which are prone to lead to disappointment (we rarely become "one soul" with our partners, unfortunately) or oppression when the inclinations of partners or friends clash, and the stronger party subjugates the will of the other in the guise of the romantic ideal of merging. In other words, romantic views of love may also be morally dangerous, and Kant's philosophy of respectful love can help us to avoid these pitfalls of romanticism.

We might of course adopt a weaker or more diluted notion of what we mean by romantic views of sex, love, and friendship, in which case we could hold, for instance, that to have a romantic view of these issues means merely to affirm that intimate, affectionate relationships with others are a great source of meaning and well-being in human life. This kind of diluted notion of a romantic view, however, would no longer be in tension with Kant's philosophy. This brings us to the third consideration mentioned above, namely, to look at what Kant actually thinks about these issues. According to Kant human beings naturally desire their own happiness (he calls this mechanism "self-love"). Kant acknowledges that having sex, enjoying nice meals, and spending time with one's friends, are all sources of natural well-being or happiness, and he holds that under moral conditions they are indeed appropriate sources of happiness. Furthermore, friendship has a morally cultivating function for Kant. Through communicating and sharing life with our friends (including respectful, mutual criticism where necessary) we learn important lessons about human interaction and may gradually grow to become morally better people. It is also evident from all of Kant's discussions on friendship that friendship cannot be reduced to "cold" morality or mere rational beneficence. Friendship involves sharing one's feelings and secrets with one's friend. It is true that Kant consistently cautions against disclosing too much to one's friend, and from this perspective his position on friendship is indeed unromantic, or perhaps it would be more accurate to say that when it comes to friendship, Kant is only cautiously romantic.

We can all ask ourselves whether we think that the ideal of friendship *should* include the notion that the friends share and communicate with each other *every thought and feeling* that each of the friends has. At least some of us have thoughts that we are anything but proud of, do not cherish, and would rather be rid of, and for those reasons choose not to disclose. Kant's idea seems to be that some of these thoughts may be such that disclosing them could lead to the friends losing respect for each other, even though he also occasionally issues more prudential warnings (i.e. were the friends to become enemies in the future, a secret could be used against the one who naively shared it). One gets the impression that Kant's view could be that as there is gradually more trust built into the friendship, the friends are able to share more intimate information with each other, thus approaching the ideals of friendship. It may be wise to leave open the question of whether there may be thoughts in the human mind that are best left altogether unuttered, undisclosed even to one's closest friends.

In any case, the notion that Kant would reduce love to a form of beneficence is quite simply misguided and not warranted by his texts. It is true that Kant allows for beneficence to be called love, but this is merely a fraction of all the different kinds or aspects of love that Kant discusses. Besides love as benevolence and beneficence, Kant's philosophy of love includes forms of love, that in essence are forms of pleasure or delight, and which may come about as an emotive or feeling-based response to the physical or moral attributes of another human being. These feelings of love may also be based on the sense of wonder one experiences while looking at a beautiful landscape or, say, a spider's web, or they may be the pleasurable emotive result of one's own beneficent behaviour towards other humans. In the last case, from a moral perspective, the feeling of love should be conditioned by humility and respect for the fundamental equality of the other – which of course may sometimes be easier said than done. Kant's philosophy of love also includes intricate discussions of religious love, and the bottom line remains that for anyone who chooses to look closely, there can be no denying that Kant's taxonomy of love is rich, nuanced, and multi-faceted (for a comprehensive account, see Rinne 2018).

Besides a general misguided charge that Kant's fully articulated ethics would involve a rejection of love or feelings, there are other more specific charges, some already mentioned, that should be taken into account. Some of these charges boil down to Kant representing and defending the conventional attitudes and mores of his day, while other charges appear inaccurate or out of context, and some seem to be valid concerns which may force us to adopt a critical stance towards Kant in the light of his own ethical theory. For instance, consider the charge that Kant's view of sexuality is "unromantic" because he does not accept sex outside marriage. There is great variability among world cultures with respect to the permissibility of non-marital sex, and for centuries a public requirement of marriage before sex has been common in the Christian cultural sphere (even though the liberality of *de facto* sexual mores has fluctuated from century to century). In recent history, attitudes in the West changed significantly following what is sometimes called the sexual revolution of the 1960s. Romantic or unromantic, Kant's general attitude towards non-marital sex reflects the historical and cultural situation in which he lived – and he does come across as a conservative. The same goes for his attitudes towards homosexuality and masturbation. In fact, when Kant tries to find a morally rational, objective justification for his condemnation of homosexuality and masturbation, he presents some of the weakest (in the sense of poor, bad, or unsuccessful) arguments to be found anywhere in his corpus. These arguments, which make questionable appeals to natural teleology as the ground of moral judgment, have been critically discussed in the previous literature (Denis 1999, Soble 2003, see also Varden 2020). Interpreters tend to agree that Kant appears to almost desperately find a rational justification for his culturally conservative views, to such an extent that he has to (or is willing to) compromise the soundness of his inferences in order to arrive at the moral conclusion predetermined by his underlying attitude. The structural problems of these arguments and Kant's use of hyperbolic language in his condemnation of homosexuality and masturbation reveal a deep, internal tension between Kant's commitment to conservative Christian mores and his own defence of enlightenment and arguably revolutionary moral theory of freedom (see also Sticker 2020).

On the other hand, the charge according to which Kant reduces marriage to a contract between two parties to use each other's sexual organs appears somewhat out of context. First, even though this is slightly beside the point, the formulation of a sexually oppressive contractual notion of marriage within legal philosophy is an unfortunate common item in the doctrines of many historical, European male philosophers. As the feminist and political theorist Carole Pateman (1988) has argued, besides Kant the historical construct of the sexual contract can be found in figures such as Hobbes, Locke, and Rousseau. This certainly does not excuse Kant, it merely shows that his notion of a contract-based, nominally equal yet *de facto* unequal marriage is a symptom of a broader cultural problem, that we still face today – namely the oppression of women. This said, it is not the case that Kant's thinking on marriage could be reduced to the sexual contract, presented in the emotionally cold "legalese" which Kant uses in the section concerning marriage right in *The Metaphysics of Morals* (for details see Brecher 2023). For a fuller and more nuanced picture of Kant's conception of marriage one must also be familiar with Kant's lectures and anthropological works, which reveal a more affectionate or emotionally astute Kant. While Kant's view of marriage is undeniably patriarchal, in his lectures and the anthropological works he uses the terminology of love and affirms excitement, pleasure, and inclination based love as belonging to a successful marriage. He maintains that the first duty of the husband is to love his spouse. (For details see Rinne 2018; cf. also Brecher 2018.) We do believe that Kant's notions of sexuality and marriage are not merely of historical interest. Through studying Kant's conception of sex and marriage, we may become better aware of the inherent moral dangers related to sexuality, dangers which concern objectifying and using another human being as a mere means – or conversely, the dangers of being objectified and used. While we should be critical of Kant's solutions to these problems, studying Kant's conceptions of sexuality and marriage can help us to better understand the conceptual and moral problems still related to these issues.

Another related, more general charge concerns Kant's sexism (and racism). While Kant argues vehemently for the universality of reason, morality, and human dignity, it is embarrassingly unclear to which extent women (and non-Europeans) are included in the sphere of rational, universal humanity. For good reason, Kant has been a target of feminist and postcolonial criticism (see e.g. Herman 1993; the articles in Schott 1997; Kneller 2006; Varden 2020; cf. also Mikkola 2011), even though some have argued that Kant in his later years changed his views about the inferiority of non-European ethnicities (Kleingeld 2007). Much of what Kant writes about women makes for a discomforting read, and it is difficult to try to excuse Kant based on what were common prejudices during his day. The ideas of respect, universal moral reason, and principled benevolence, all of which

Kant advocated, seem to be in stark contrast with his mockery of (especially educated) women. Women's education was a hot topic around Europe during the latter part of the 18th century, and Kant appeared to have remained steadfast in thinking that the idea of women's education was more or less ridiculous. This was not the case with progressive men of his day, like the mayor of Königsberg, Theodor Gottlieb von Hippel, whom Kant personally knew and had discussions with. (See Petschauer 1986.) Kant's deleterious remarks on women's education are also roughly contemporaneous with Mary Wollstonecraft's career and her *Vindication of the Rights of Woman* (2014 [1792]). Where Kant expressed certain doubts concerning the capacities of women or thought that education might make women less feminine and was therefore problematic in their case (see Baron 1997), Wollstonecraft held that if reason was universal or gender-neutral (as she thought it was), the cause for women's underperformance in society could only be attributed to their lack of rights and education, and concluded that therefore women ought to have access to the same rights and education as men. It should not take anything away from Wollstonecraft's courage and brilliance when we note, that an inference like hers is nowhere to be found in Kant.

III

The aim of our collection of essays is to help us understand how the notions of sex, love, and friendship function in Kant's philosophy, both individually and in conjunction with each other. As may have already become obvious from our argumentation above, the concepts of sex, love, and friendship are more pertinent to Kant than often thought. They play an integral role in his conception of human life. The three notions are closely interrelated, and to an extent, overlapping. In different areas of his philosophy, Kant acknowledges that from the crudest impulses of nature to the highest ideals of virtue and morally deserved happiness, the phenomenon of love permeates human existence. An understanding of how sex, love, and friendship function in Kant's practical philosophy is necessary for a comprehensive understanding of his ethical project; and as recent scholarship has come to realise, Kant's engagement with the issues surrounding sex, love, and friendship comprises substantial contributions to the philosophical discussion of these topics. In the context of a new appraisal of Kant's late work *The Metaphysics of Morals*, recent years have seen a growing interest in Kant's discussion of specific moral issues including those surrounding personal relationships and the role of feelings in moral life. As the extant lecture notes taken by his students testify, Kant thought about many of these matters for several decades and continually refined his views up to the publication of *The Metaphysics of Morals*.

Kant develops a concept of sexual objectification and proposes, as a solution to the problem of objectification it poses, a novel conception of legal marriage that differs from the natural law theories of his time in several key aspects. Scholars are divided as to what exactly, according to Kant, is the ground of objectification, whether marriage can be a remedy for it, and what alternative approaches to sex within a Kantian framework would look like. In Kant's ethical writings we discover a nuanced taxonomy of different kinds of love, their relation to other feelings and their implications for moral agency in general. At the most general level, Kant divides love into 'love of benevolence' (*Liebe des Wohlwollens*) and 'love of delight' (*Liebe des Wohlgefallens*), such that love of benevolence is goodwill directed to the well-being of its object, and love of delight is a pleasure taken in the physical or moral perfections, or even the sheer existence, of the object. Kant argues that 'love of human beings' is one of the requisite predispositions to morality and he takes 'duties of love' to be an essential class of our duties towards others and to constitute an integral part of virtue. In the *Doctrine of Virtue*, Kant argues that benevolent love implies making the ends of others one's own. While there is consensus among interpreters that Kantian morality requires benevolence to be constrained by respect for the other person, there has been only little discussion about the specific emotional requirements we have to submit to when rationally promoting the ends of others. Finally, while there has emerged a lively discussion about the role of love in different areas of Kant's ethics, there is still room for establishing a more comprehensive overall account of the role of love in Kant's practical philosophy.

Kant regards friendship as a moral ideal: a union of two persons based on a connection of mutual love and respect. He argues that engaging in friendship aids in developing virtue and makes agents deserving of happiness, but at the same time warns against friends drawing too close to each other. So far no attempt has been made by interpreters to situate Kant's cautionary remarks within his moral anthropology and relate them to his account of the human being's unsocial tendencies in particular. Moreover, there is ongoing controversy as to whether Kant takes moral friendship to be properly realizable or an unattainable ideal. It is still unclear how exactly, in Kant's eyes, moral friendship facilitates our aspiration towards the highest good (which according to Kant consists in happiness proportioned to virtue).

The papers in our collection address the issues just mentioned, approaching these topics from historical, philosophical, and exegetical perspectives. Some of our authors write thinking mainly *about* Kant, whereas others could be more accurately described as drawing *from* Kant or thinking *with* Kant, and yet others are arguing *against* Kant. The volume thus offers a set of perspectives and styles of engaging with the history of philosophy. There are many plausible ways of conducting research on Kant's philosophy, and our volume reflects the methodological diversity within the field. We hope our collection will spark further interest and debate in the study of sex, love, friendship, and Kant's philosophy, and that our volume will come to mark an accessible reference point for future discussions within our chosen terrain.

In preparation for the collection, we held a three-day workshop at the University of St Andrews on 21–23 July 2017. The workshop brought together scholars working on different aspects of sex, love, and friendship in Kant to present their work, exchange and develop ideas, and to establish points of contact between their individual research approaches. We are very grateful to the Scots Philosophical Association and the Mind Association for the generous support we received for this purpose as well as to the Aristotelian Society and the UK Kant Society. We are also very grateful to the Department of Philosophy of the University of St Andrews for hosting the workshop and especially to Jens Timmermann for his support during all stages of the project.

IV

In the opening essay, **Robert B. Louden** (Southern Maine) engages recent interpreters who view Kant's discussion of sex and marriage in a more sympathetic light. In contrast to these approaches, he argues that the first sharp criticisms of Kant's conception of marriage by his contemporaries Schütz and Bouterwek were already correct. According to Louden, Kant's claim that within marriage persons can rightfully possess each other as things is profoundly inconsistent with his basic moral philosophical distinction that Kant asserts in the *Groundwork* and elsewhere between persons, who have unconditional worth, and things, which have only relative worth. Louden submits that Kant's concept of 'a right to a person akin to a right to a thing', which is introduced in the *Doctrine of Right*, blurs the more fundamental distinction of persons and things. Without this distinction, argues Louden, Kant's entire ethical theory falls apart: for if reason cannot find anything of absolute worth, then the establishment of a supreme practical principle that holds unconditionally would fail.

In his paper, **Martin Brecher** (Mannheim) picks up on recent attempts to develop a justification of same-sex marriage using Kant's sexual morals. These approaches embrace Kant's notion of sexual objectification to morally justify the legal institution of marriage, while purging out Kant's notorious claims about 'unnatural' (i. e., non-heterosexual) sex. The paper challenges such approaches from an exegetical point of view, arguing that Kant's theory of sexuality is more cohesive. In particular, both the problem of sexual objectification and the (as Kant sees it) problem of 'unnatural' sex stem from a single root: the 'animality' of sexual desire. This gives rise to the two moral requirements of marriage and adherence to the natural purposiveness of sex, the fulfilment of both of which is, according to Kant, necessary to avoid violating our dignity as moral beings by acting on this animal impulse. As Brecher points out, a faithful and coherent interpretation of Kant's theory of sexuality makes it look a lot less tenable with respect to present-day discussions than some interpreters suggest, prompting us to consider in more detail the ways we engage with Kant's account in present-day theorising.

For Kant, obviously, sexual relations are morally problematic and involve dangers of objectification. Instead of disregarding Kant's theories of sexuality as merely representing the cultural and religious biases of his time, **Melissa Fahmy's** (Georgia) contribution to this volume aims to vindicate the Kantian view that sexual relations are indeed inherently morally problematic – but for reasons other than Kant himself thought. The moral problems related to sexuality may not be so much connected to succumbing our humanity to animality, but rather to those aspects that make human sexual activity distinct from animal sexual activity. One important aspect that Fahmy focuses on is the fact that agents often engage in sexual activities for reasons that may be unknown to the participants themselves. According to Fahmy, this makes the acquiring of proper informed consent problematic and can lead to using the other as a mere means. Problematising the notion of consent, Fahmy formulates some basic guidelines for good Kantian sex by drawing on the demands of self-respect and consideration of the happiness of others. These guidelines in particular involve self-reflection and self-scrutiny as well as being forthright with the other, establishing transparency and thus enabling normatively meaningful consent that can ensure respect for the dignity of both partners.

In his mature main treatise on moral philosophy, *The Metaphysics of Morals*, Kant lays out a distinct set of ethical duties, which he calls 'duties of love'. Duties of love involve making another person's end of happiness one's own end. According to **Jeanine Grenberg** (St. Olaf), the successful fulfilment of these duties requires that one acquires a particularly high level of moral character, called 'inner freedom' or 'autocracy', which especially involves self-mastery of one's affects, inclinations and passions. In her contribution, Grenberg investigates this concept and argues that the person of inner freedom – i. e. one who is not ruled by his or her emotions – is best equipped for loving others ethically. In order to properly make another person's ends one's own the agent has to maintain attentiveness to and loving concern for the situation of the other. Grenberg highlights her idea by analysing the characters of Anne and Mary Elliot in Jane Austen's *Persuasion* who are perfect examples, respectively, of having and not having the state of inner freedom required for becoming a loving person.

Dieter Schönecker's (Siegen) article focuses on Kant's notion of love of human beings as it appears in section XII of the "Introduction to the Doctrine of Virtue". Kant is often remembered for prioritising respect for the moral law over everything else in his ethics, and it is striking that in the "Introduction", Kant appears to hold that – beside moral feeling, conscience and self-respect – there is a moral predisposition of love of human beings embedded in the human mind. Schönecker argues that the four moral predispositions not only are the basis for moral motivation, but that they are also necessary conditions to become aware of the necessitation of the categorical imperative and therefore necessary for grasping the moral law as a categorical imperative. In explaining the role that love of human beings plays as a moral predisposition, Schönecker elaborates further on the distinction between love of benevolence and love of delight and argues that the love of human beings at issue in the "Introduction" can only be identified with love of delight, and not with benevolence or an inclination to beneficence.

The ethical life is not merely about respect for the moral law, but includes our emotions and emotive dispositions, and the cultivation of our emotive capacities in social relationships. Besides Kant's general division of love into love of benevolence and love of delight (mentioned earlier in this introduction), there are various aspects of love in Kant's writings, such as self-love, sexual love, love of God, love of one's neighbour, and love in friendship, which taken together with the general division form the conceptual structure of love in Kant's philosophy. In his article, **Pärttyli Rinne** (Aalto) provides a concise overview of some of the main features of this conceptual structure. While the aspects of love can be plausibly assembled into an ascending structure beginning with the crudest impulses of human nature and ending with the highest ideals of morality, Rinne claims that it can also be highly illuminating to understand Kant's concept of love through the Stoic metaphor of an 'expanding circle' of concern and affection. By constructing an 'expanding circle model' of love in Kant, Rinne highlights the *continuity* between Kant's different notions of love. While the 'ascent model' and the 'expanding circle model' emphasise different perspectives to phenomena of love, Rinne shows that they are not mutually exclusive, but rather complement each other.

The ideals of friendship are key for Kant's overall ethical doctrine, and he developed his philosophy of friendship over the course of several decades. Despite the importance of the concept of friendship for Kant, as **Kate Moran** (Brandeis) shows, he also cautions against too much emotional proximity in friendships, advocates retaining a certain amount of distance within these relationships and even warns against acting beneficently towards one's friends. How can Kant's insistence on the importance and value of friendship be reconciled with the striking realism he displays about human psychology when it comes to being benefactor or recipient? Moran argues that Kant's reservations are not simply meant as guards against negative or unpleasant feelings in one's relationship to others. According to Moran, these reservations can be better understood by investigating Kant's notion of misanthropy. Utilising Adrienne Martin's concept of 'normative hope', Moran argues in our volume that Kantian misanthropy is a defence mechanism against a disappointment of this hope, and that avoiding such normative disappointment may be essential for preserving one's moral attitude towards humanity.

In the final essay of the volume, **Kiran Bhardwaj** (Andover) proposes that striving for or engaging in moral friendships may serve as a bridge between human imperfection and the highest good. Bhardwaj discusses Kant's taxonomy of different kinds of friendships, which can be found in the *Metaphysics of Morals* as well as in the lecture notes, and argues that moral friendship is a necessary vehicle not only for developing one's own virtue, but also for promoting the happiness of others. Without such friendships, it seems, we may not be able to meaningfully strive for the highest good as happiness proportionate to virtue. Bhardwaj takes the position that, although Kant considers perfect friendship an ideal, moral friendships can indeed be sometimes achieved, and she sees these friendships as a 'microcosm' for what a kingdom of ends might look like more generally. Friendship thereby also serves an important motivational function by supporting our hopes for what is possible as a result of our moral actions.

References

Baron, Marcia, 1995, *Kantian Ethics Almost Without Apology*, Ithaca: Cornell University Press.

Baron, Marcia, 1997, "Kantian Ethics and Claims of Detachment", in: Robin Schott (ed.), *Feminist Interpretations of Immanuel Kant*, University Park, PA: The Pennsylvania State University Press, 145–170.

Baron, Marcia/Fahmy, Melissa, 2009, "Beneficence and Other Duties of Love in *The Metaphysics of Morals*", in: Thomas Hill (ed.), *The Blackwell Guide to Kant's Ethics*, Malden, MA/Oxford: Wiley-Blackwell, 211–228.

Brecher, Martin, 2018, "Ein Zwangsrecht auf Geschlechtsverkehr? Das kantische Vernunftrecht und die 'eheliche Pflicht'", *Aufklärung*, 30, 93–118.

Brecher, Martin, 2023, *Vernunftrecht und Verdinglichung. Eine Rekonstruktion von Kants Eherecht*, Berlin/Boston: de Gruyter.

Carnap, Rudolf, 1937, *Logical Syntax of Language*, London: Kegan Paul.

Cohen, Alix, 2009, *Kant and the Human Sciences. Biology, Anthropology and History*, Basingstoke/New York: Palgrave Macmillan.

Cohen, Alix (ed.), 2014, *Kant's Lectures on Anthropology. A Critical Guide*, Cambridge: Cambridge University Press.

Denis, Lara, 1999, "Kant on the Wrongness of 'Unnatural' Sex", *History of Philosophy Quarterly*, 16/2, 225–248.

Denis, Lara, 2001, "From Friendship to Marriage: Revising Kant", *Philosophy and Phenomenological Research*, 63/1, 1–28.

Fahmy, Melissa, 2010, "Kantian Practical Love", *Pacific Philosophical Quarterly*, 91, 313–331.

Frierson, Patrick, 2014, "Affects and Passions", in: Alix Cohen (ed.), *Kant's Lectures on Anthropology. A Critical Guide*, Cambridge: Cambridge University Press, 94–113.

Grenberg, Jeanine, 2014, "All You Need Is Love?", in: Alix Cohen (ed.), *Kant on Emotion and Value*, Basingstoke: Palgrave Macmillan, 210–223.

Grenberg, Jeanine, 2015, "Love", in: Lara Denis and Oliver Sensen (eds.), *Kant's Lectures on Ethics. A Critical Guide*, Cambridge: Cambridge University Press, 239–255.

Guyer, Paul, 2010. "Moral Feelings in the *Metaphysics of Morals*", in: Lara Denis (ed.), *Kant's Metaphysics of Morals. A Critical Guide*, Cambridge: Cambridge University Press, 130–152.

Hahn, Hans, 1930, "Die Bedeutung der wissenschaftlichen Weltauffassung, insbesondere für Mathematik und Physik", *Erkenntnis*, 1/1, 96–105.

Herman, Barbara, 1993, "Could it Be Worth Thinking about Kant on Sex and Marriage?", in: Louise Antony and Charlotte Witt (eds.), *A Mind of One's Own. Feminist Essays on Reason and Objectivity*, Boulder: Westview Press, 53–72.

Horn, Christoph, 2008, "The Concept of Love in Kant's Virtue Ethics", in: Monika Betzler (ed.), *Kant's Ethics of Virtue*, Berlin: de Gruyter, 147–173.

Jacobs, Brian/Kain, Patrick (eds.), 2007, *Essays on Kant's Anthropology*, Cambridge: Cambridge University Press.

Jauch, Ursula Pia, 1988, *Immanuel Kant zur Geschlechterdifferenz*. Wien: Passagen.

Kleingeld, Pauline, 2007, "Kant's Second Thoughts on Race", *The Philosophical Quarterly*, 57/229, 573–592.

Kneller, Jane, 2006, "Kant on Sex and Marriage Right", in: Paul Guyer (ed.), *The Cambridge Companion to Kant and Modern Philosophy*, Cambridge: Cambridge University Press, 447–476.

Langton, Rae, 2009, *Sexual Solipsism. Philosophical Essays on Pornography and Objectification*, Oxford: Oxford University Press.

Louden, Robert B., 2000, *Kant's Impure Ethics*, Oxford: Oxford University Press.

Louden, Robert B., 2011, *Kant's Human Being*, Oxford: Oxford University Press.

Mikkola, Mari, 2011, "Kant on Moral Agency and Women's Nature", *Kantian Review*, 16/1, 89–111.

Munzel, G. Felicitas, 1999, *Kant's Conception of Moral Character: The "Critical" Link of Morality, Anthropology, and Reflective Judgment*, Chicago: University of Chicago Press.

Munzel, G. Felicitas, 2012, *Kant's Conception of Pedagogy. Toward Education for Freedom*, Evanston, IL: Northwestern University Press.

Pateman, Carole, 1988, *The Sexual Contract*, Stanford: Stanford University Press.

Petschauer, Peter, 1986, "Eighteenth-Century German Opinions about Education for Women", *Central European History*, 19/3, 262–292.

Reath, Andrews, 2006, "Kant's Theory of Moral Sensibility: Respect for the Moral Law and the Influence of Inclination", in: Andrews Reath, *Agency and Autonomy in Kant's Moral Theory. Selected Essays*, Oxford: Oxford University Press, 8–32.

Rinne, Pärttyli, 2018, *Kant on Love*, Berlin/Boston: de Gruyter.

Schott, Robin (ed.), 1997, *Feminist Interpretations of Immanuel Kant*. University Park, PA: The Pennsylvania State University Press.

Schönecker, Dieter, 2010, "Kant über Menschenliebe als moralische Gemütsanlage", *Archiv für Geschichte der Philosophie*, 92/2, 133–175.

Sigmund, Karl, 2017, *Exact Thinking in Demented Times. The Vienna Circle and the Epic Quest for the Foundations of Knowledge*, New York: Basic Books.

Singer, Irving, 2009, *The Nature of Love. Volume 2: Courtly and Romantic*, Cambridge, MA: The MIT Press.

Skinner, B.F., 2005, *Science and Human Behavior*, Cambridge, MA: The B.F. Skinner Foundation.

Soble, Alan, 2003, "Kant and Sexual Perversion", *The Monist*, 86/1, 55–89.

Sticker, Martin, 2020, "The Case Against Different-Sex Marriage in Kant", *Kantian Review*, 25/3, 441–464.

Timmermann, Jens, 2016, "Kant über Mitleidenschaft", *Kant-Studien*, 107/4, 729–732.

Varden, Helga, 2020, *Sex, Love, and Gender. A Kantian Theory*, Oxford: Oxford University Press.

Watson, John, 1913, "Psychology as the Behaviourist Views It", *Psychological Review*, 20, 158–177.

Wilson, Holly L., 2006, *Kant's Pragmatic Anthropology. Its Origin, Meaning, and Critical Significance*, Albany, NY: State University of New York Press.

Wollstonecraft, Mary, 2014 [1792], *A Vindication of the Rights of Woman*, New Haven: Yale University Press.

Wood, Allen, 2008, *Kantian Ethics*, Cambridge: Cambridge University Press.

Robert B. Louden

What's So Special About Legalized Sex?
(Or, How Can Two Wrongs Make a Right?)

Abstract: In this essay I reassess a long-standing sore point within Kant's moral and legal philosophy – viz., his position on heterosexual sex and marriage. My own standpoint is consciously retrograde. In opposition to recent revisionist efforts by feminist scholars to defend Kantian models of marriage, I believe early critics of Kant such as Christian Gottfried Schütz and Friedrich Bouterwek were right: his position on sex and marriage is not salvageable. Human sexual activity is not inherently or necessarily objectifying, humans do not devolve into animals bereft of rationality, free will, and responsibility when they engage in sex, and the institution of marriage does not necessarily resolve the inherent problems Kant sees in sex. Finally, his notorious effort to forge a third division of private law – "personal right of the thingly kind" – is not only enigmatic but ultimately incoherent.

> Love and marriage, love and marriage,
> Go together like a horse and carriage.
> This I tell ya, brother, you can't have one without the other....
> Try, try, try to separate them, it's an illusion.
> Try, try, try and you only come to this conclusion:
> Love and marriage, love and marriage,
> Go together like a horse and carriage.
> Dad was told by mother you can't have one
> You can't have none.
> You can't have one without the other.
>
> – Frank Sinatra, *Love and Marriage*

> If a man and a woman want to enjoy each other's sexual attributes they must necessarily marry [*müssen sie sich nothwendig verehlichen*].
>
> – Kant, *The Metaphysics of Morals* (6:278)

Kant's views on sex and marriage certainly rank among his most severely and frequently criticized positions on applied ethics issues – perhaps topped only by his well-documented racism. However, in the latter case, several commentators have argued recently that in his later years Kant finally saw the errors of his ways and came around to a much less objectionable position.[1] No such "second

---

1 See Kleingeld 2007, Muthu 2003, 184, and Shell 1996, 387 n. 23. However, nowhere in any of his

https://doi.org/10.1515/9783111291130-003

thoughts" arguments are likely to be forthcoming when it comes to his beliefs about sex and marriage. Also – here too, unlike his positions on other applied moral issues such as punishment or homosexuality[2] – Kant's views on heterosexual sex and marriage were strongly criticized right from the start by his contemporaries. They do not just appear objectionable when viewed through the lens of current moral attitudes. For instance, Christian Gottfried Schütz (1747–1832), who corrected the proofs to the second edition of Kant's *Anthropologie in pragmatischer Hinsicht* (see letter from Schütz of May 22, 1800, Br 12:307),[3] remarks, in another letter written to Kant: "You cannot really believe that a man makes a thing out of a woman [*zur Sache macht*] by engaging in *marital* cohabitation with her, and vice versa. You seem to think marriage is no more than a *mutuum adiutorium* [mutual subordination]" (Kant to Schütz, July 10, 1797, Br 12:180).[4] Michel Foucault cites this same text in his own early work, *Introduction to Kant's Anthropology* (1961), first published posthumously in both French and English in 2008, remarking that Schütz "was concerned to find, reading Kant's *Metaphysics of Morals*, ownership amongst individuals so closely modeled on the main forms of rights over things. [...] Schütz refused to accept that in matrimony 'the woman becomes a thing which belongs to the man'" (Foucault 2008, 40). And, as I remarked in an earlier essay on Foucault's interpretation of Kant's anthropology, "if we read between the lines a bit, we may be able to detect intimations of Foucault's own later interests in practices of power in this discussion" (Louden 2013, 168).

Hegel, in his *Philosophy of Right*, also strongly criticizes Kant's position, when he claims that "*marriage* cannot be subsumed under the concept of contract, this subsumption – which can only be described as a disgrace, one must say [*Schändlichkeit, muß man sagen*] – is proposed by *Kant* (*Metaphys. Anfangsgründe der Rechtslehre*)" (Hegel 1970, 157/§ 75, see also 310/§161 *Zusatz*).[5] And so it went for many

---

published writings or lectures does Kant explicitly disavow his racism. For skepticism concerning Kant's alleged "second thoughts" on race, see Louden 2011, 131–135 and Louden 2015, 522 f.

2 In this essay I will not discuss Kant's notorious claim that sex "with a person of the same sex" is "*unnatural*" (MS 6: 277). But it should also be noted that in recent years several commentators have tried to use Kant's conception of heterosexual marriage to defend same-sex marriage. For discussion and references, see Altman 2010, Sticker 2016, and Arroyo 2017.

3 Given the well-documented textual problems in Kant's *Rechtslehre*, one might well wish that Schütz had also handled the proofreading for this text as well. For discussion, see Mautner 1981, Ludwig 1986, xiii–xxiv, and Gregor 1996, 355–357.

4 Kant cites from Schütz 's earlier letter to Kant, but this earlier letter is not included in the Academy Edition collection of Kant's *Briefe* – presumably because it has not survived.

5 Strictly speaking, in his *Rechtslehre* Kant does not subsume marriage "under the concept of contract". He discusses contract law (*persönliches Recht*) in Section II of Part I of the *Rechtslehre* (MS 6:2776), whereas marriage law is discussed in Section III (MS 6:276–286). In Kant's view, contract

years. Kant's position on marriage "is shallow and even repulsive" (Aris 1936, 102), "notorious, an embarrassment to moral philosophers and philosophers of law alike" (Mendus 1992, 175), etc. But the tide began to turn after the appearance of Barbara Herman's influential 1993 essay, "Could It Be Worth Thinking About Kant on Sex and Marriage?" Writing partly under the influence of feminist theorists Andrea Dworkin and Catherine MacKinnon, whose views, she suggests, are "very Kantian" (Herman 1993, 56), Herman argues that Kant is correct in holding "that sexual activity is unavoidably morally problematic" (Herman 1993, 63). Suddenly, scores of commentators started not only thinking about Kant on sex and marriage, but many also began to "forge a Kantian ideal of [...] 'moral marriage'" (Denis 2001, 27; cf. 3), arguing that "the kind of marriage contract Kant advocates need not be regarded as deeply flawed" (Wilson 2004, 118), that Kant's views on sex and marriage "are relevant and instructive for contemporary discussions of sexual ethics" (Brake 2005, 59), that "Kantian marriage can indeed survive the criticisms it has received by contemporary thinkers" (Papadaki 2010, 292), and that "there is value in retrieving and reconsidering [...] [Kant's model of marriage] even today" (Kneller, 2006, 470).

The present essay is consciously retrograde. I think Schütz was correct in criticizing Kant's account of sex and marriage back in 1797, and I also believe that Friedrich Bouterwek, in his 1797 review of the *Rechtslehre*,[6] was right in arguing that Kant's "new phenomenon in the juristic sky" (AA 20:449; see also MS 6:359) – viz., the strange concept of "personal rights of the thingly kind" (see MS 6:276) which he forged to try to explicate his model of marriage – not only does not represent an advance in thinking about sex and marriage, but is also fundamentally inconsis-

---

law and marriage law constitute two distinct divisions of private law. Property law (*Sachenrecht*), discussed in Section I of the *Rechtslehre* (see MS 6:260–270), is the third division. In Kant's scheme, marriage (along with laws concerning parent-child relations and those concerning families and domestic servants) is subsumed under a third distinct division of private law, awkwardly described in the title of Section III as "*Von dem auf dingliche Art persönlichen Recht*" (MS 6:276) – literally, "Of Personal Right of the Thingly Kind", or (in Mary Gregor's translation) "On Rights to Persons Akin to Rights to Things" or (in John Ladd's rendering) "Personal rights of a real kind [Domestic Rights]". As one writer remarks, this is "a most enigmatic formulation" (De Laurentiis 2000, 309). Gregor, in a note to her translation, writes: "this third division of rights is an innovation on Kant's part, and there is no English term for it corresponding to 'property' and 'contract'" (Gregor 1996, 426 n. b). Similarly, Ladd notes in his Translator's Introduction that Kant feels forced here "to invent a new kind of right" (Ladd 1999, xxxiv). In the present essay I shall be criticizing Kant's innovation. On my view, it is not only enigmatic but ultimately incoherent.

6 Bouterwek's review of Kant's *Rechtslehre* was first published in the *Göttingische Anzeigen* on February 18, 1797, and is reprinted in AA vol. 20:445–453. I discuss it below in "A Supernova or a Shooting Star?"

tent with one of the core tenets of Kant's moral philosophy. Persons (even persons who are married to one another) cannot "possess each other as things" (Bouterwek 1799, 1199), for persons and things are qualitatively different substances with radically different moral and legal properties. Although Kant's views on this topic are certainly "worth thinking about" (Herman 1993, 49 – I would not be writing this essay if I did not believe so), I see little in them that can or should be salvaged. And while the fundamental criticisms of Kant's views on sex and marriage that I shall be presenting are not new (they track back to Schütz and Bouterwek), I do hope to convince the reader that they are nevertheless sound.

The Nature of Human Sexual Activity (According to Kant)

As noted earlier, Herman sees Kant as being committed "to the uncomfortable claim that sexual activity is unavoidably morally problematic" (Herman 1993, 63), and this "pessimism" about human sexuality (Kneller 2006, 458) is a feature that resonates strongly in many of the recent quasi-defenses of his position. Indeed, if we look at some of Kant's own statements, "morally problematic" and "pessimism" are underdescriptions of his actual position. Here are a few examples:

> there lies in this inclination a degradation of the human being [*Erniedrigung des Menschen*]; for as soon as anyone becomes an object of another's appetite, all motives of a moral relationship fall away [...]. This is the reason why we are ashamed of possessing such an impulse, and why all strict moralists [...] have sought to repress and dispense with it [*unterdrücken und zu entbehren*]. [...] [T]his inclination is a *principium* for the degradation of humanity. [H]umanity is here set aside. [...] [E]ach partner dishonors the humanity of the other. [...] Thus humanity [...] is dishonored and put on a par with animal nature. [...] All philosophers censure this inclination [...]. [T]here is something contemptible in the act itself, which runs counter to morality [*in der Handlung selbst etwas verächtliches, was wider die Moralität läuft*]. (Mo-Collins 27:384–386)

> [I]t seems as though all sexual inclination would run counter to morality. [...] In the first place, sensual congress of the sexes is a phenomenon in the human being that is entirely similar in function to that of animals; this bodily act of physical nature also engenders shame [*Scham*] and turns it into an obscene act [*obscönen Handlung*], i. e., one that in public presentation would awaken repugnance [*Widerwillen*], accompanied by the notion of *impudicitia* [lewdness]. Now if the act of intercourse were permissible, in and of itself, there would be no explaining the shame; and it rests on nothing else but this, that in presenting ourselves to the other as an object of enjoyment we feel that we are debasing [*herabsetzt*] humanity in our own person and making ourselves similar to the beasts. (MS-Vigilantius 27:638; cf. VAMS 23:359, 20:463)

On Kant's view, human sexual activity is more than "morally problematic". It is "contemptible" and "runs counter to morality". It runs counter to morality because it puts us "on a par with animal nature", and this is partly why "all strict moralists [...] have sought to repress and dispense with it". As Kneller aptly notes, right before citing the same passage from Vigilantius that I have cited above, Kant believed that "during sex both partners reduce themselves to animals bereft of free will and responsibility. For him, a sign of this is the shame and secrecy attached to sexual activity" (Kneller 2006, 458). And because he holds that sexual activity reduces humans to animals, sex for Kant (again, to quote Kneller) is an instance of "moral devolution" (Kneller 2006, 465).

Is there a way out of this degradation of humanity – other than universalized celibacy, which, at least in Kant's day, would have soon led to the extinction of the human race? One solution he does not consider is the possibility of sexual reproduction via artificial means. Kant would of course be opposed to selling one's eggs or sperm for profit (a person "is not entitled to sell a tooth, or any of his members. [...] Human beings have no right [...] to hand themselves over for profit": Mo-Collins 27:386; cf. MS-Vigilantius 27:602, GMS 4:429), but provided that there is no buying and selling involved, I think he would be a strong advocate of human sexual reproduction via artificial means. For it would solve the degradation of humanity problem while still enabling the human species to reproduce. And this technological fix to the moralist's dilemma, while not a new idea, appears at present to be finally working its way out of fiction and into reality. For instance, Henry Greely opens his recent book, *The End of Sex and the Future of Human Reproduction* (2016) with the following prediction:

> I expect that, sometime in the next twenty to forty years, amongst humans with good health coverage, sex, [...] will largely disappear, or at least decrease markedly. Most of those people will no longer use sexual intercourse to conceive their children. Instead of being conceived in a bed, in the backseat of a car, or under a "Keep off the Grass" sign, children will be conceived in clinics. Eggs and sperm will be united through in vitro fertilization (IVF). The DNA of the resulting embryos will then be sequenced and carefully analyzed before decisions are made (passive voice intentional) about which embryo or embryos to transfer to a womb for possible development into one or more living, breathing babies. (Greely 2016, 1 f.)

But this kind of twenty-first century technological fix was of course not yet available in Kant's era. So he is stuck with trying to legitimize old-fashioned sexual activity. And the strategy he settles on is a juridical one. Only through the legal institution of marriage can human sexual activity be made morally permissible: "the marriage contract [*Ehevertrag*] is not an arbitrary [*kein beliebiger*] choice but a necessary contract by the law of humanity; that is, if a man and a woman want to enjoy each other's sexual attributes they *must* necessarily marry, and this is necessary in accordance with pure reason's laws of right" (MS 6:277 f.). "Marriage is [...] the sole condition [*die einzige Bedingung*] for making use of one's sexual inclination" (Mo-Collins 27:388). Legalized sex, Kant believes, does not run counter to morality, even though "there is something contemptible in the [sexual] act itself, which runs counter to morality". And Kant's juridical strategy is another part of the current appeal of his position. As Herman notes: "to those who see the law as a positive avenue for radical social change, Kant may provide an unexpected source of theoretical insight and support" (Herman 1993, 65). But what makes sex within a legal marriage necessarily different from sex outside of marriage? Before examining some of the details of how exactly this juridical strategy is supposed to work and Kant's defense of it, let us take a closer look at how he conceptualizes human sexual activity.

Persons and Things, Proprietors and Property

According to Kant, human sexual activity is "fundamentally immoral" (Brake 2005, 61) rather than merely morally problematic because it involves a temporary forfeiture of our humanity. When humans engage in sex they devolve into a merely animal state, void of reason, free will, and responsibility. But in describing human sexual activity Kant also makes heavy use of his famous distinction between persons and things. When humans engage in sex, they temporarily lose their status as persons and devolve into things.[7] Kant states this repeatedly in lecture transcriptions from his ethics classes as well as in the *Rechtslehre*. Here are a few examples: "as soon as anyone becomes an object of another's appetite, all motives of moral relationship fall away, as object of the other's appetite that person is in fact a thing [*ist er nämlich eine Sache*]" (Mo-Collins 27:384 f.). "In this act [viz., sexual activity] a

---

7 Kant's position that humans treat each other as things rather than persons when they engage in sex is a clear link to contemporary feminist accounts of sexual objectification, and this link also helps to explain the recent revival of interest in his views on sex and marriage. However, there are at least two major differences between Kant and feminism on this point: (1) On Kant's view, sexual objectification is necessarily symmetrical. When engaging in heterosexual activity men treat women as objects, but women also treat men as objects (consensual objectification). Feminists view sexual objectification as asymmetrical – men are exclusively the objectifiers; women, the objects. (2) On Kant's account, human sexual activity necessarily involves objectification, whereas feminists view objectification as a social construction, something that can be changed through social transformation. For discussion, see Brake 2005, 83–89 and Nussbaum 1999, 213–239, esp. 224–227. See also Wood 1999, 396 f. n. 11, who argues convincingly that the Kantianism of Andrea Dworkin's view of sex can be traced back to Beauvoir's and Sartre's appropriation of Kant's analysis of sex.

human being makes himself into a thing [*macht sich* [...] *selbst zur Sache*], which conflicts with the right of humanity in his own person" (MS 6:278).

Persons (the complete set of which includes not just humans but all rational beings: "every other rational being also represents its existence in this way" – GMS 4:429) are ends in themselves; i.e., "something that may not be used merely as a means" (GMS 4:428), whereas things "have only a relative worth, as means" (GMS 4:428). For Kant, this distinction between persons and things (*Personen und Sachen*) is qualitative, not quantitative. Persons and things differ not merely by degree but in kind. An entity that is a mere thing can never become a person, for it lacks the necessary capacities of rationality, free will, and responsibility. Kant highlights this crucial distinction earlier in the *Rechtslehre* when he writes: "A *person* [*Person*] is a subject whose actions can be *imputed* to him. *Moral* personality is therefore nothing other than the freedom of a rational being under moral laws. [...] A *thing* [*Sache*] is that to which nothing can be imputed" (MS 6:223).

Furthermore, without this distinction between persons and things – i.e., if there are no persons with absolute worth – then all worth becomes "conditional, and hence contingent", and "then no supreme practical principle of reason could be found at all" (GMS 4:428). In other words, without the crucial and fundamental distinction between persons and things, Kant's entire ethical theory project falls apart. If the qualitative distinction between persons and things is not granted and sustained, then there is no way to establish "the supreme principle of morality" (GMS 4:392). So perhaps we should forego sexual activity after all, and hope that Greely's earlier-mentioned IVF scenario for human reproduction kicks in quickly?

And while entities that are persons have the ability to temporarily (or even permanently) devolve into things by relinquishing their capacities of rationality, free will, and responsibility, to do so is categorically forbidden in Kant's ethics. Persons must never treat themselves or any other persons as things. This is the main point of the end in itself formula of the categorical imperative: "*So act that you use humanity in your own person as well as in the person of any other, always at the same time as an end, never merely as a means*" (GMS 4:429).

Thus we reach the same conclusion articulated earlier regarding the fundamental immorality of human sexual activity by means of a slightly different route. Human sexual activity is fundamentally immoral because it is a clear violation of the end in itself formula of the categorical imperative. When humans[8] engage in sex they are using persons (themselves as well as their partner) as things,

---

8 Again, not just humans but all rational beings. Extraterrestrial rational beings who engage in sex will also need to get legally married if they wish to avoid acting in a fundamentally immoral manner.

and the use of a person as a thing "clashes with a fundamental principle of Kant's ethics" (Brake 2005, 65; cf. Kneller 2006, 458, Mendus 1992, 176).

Another fundamental and related aspect of Kant's distinction between persons and things – one that also plays a key role in his discussion and defense of marriage – is the difference between property and proprietorship. Things can be owned as property, but persons cannot. And persons can become proprietors or owners of property, whereas things cannot. Kant also makes this point repeatedly in numerous texts. Here are a few examples:

> The human being cannot dispose over himself, because he is not a thing [keine Sache ist]. He is not his own property [Eigenthum] – that would be a contradiction; for so far as he is a person, he is a subject, who can have ownership of other things [Eigenthum an anderen Dingen]. But now were he something owned by himself, he would be a thing over which he can have ownership. He is, however, a person who is not property, so he cannot be a thing such as he might own; for it is impossible, of course, to be at once a thing and a person [Sache und Person zugleich], a proprietor and a property [ein Eigenthümer und ein Eigenthum] at the same time. (Mo-Collins 27:386; cf. VAMS 20:458 f.)

> [T]he human being [...] cannot [...] make himself the physical property of others, i. e., give up his freedom and personality so entirely that the other can treat him as a thing [als Sache behandlen] (MS-Vigilantius 27:602).

> The human being [...] is not a thing, hence not something that can be used merely as a means, but must in all his actions be considered as an end in itself. Thus the human being in my own person is not at my disposal (GMS 4:429).

> [A] human being cannot have property in himself, much less in another person (MS 6:359).

These clear distinctions between persons and things and proprietors and property resurface in Kant's discussion of marriage in a way that has puzzled many commentators. For he explicitly uses the language of possession and property to refer to the marriage partners, who themselves are persons. In marriage, "one person is acquired by the other as if s/he were a thing [gleich als Sache erworben]" (MS 6:278). In the Vigilantius transcription he is even more blunt: in "the institution of matrimonium", "[t]hey both acquire each other completely [beyde sich ganz erwerben], and one becomes the other's property [Eigenthum]" (MS-Vigilantius 27:638 f.). And this is also what the peculiar language of the title of Section III, Part I of the Rechtslehre (viz., "On Personal Rights of the Thingly Kind [Von dem auf dingliche Art persönlichen Recht]" (MS 6:276) is meant to flag. Kant is discussing relationships between moral persons (husband and wife, parent and child, head of household and domestic servants), yet he also describes these relationships as ones involving ownership and property. In each case, his root assumption is that when protected by the cover of law, relationships which would otherwise be morally impermissible are somehow transformed into legitimate and morally permissible ones. But how is this assumption to be justified?

In the *Rechtslehre* he offers the following argument to support his claim that in marriage the spouses are each other's legitimate property, and one may assume that a similar argument would also apply to children and servants:

> That this *personal right* [*persönliche Recht*] is, however, at the same time a right of the thingly kind [*auf dingliche Art*] rests on the fact that if one of the marriage partners [*Eheleute*] has left or given her/himself into someone else's possession, the other partner is justified, always and without question, in bringing her/his partner back under her/his control, just as if she/he were a thing [*gleich als eine Sache*]. (MS 6:278)

In other words, if your spouse (or servant or child) decides to leave for whatever reason, you are always entitled to retrieve your missing property. But this is a question-begging argument[9] – viz., it merely accepts as true the claim that persons can be property, and this is precisely what needs to be justified. And as we saw earlier, Kant himself is adamant that persons are not things, and that persons cannot be owned as property. As Papadaki remarks:

> When it comes to marriage, Kant seems to ignore his previously expressed conviction that it is impossible for one to be both a proprietor and a property. The husband and wife, he tells us, are each other's proprietors and properties at the same time. Kant's definition of marriage, then, becomes paradoxical. It is conceptually impossible to be both a person (proprietor) and a thing (property), yet spouses achieve their "romantic blending"[10] through being each other's properties and proprietors (Papadaki 2010, 281).

Parts and Wholes: All of Me

All of me
Why not take all of me…
You took the part that once was my heart
So why not take all of me.

   – Billie Holiday, *All of Me*

What exactly is Kant's proposed solution to the problem of human sexual activity, and how is it supposed to work? How does the institution of marriage, or legalized sex, transform sex from a fundamentally immoral activity into a morally permis-

---

9 Cf. Bouterwek's remark in his 1797 review of Kant's *Rechtslehre*: "Is it possible that a thinker of the first rank does not see the circle in this argument?" (AA 20:449).
10 Papadaki borrows this phrase from Herman (see Herman 1993, 61). I will come back to it later.

sible one? In the *Rechtslehre*, Kant claims that "there is only one condition" under which sexual activity that does not conflict with the right of humanity in one's own person "is possible"; *viz.*, "that while one person is acquired by the other *as if a thing* [*gleich als Sache*], the one who is acquired reciprocally acquires the other; for in this way each reclaims her/his self and restores it to her/him self" (MS 6:278; cf. Mo-Collins 27:388.) But does this reclamation-of-oneself claim make any sense? How can two wrongs make a right?[11] Outside of the sexual sphere, they clearly don't. If I use you as a mere means, and you in turn (or simultaneously) use me as a mere means, we have both acted wrongly. In normal moral arithmetic, two wrongs do not make a right. But on Kant's view, in the special case of marriage, they somehow do. Persons are not things or property, and thus "a human being cannot have property in himself, much less in another person" (MS 6:359). But when two people become married to each other, each "becomes the other's property" (MS-Vigilantius 27:638), and thus it appears that the institution of marriage itself is immoral. Rather than solve the problem of the immorality of sexual activity, the institution of marriage simply affirms it. As Brake remarks, "if I cannot give myself to someone in the first place, how can I get myself back from him?" (Brake 2005, 72).

Another mysterious chapter in Kant's marriage story – one that is intended to resolve the paradox described above – involves the move from parts to wholes, from body parts (viz., sexual organs) to whole bodies. The institution of marriage is a contract between a man and a woman for the "reciprocal use" and "lifelong possession" of each other's "sexual organs and capacities" (MS 6:277). But in gaining legal access to, and lifelong possession of, a specific body part one also acquires the entire person, since "it is evident that if someone concedes a part of her/himself to another, s/he concedes her/himself entirely. It is not possible to dispose over a part of oneself, for such a part belongs to the whole" (Mo-Collins 27:387). Kant makes this same move from parts to whole in the *Rechtslehre*: "for a human being the acquisition of a body part [*Erwerb eines Gliedmaßes*] is at the same time the acquisition of the whole person, since a person is an absolute unity" (MS 6:278). But how and why does a right over a part of a body entail a right over the whole body? This is another dubious move in his argument. If I legally contract to use your foot, say, for a photo shoot for my shoe company, this doesn't mean that I thereby possess all of you. What Kant wants is a marriage commitment where each partner "dedicates oneself to the other" through "good or ill fortune and all of one's circumstances" (Mo-Collins 27:388) – or, as the traditional Protes-

---

11 Cf. Wood 1999, 258, and de Laurentiis 2000, 312, who also invoke this disreputable maxim in discussing Kant's views on marriage.

tant wedding vow has it, "for better, for worse, for richer, for poorer, in sickness and in health". But he tries to force this conclusion on the reader by means of an implausible "you-can't-have-a-part-without-possessing-the-whole" premise.[12] Furthermore, there are several additional problems with Kant's "unity of wills" solution, as Herman notes in the following passage:

> Although one sees what Kant may have wanted – a kind of romantic blending of self into a new and larger self – it is not possible for him to get what he wants. If the problem with sex is that we are embodied selves, and use of the body implies title over a self, things are not great-ly improved if we become parts of a new self that has two bodies (and sex would then be what?). The threat to the autonomous agent would seem to be increased rather than resolved in the surrender to the new union of persons [...]. (Herman 1993, 61)

At one level, Kant's attempt to legitimate human sexual activity through the insti-tution of marriage is an old, familiar story, aptly summarized by Frank Sinatra in his song, *Love and Marriage* ("you can't have one without the other"). But in Kant's case the stakes are raised considerably (and the resultant paradoxes are left unre-solved) by his heavy reliance on the person/thing dichotomy.

A Supernova or Merely a Shooting Star?

As noted earlier (see n. 5), Kant divides private law into three parts. The first two divisions – *Sachenrecht* (property law) and *persönliches Recht* (contract law) – are familiar territory for many readers. There are laws dealing with "a (corporeal) *thing* [*Sache*] external to me" (MS 6:247) – aka property, and there are also laws dealing with "another's choice to perform a specific deed (*praestatio*)" (MS 6:247) – aka contracts. But Kant also holds that there exists a third distinct kind of "external object of my choice" (MS 6:247). This third type of external object of choice – under which Kant places not only sexual activity and marriage but also "parental right [*Das Elternrecht*]" (MS 6:280) (the rights and duties of parents

---

12 Christine Korsgaard argues that Kant's theory of marriage "is based on Rousseau's theory". Marriages, "like the state, depend on the formation of a General Will" (Korsgaard 2009, 189). In marriage, "what is exchanged is a part of one's practical identity, and what results is a transfor-mation of that identity" (Korsgaard 1996, 215 n. 14). I think she may be right in pointing to Rous-seau's theory of the general will as a source of Kant's model of marriage, but her claims offer little support for Kant's model. The resulting larger agent that issues from the marriage contract is fun-damentally problematic for several reasons. See, e.g., Herman's doubts about "the romantic blend-ing of self into a new and larger self" (Herman 1993, 61), which I discuss briefly at the end of this section.

with respect to their children) and the "right of a head of the household [*Das Hausherrenrecht*]" (MS 6:282) (the rights and duties of heads of household with respect to servants) – requires, Kant holds, a special concept. This third type of external object of choice dealing with domestic rights is neither a property right nor a contract right, but one involving an awkward hybrid of persons and things. Thus Kant entitles the third section of Part I – *"Von dem auf dingliche Art persönlichen Recht"* (MS 6:276) – literally, "of personal right of the thingly kind".

Gregor and Ladd, in their respective English translations of Kant's *Rechtslehre*, both comment briefly on some the challenges posed to translators by Kant's introduction of a third kind of right (for references, see n. 5), and in fact Kant's innovation was noted in one of the very first reviews of the *Rechtslehre* – viz., Friedrich Bouterwek's,[13] first published in the *Göttingische Anzeigen* No. 28 (February 18, 1797). Bouterwek writes:

> *Von dem auf persönliche Art dinglichen Rechte.* p. 105.[14] This is then the new phenomenon in the juristic sky. With this Kant has in mind the category of reciprocity [*Wechselwirkung*] by which he is so well known. Here we find, completely unexpectedly, marriage right, parental right, and household right. (Relations of heads of household to their servants.) The man acquires a wife, the couple acquire children, and the family (children included?) acquire servants. This properly acquired right [*wohlerworbene Recht*] is not merely a right to a person [*persönliches Recht*]; for – – – the man can lay claim to his runaway wife, the father to his runaway child, and the master to his runaway servant. (Is it possible that a thinker of the first rank does not see the circle in this argument? *If* it is true that the husband can as it were claim his wife and so forth, then the relation of marriage partners and so forth to one another is certainly more than personal. Now the greater part of the juristic world, and among others also this reviewer, deny the hypothetical premise, and consequently also the Kantian conclusion.) (AA 20:449 f.)

Kant added an Appendix to the 1798 edition of the *Rechtslehre*, at the beginning of which he credits Bouterwek's review as the stimulus which led him to write the

---

13 Friedrich Bouterwek (1766–1828), was a philosopher, aesthetician, and poet at the University of Göttingen. In his letter to Bouterwek of May 7, 1793, Kant thanks him for his decision to offer a course on the *Critique of Pure Reason*, praising his "poetic mind that would have the intellectual power to explain the pure concepts of the understanding and make these principles more readily communicable" (Br 11:432). And in *Toward Perpetual Peace* Kant cites a line from one of Bouterwek's poems (ZeF 8:367). A complete translation of Bouterwek's Review is available in Westphal (2014), and selected passages from it are printed in italics in Kant (2016, 341–354). In the following citations from Bouterwek I have borrowed a few phrases from Westphal's translation. For further information about Bouterwek, see Zinkstok (2016).

14 Literally, "Of Thingly Rights of the Personal Kind". Note that Bouterwek has reversed the order of the terms "person" and "thing" in Kant's original section title. Is this accidental or intentional? And does reversing the order of the terms make a substantive difference?

addition: "I take the occasion for these remarks chiefly from the review of this book in the *Göttingen Journal* (No. 28), 18 Feb. 1797). In this review the book was examined with insight and rigor, but also with appreciation" (MS 6:356). Similarly, in a letter to Johann Heinrich Tieftrunk of October 13, 1797, Kant writes: "The Göttingen Review (in issue No. 28) taken as a whole is not unfavorable to my system. It induces me to publish a *Supplement,* so as to clear up a number of misunderstandings, and perhaps eventually to complete the system" (Br 12:207). Although Kant's response to Bouterwek is cursory and unsystematic (and, as Gregor remarks, "Kant's quotations [from Bouterwek's review] are not always accurate" – Gregor 1996, 638 n. 37), he does devote special attention to Bouterwek's criticism of his "new phenomenon". As he writes later in the Appendix: "We must now examine whether this concept, this "new phenomenon in the juristic sky", is a *stella mirabilis* (a phenomenon never seen before, growing into a star of the first magnitude but gradually disappearing again, perhaps to return at some time) or merely a *shooting star.*" (MS 6:358 f.)

Kant clearly believes that his new concept is a supernova – "a star of the first magnitude" – but I am inclined to side with Bouterwek in viewing it as a mere shooting star – a phenomenon that merely makes a brief appearance and then disappears. Part of my argument here is empirical and historical. Kant's "third way" simply did not catch on. I am not aware of any subsequent legal theorist who defends the necessity of a third distinct kind of external object of choice. In post-Kantian legal theory, *Eherecht* (along with Kant's other two subdivisions of domestic right, *Elternrecht* and *Hausherrenrecht*) are simply not understood in the strange manner proposed by Kant.

But there is also an important conceptual component to my argument, one that I have stressed at earlier points in this essay. *Sachen* and *Personen* are qualitatively distinct entities in Kant's practical philosophy, and because of this qualitative difference, they are not to be mixed under any circumstances. We are forbidden to treat persons as things, and vice versa. Once one tries to blur their boundaries – as Kant unfortunately does in §§ 22–30 of the *Rechtslehre* – his whole program in moral philosophy loses its foundation, because now there is no longer a way to justify "a supreme practical principle" (GMS 4:428). Kant's "defense of a strange, newly added type of right [*befremdlichen, neu hinzukommenden, Rechtstitels*] which has recently been added to the doctrine of natural law" (MS 6:361) therefore fails. It was merely a shooting star.

Conclusion

I have tried to show that the arguments Kant presents in defense of his position that sex within marriage is nonobjectifying are unsuccessful. But in drawing attention to and defending some of the very first criticisms of Kant's views on sex and marriage made by his contemporaries, several broader conclusions also become evident. First, human sexual activity is not inherently or necessarily objectifying. Humans do not necessarily treat themselves as things when they engage in sex with each other. All human activity is potentially objectifying, and while sexual activity often does involve objectification (indeed, more so than most if not all of our other behavior), it is not inherently or necessarily always objectifying.[15] This was part of Schütz's point to Kant back in 1797, a point that Kant simply evades in his reply when he writes: "the question is whether a marital cohabitation is possible, and how" (Kant to Schütz, July 19, 1797, Br 12:182). And it also lies in the background of Bouterwek's complaint about the circularity in Kant's argument that a husband can reclaim his runaway wife because she is her property – a complaint that Kant does not even respond to. Second, and related, humans do not necessarily devolve into animals bereft of rationality, free will, and responsibility when they engage in sexual activity. Sexuality is one of many activities that humans share in common with animals, but it is possible for humans to hold onto their rationality, free will, and responsibility when engaging in sex. Kant is unfortunately too close to Augustine's mistaken claim that our sexual organs "will not obey the direction of the will" (Greenblatt 2017, 26). Human sexual desire is extremely powerful, but whether and how we choose to act on this desire can and should be directed by the will.

Third, whether an action is objectifying or not depends on its maxim (cf. GMS 4:399). If agents incorporate maxims of respect for their partners as well as themselves in their actions, then their actions are not objectifying. And it is possible (though admittedly not always easy) for humans to "act with respect in sexual situations" (Brake 2005, 89). While Kant does not claim that acting with respect in sexual situations is impossible, he does hold that it is only possible within the juridical institution of marriage or legalized sex. As Herman notes, he seeks to "construct moral regard" by making the acceptance of obligations with respect to the welfare of one's marriage partner a condition of sexual activity (Herman 1993, 63). While I think Kant is overly optimistic on this matter (we all know legally married people who do not respect their partners and have not succeeded in constructing moral regard for one another), my argument in the present paper is not anti-

---

15 On this point I have also been influenced by both Brake's and Nussbaum's discussions (see esp. Brake 2005, 60; Nussbaum 1999, 239).

marriage. There often is something special about legalized sex. To put it in more Kantian terms: just as citizens who live in democratic regimes where the rule of law is respected can be said to live under a "moral veneer" whereby "the development of the moral predisposition to immediate respect for right is actually greatly facilitated" (ZeF 8:375 f. n.), so lovers who publicly commit themselves to each other's "good or ill fortune", and who vow that "neither will be subject to happiness or misfortune, joy or pleasure, without the other taking a share in it" (Mo-Collins 27:388) have placed themselves under a moral veneer where their capacity for mutual respect is greatly facilitated. By means of the juridical strategy of marriage, "a great step is taken *toward* morality (though it is not yet a moral step)" (ZeF 8:376n.). But of course there is no guarantee that the juridical strategy will in fact result in a moral step.[16]

References

Altman, Matthew, 2010, "Kant on Sex and Marriage: The Implications for the Same-Sex Debate", *Kant-Studien*, 101, 309–330.

Aris, Reinhold, 1936, *History of Political Thought in Germany from 1789 to 1815*, London: Frank Cass & Co. Ltd.

Arroyo, Christopher, 2017, *Kant's Ethics and the Same-Sex Marriage Debate – An Introduction*, Cham: Springer.

Bouterwek, Friedrich, 1799, Rezension von Kants *Metaphysische Anfangsgründe der Rechtslehre*, *Göttingische Anzeigen von gelehrten Sachen*, 28 (29. Juli 1799), 1197–1200.

Brake, Elizabeth, 2005, "Justice and Virtue in Kant's Account of Marriage", *Kantian Review*, 9, 58–94.

De Laurentiis, Allegra, 2000, "Kant's Shameful Proposition: A Hegel-Inspired Criticism of Kant's Theory of Domestic Right", *International Philosophical Quarterly*, 40, 297–312.

Denis, Lara, 2001, "From Friendship to Marriage: Revising Kant", *Philosophy and Phenomenological Research*, 63, 1–28.

Foucault, Michel, 2008, *Introduction to Kant's Anthropology*, edited by Roberto Nigro, translated by Robert Nigro and Kate Briggs, Los Angeles: Semiotext(e).

---

16 For related discussion, see Louden 2000, 149 and Louden 2007, 208 f. The roots of this essay lie in an informal talk I gave at a workshop on Kant's *Rechtslehre*, held at Boston College in July 2012. I would like to thank Susan Shell for inviting me to participate in the workshop, and fellow participant Howard Williams for encouraging me to further develop my remarks. A first draft of the essay was written in July 2016, while I was visiting professor at Universidade Federal de Santa Catarina in Florianopolis, Brazil. I would like to thank my host Maria Borges for making this visit possible. Thanks also to Jens Timmermann, Martin Brecher, and Pärttyli Rinne, for their invitation to participate in the Kant on Love, Sex, and Friendship Workshop held at St Andrews in July 2017 – particularly to Martin, for his helpful comments on an earlier draft. A later version of the paper was also presented as an invited lecture at John Cabot University in Rome in March, 2018 – many thanks to Tom Bailey for making this visit possible.

Greely, Henry T., 2016, *The End of Sex and the Future of Human Reproduction*, Cambridge, MA: Harvard University Press.

Greenblatt, Stephen, 2017, "The Invention of Sex: St. Augustine's Carnal Knowledge", *The New Yorker*, June 19, 2017, 24–28.

Gregor, Mary J. (ed. and trans.), 1996, Immanuel Kant, *Practical Philosophy*, Cambridge: Cambridge University Press.

Hegel, Georg Wilhelm Friedrich, 1970, *Grundlinien der Philosophie des Rechts*, edited by Eva Moldenhauer and Karl Markus Michel, Frankfurt a. M.: Suhrkamp.

Herman, Barbara, 1993, "Could It Be Worth Thinking About Kant on Sex and Marriage?", in: Louise M. Antony and Charlotte Witt (eds.), *A Mind of One's Own: Feminist Essays on Reason and Objectivity*, Boulder, CO: Westview Press, 49–68.

Kant, Immanuel, 2016, *Lectures and Drafts on Political Philosophy*, edited by Frederick Rauscher, translated by Frederick Rauscher and Kenneth R. Westphal, Cambridge: Cambridge University Press.

Kleingeld, Pauline, 2007, "Kant's Second Thoughts on Race", *Philosophical Quarterly*, 57, 573–592.

Kneller, Jane, 2006, "Kant on Sex and Marriage Right", in: Paul Guyer (ed.), *The Cambridge Companion to Kant and Modern Philosophy*, Cambridge: Cambridge University Press, 447–476.

Korsgaard, Christine M., 2009, *Self-Constitution: Agency, Identity, and Integrity*. Oxford: Oxford University Press.

Korsgaard, Christine M., 1996, *Creating the Kingdom of Ends*. Cambridge: Cambridge University Press.

Ladd, John (trans.), 1999, Immanuel Kant, *Metaphysical Elements of Justice*, Indianapolis: Hackett.

Louden, Robert B., 2000, *Kant's Impure Ethics: From Rational Beings to Human Beings*, New York: Oxford University Press.

Louden, Robert B., 2007, *The World We Want: How and Why the Ideals of the Enlightenment Still Elude Us*, New York: Oxford University Press.

Louden, Robert B., 2011, *Kant's Human Being: Essays on His Theory of Human Nature*, New York: Oxford University Press.

Louden, Robert B., 2013, "El Kant de Foucault", *Estudos Kantianos*, 1, 163–182.

Louden, Robert B., 2015, "The Last Frontier: Exploring Kant's Geography", in: Robert R. Clewis (ed.), *Reading Kant's Lectures*, Berlin/Boston: de Gruyter, 505–525.

Ludwig, Bernd, 1986, "Einleitung", in: Immanuel Kant, *Metaphysisiche Anfangsgründe der Rechtslehre*, edited by Bernd Ludwig, Hamburg: Felix Meiner.

Mautner, Thomas, 1981, "Kant's *Metaphysics of Morals:* A Note on the Text", *Kant-Studien*, 72, 356–359.

Mendus, Susan, 1992, "Kant: 'An Honest but Narrow-Minded Bourgeois'?", in: Howard Lloyd Williams (ed.), *Essays on Kant's Political Philosophy*, Chicago: University of Chicago Press, 166–190.

Muthu, Sankar, 2003, *Enlightenment against Empire*. Princeton: Princeton University Press.

Nussbaum, Martha C., 1999, *Sex and Social Justice*, New York: Oxford University Press.

Papadaki, Linda, 2010, "Kantian Marriage and Beyond: Why It Is Worth Thinking about Kant on Marriage", *Hypatia*, 25, 276–294.

Shell, Susan Meld, 1996. *The Embodiment of Reason: Kant on Spirit, Generation, and Community*, Chicago: University of Chicago Press.

Sticker, Martin, 2016, "Kant's Case Against Traditional Marriage", 13th Annual Meeting of the Eastern Study Group of the North American Kant Society, Yale University.

Westphal, Kenneth R., 2014, Translation of Friedrich Bouterwek's Review of Kant, *Metaphysical Foundations of the Doctrine of Right*, Kantian Studies Online, 240–261.

Wilson, Donald, 2004, "Kant and the Marriage Right", *Pacific Philosophical Quarterly*, 85, 103–123.

Wood, Allen W., 1999, *Kant's Ethical Thought*, Cambridge: Cambridge University Press.

Zinkstok, Job, 2016, "Bouterwek, Friedrich (1766–1828)", in: Heiner F. Klemme and Manfred Kuehn (eds.), *The Bloomsbury Dictionary of Eighteenth-Century German Philosophers*, London: Bloomsbury, 91–94.

Martin Brecher

Animal Desire and Rational Nature: Kant's Argument for Marriage and the Problem of 'Unnatural' Sex

Abstract: While many interpreters endorse both Kant's worry about objectifying tendencies in human sexuality and his argument that legal marriage can avert sexual objectification, they at the same time reject Kant's notorious and spurious claim that sexual acts are moral only if in line with the 'natural end' of procreation, while 'unnatural' sex would violate our humanity. However, from an exegetical point of view, such a divisional approach is unconvincing. I shall argue that, for Kant, both the problem of sexual objectification and the (as Kant sees it) problem of 'unnatural' sex stem from a single root: the specific character of sexual desire and action. Kant's views about the moral problems of sex result from his anthropological theory of sexuality as part of our 'animality', and they cannot be partitioned as easily. Consequently, proponents of Kantian arguments for same-sex marriage need to undertake more radical revisions of Kant's theory of sexuality.

1 Introduction

The idea of autonomy is at the centre of Kant's moral philosophy and informs his system of practical philosophy.[1] The notion of autonomy, the special status it accords the human being, the fundamental rights it grounds, and the particular demands that it imposes on our actions make Kant's moral philosophy a particularly rich and attractive resource for present-day issues in moral theory and practical ethics as well as in legal and political philosophy. Thus, in recent years, Kant's treatment of particular moral questions has received increasing attention. In particular, Kant's account of sex and marriage, which had been discarded by generations of readers as legalistic and obscure, if not outright absurd, is now a subject of nuanced discussion not only in Kant scholarship, but also in philosophical debates

---

1 Interpreters, however, are at odds as to which degree this holds and in particular whether or not there are major fractions between the moral foundations developed in the *Groundwork* and the second *Critique* on the one hand and Kant's legal and political philosophy on the other. In what follows, I will assume the coherence and unity of Kant's practical philosophy, an assumption I share with the interpretations of Kant's sexual morals with which I engage below.

https://doi.org/10.1515/9783111291130-004

about sex and sexual relationships more generally.[2] Notably, some philosophers who are engaged in the contemporary debate about same-sex marriage turn to Kant and draw on his sexual morals for developing a conception of marital relationships that could serve as a suitable basis for a modern marriage law no longer limited to different-sex couples.[3]

What makes Kant's views on sex and marriage particularly interesting for present-day theorizing is his idea that sex poses a particular moral problem, the problem of sexual objectification. Kant argues that unless a sexual act is subject to particular legal and moral conditions (most importantly, legal marriage) the agents involved treat themselves as things, as mere means, so that the action runs counter to our dignity as rational, autonomous agents. Considered thus far, Kant's concept of marriage and its deduction from the problem of sexual objectification is just as applicable to same-sex relationships as it is to different-sex relationships. Hence, proponents of same-sex marriage, as Altman submits, "can concede to their opponents that marriage is an important moral institution and conclude on that basis that [...] it ought to be available to same-sex partners as well" (Altman 2010, 310).[4] However, while Kant argues that legal marriage as such does not require the pursuit of 'begetting and bringing up children', he still agrees with traditional accounts of sexual morals in that he notoriously considers all non-heterosexual sex acts as 'unnatural' and as violating our dignity as rational beings, branding them as 'unnatural carnal vices' (RL 6:277; Mo-Collins 27:390). Consequently, Kant still considers marriage as necessarily being a "union of two persons of *different* sexes" (RL 6:277; emphasis added).[5]

---

2 See, e.g., Soble 1998, Nussbaum 1999, Halwani 2010, Brake 2012.

3 See, most notably, Altman 2010 and 2011, Arroyo 2017, Varden 2017 and 2020.

4 Cf. Schaff 2001, 453: "On Kant's own argument, if 'marriage,' or some sufficiently legal recognition of union, is allowed between same-sex couples, then the debasement of persons would not take place". Similarly, Barbara Herman has pointed out that Kant's "critique of sexuality would apply equally to same-sex sexual relations" and that there is in Kant's conception of marriage right "no conceptual barrier to same-sex marriage and a strong argument for it" (Herman 1993, 65 f. notes 6 and 22). Other interpreters also hold that Kant's marriage right is at least "consistent with a defense of same-sex marriage" (Sadler 2013, 213 cf. also D. Wilson 2004, 116 f.).

5 In general I shall use the English translations from the *Cambridge Edition of the Works of Immanuel Kant*. Quotations from the *Groundwork* are taken from Jens Timmermann's revised translation. A note on the *Lectures on Ethics:* The text of the Kaehler lecture notes, edited by Werner Stark in 2004, is much more reliable than that of the Collins notes in volume 27 of the Academy Edition. However, since the Collins notes are available in English translation (which, alas, is in itself not always very reliable), I shall quote from the Collins notes where there is no difference in the text between Collins and Kaehler, but I shall provide additional references to the Kaehler text (giving the manuscript pages). In general, I shall indicate when I modify translations or when I have translated texts myself. I am grateful to Jens Timmermann for helpful suggestions and corrections.

While proponents of Kantian same-sex marriage endorse Kant's argument that legal marriage is necessary to avoid the problem of objectification, they reject Kant's claim that certain forms of sex are 'unnatural' and hence immoral, arguing that "Kant's appeal to what is natural is not only unjustified, but also irrelevant" (Altman 2010, 326). However, such a 'divisional' interpretative approach to Kant's account of sex can be challenged from an exegetical point of view. Indeed, the aim of my paper will be to show that Kant's claims about morally legitimate sex build on a unified view of sexual action and desire grounded in Kant's anthropological theory of sexuality. As I shall argue, for Kant both the problem of sexual objectification and the (as he sees it) problem of 'unnatural' sex stem from a single root: the specific character of sexual desire and action which he considers as part of our 'animality'. Hence, Kant's worries about the moral problems inherent in what he considers 'natural' and 'unnatural' sex, respectively, cannot be separated as easily as one might wish.[6]

In developing my account I will first, in section 2, discuss Kant's notion of sexual objectification. This notion constitutes the basis for Kant's account of marriage: by recourse to it Kant justifies (i.e., deduces) his concept of legal marriage. By unfurling Kant's view of the 'use of one's sexual organs' (*Geschlechtsgebrauch*) and of sexual desire as its natural determining ground, I will show that Kant takes the problem of objectification to have its root in the specific character of our 'animal' sexual desire.

In section 3, I will turn to Kant's discussion of what he considers 'unnatural' sex. First, I will show that Kant regards 'unnatural' sex as morally problematic because he thinks that in any sexual act that is not directed towards the 'natural end' of procreation, agents use themselves as mere means for the gratification of their animal sexual desire. Secondly, I will clarify why Kant thinks that the fact that procreation is the 'natural end' of sex can have moral significance; in particular, I will argue that we should understand Kant as claiming that insofar as sex can be judged purposively, it can be considered as conforming to reason. This is why Kant thinks that limiting sexual action by considerations of procreation is a *pro tanto* requirement for making sex formally conform to the demands of reason.

My paper will arrive at a somewhat paradoxical result: While I argue that Kant's account of the morality of sex is much more coherent than many interpreters think, this has the consequence of making Kant's sexual morals look a lot less tenable in light of present-day concepts of human sexuality. In the concluding sec-

---

6 To avoid any misunderstanding: my interpretation does not imply any agreement with Kant's views about sex in general or about what he considers 'unnatural' sex in particular.

tion of the paper, I will very briefly touch on options for revising Kant's theory and in particular his notion of the 'natural end' of sexual acts.

2 Sexual Desire, the Problem of Objectification, and the Safe Haven of Marriage[8]

Kant famously argues, in the *Metaphysics of Morals* as well as in his earlier lectures on ethics and natural law, that lifelong and monogamous marriage is the only type of sexual relationship that is "in accordance with law" (RL § 24, 6:277; cf. MS-Vigilantius, 27:638 f.). Agents who want to engage in sexual intercourse, that is, who want "to enjoy each other's sexual attributes", "*must* necessarily marry, and this is necessary in accordance with pure reason's laws of right" (RL 6:278). In contrast to traditional accounts of marriage still prevalent in the late eighteenth century, Kant does not justify the legal necessity of marriage with respect to the "end of begetting and bringing up children".[7] Instead Kant submits that sexual intercourse outside of marriage involves objectification and thereby a violation of our humanity. Kant argues that – *prima facie* – an agent makes himself or herself 'into a thing' if he or she engages in sexual intercourse with another agent. Only within marriage is it possible for the partners to have sex with each other without objectification (RL 6:278; cf. Mo-Collins, 27:388).

Making oneself into a thing amounts to a violation of humanity in one's own person; specifically, making oneself into a thing by allowing another person to use oneself as a thing amounts to a violation of the *right* of humanity in one's own person: "In this act a human being makes himself into a thing, which conflicts with the right of humanity in his own person" (RL § 25, 6:278; translation modified).[8]

---

7 See, for instance, Kant's textbook authors Baumgarten (*Ethica*, § 272) and Achenwall (*Ius naturae*, pars posterior, § 42). The same holds for, e. g., Pufendorf (*De officio*, II 2 § 2) and Wolff (*Deutsche Politik*, § 16, and *Institutiones*, § 856), but also for Crusius (*Anweisung vernünfftig zu leben*, § 563) with whose moral theory Kant also engages.

8 "[T]his act" is the giving oneself to another person for the use of one's sexual organs (see RL 6:278). For Kant, consent is a necessary condition for morally legitimate sex. This follows from the general demand that "rational beings [...] are always to be esteemed at the same time as ends, i. e. only as beings who must, of just the same action, also be able to contain in themselves the end" of this action (GMS 4:431). In the context of right, using the body of another person without her consent infringes on her innate right to freedom, her 'inner mine' (RL, 6:236, 6:248), and this straightforwardly violates the universal principle of right (RL 6:230). Hence, rape (*Nothzucht*) is a punishable crime (RL, Appendix, 6:363). In his discussion of sexual morality, Kant presupposes that the sexual acts are consensual and he is merely concerned with the specific conditions that

To properly understand this claim, we have, first, to consider what Kant understands by violations of the right of humanity in our own person (2.1) and, secondly, why he considers sex as posing an inherent risk to our dignity as autonomous agents (2.2). Finally, we will briefly turn to marriage as the solution to this problem (2.3).

2.1 Non-Marital Sex as a Violation of the Right of Humanity in Our Own Person

Humanity is the defining mark of human beings as rational, autonomous beings. In virtue of our humanity we are persons, free agents subject only to the moral law, which according to Kant is the law of our own pure reason (MS 6:223, 6:239; KpV 5:87, 5:131 f.). Being a person entails a certain normative status. It places certain constraints on the ways in which we can act towards others, but also on the ways in which we may act towards ourselves: "man can be his own master (*sui iuris*) but cannot be the owner *of himself* (*sui dominus*) (cannot dispose of himself as he pleases) [...] since he is accountable to the humanity in his own person" (RL § 17, 6:270). In Kant's system of duties, the right of humanity in our own person is what corresponds to the inner duty of right. For this type of duty Kant refers to the (Pseudo-)Ulpian formula from Roman Law, *honeste vive* (literally, "lead an upright life"[9]), which he glosses as the imperative: "Do not make yourself a mere means for others but be at the same time an end for them." (RL 6:236)[10] The inner duty of right is characterized by three specific properties: first, as an inner duty, it is a *duty to oneself*; secondly, as a duty of right, it is *a perfect duty*, precisely circumscribing which actions are permitted or prohibited; and, finally, again as a duty of right, it governs *the agent's external relation to other agents:* for right concerns "the external and indeed practical relation of one person to another, insofar as

---

make this consent legitimate. As I have argued elsewhere, Kant's marriage right does not entail a coercible right to sexual intercourse (Brecher 2018a). Hence, in what follows, when I speak of sexual acts I always mean consensual sexual acts.

9 I am grateful to Jens Timmermann for suggesting this formulation.

10 The correspondence of inner duty of right and the right of humanity in our own person is also presented in the table that presents the division of the metaphysics of morals 'in accorance with the objective relation of law to duty' (6:240). In the Introduction to the *Doctrine of Right*, Kant says that the inner duty of right "will be explained later as obligation from the right of humanity in our own person" (6:236). However, he does not present such an explanation in any substantive form. However, at the beginning of the main part of the *Doctrine of Virtue*, Kant presents an explanation of duties to oneself as "obligation[s] to [one]self (to the humanity in [one's] own person)" (TL § 3, 6:418).

their actions, as *facta,* can have (direct or indirect) influence on each other" (RL § B, 6:230; translation modified). The inner duty of right is thus a duty that I have to myself, but with respect to my external relation to other agents. Specifically, it requires that I refrain from any kind of interaction with others that would infringe on my freedom or be detrimental to my being a person. The inner duty of right prohibits making *oneself* a mere means *for others* (cf. the quote from 6:236 above).

One normative consequence, as Kant points out, is that contracts that infringe on the personhood of at least one of the parties are invalid, "null and void", lacking any binding force (e. g., RL § 30, 6:283; cf. § 26, 6:279, and Appendix, 6:360). A case in point is selling oneself into slavery. Such an agreement is invalid, for

> a contract by which one party would completely renounce its freedom for the other's advantage would be self-contradictory, that is, null and void, since by it one party would cease to be a person and so would have no duty to keep the contract but would recognize only force (RL § 30, 6:283).

Similarly, Kant considers contracts for sexual services as well as agreements to enter into sexual relationships other than lifelong monogamous marriage to violate the inner duty of right. In all of these cases, at least one of the persons involved "would be surrendering herself as a thing to the other's choice" (RL § 26, 6:279), would "make[] herself into a mere thing" (6:278; cf. 6:359 f.).[11] Such agreements – Kant in particular mentions polygamy, prostitution (*"pactum fornicationis"*), concubinage and morganatic marriage (*Ehe zur linken Hand*) – are not legally valid, and "either party can cancel the contract with the other as soon as it pleases without the other having grounds for complaining about any infringement of its rights" (6:279).

For Kant, the problem of sexual objectification arises from an agent consenting to another person acting toward her (or him) in a certain way, to that person using her (or his) body in a certain way. As the quotations above show, the agent makes *herself* (or *himself*) into a thing by her (or his) consent. This consent, however, is problematic because of the way the other person will then (consensually) use her (or him). The use of the body is a use of the person, because, as Kant repeatedly stresses, from a practical point of view we cannot separate the body or parts of it from the subject, for "a person is an absolute unity" (RL 6:278; cf. 6:279). By engaging in sexual intercourse the agent allows herself (or himself)

---

11 The feminine pronoun is used in the translation of these passages because *Person* is grammatically feminine in German. It should be kept in mind, however, that Kant is speaking about persons of either sex.

– *prima facie* – to be treated in a way that is incompatible with her (or his) personality, that is, with being a person. Why does sex have this moral implication?

2.2 Sexual Desire and the Grounds of Objectification

As I will now argue, the reason why Kant regards sex as – again, *prima facie* – incompatible with our personality, our being autonomous agents, lies in the nature of the sexual act. In the ethics lecture notes from the 1770s Kant rejects consequentialist accounts of sexual morals[12] and argues that the relevant problem is to be found "in the act itself":

> All philosophers censure this inclination only for its pernicious effects, and the ruin it brings, partly to the body, and partly to the general welfare, and see nothing reprehensible in the act as such [...] Yet here there is something contemptible in the act itself, which runs counter to morality. (Mo-Collins, 27:386; cf. Mo-Kaehler, 300)

In line with this view, Kant in the *Doctrine of Right* derives the problem of objectification from the specific character of the reciprocal bodily use in sexual intercourse. What by nature differentiates sex from other actions, he argues, is that it is a form of enjoyment: "[T]he natural use that one sex makes of the other's sexual organs is enjoyment [*Genuß*], for which one gives itself up to the other." (RL § 25, 6:278)

However, without further elaboration one is left puzzled: for why should sex be considered as specifically different from other forms of enjoyment we may provide each other through the use of our bodies, without (at least *ceteris paribus*) thereby degrading ourselves?[13] In the *Doctrine of Right*, Kant does not provide

---

12 The case in point of such an consequentialist approach to sexual morality can be found in Wolff's *Deutscher Politik* (§§ 28 ff.) where Wolff provides a long list of the bad consequences that may result from unchaste behaviour – from neglecting one's studies and wasting money through to infanticide.

13 This question has been raised by early critics of Kant's notion of sex, in particular, by Friedrich Bouterwek (1797 and 1799; see Bouterwek 2014 for translations of both reviews) and Christian Gottfried Schütz. Schütz first articulated his worries in a letter to his and Kant's common friend Johann Schultz that was then passed on to Kant (see Schultz's own reply to Schütz; printed in F.K.J. Schütz 1834, vol. II, 465–468). The original letter is lost but Kant paraphrases Schütz's criticisms in his response (Br 12:181–183). In 1799 Schütz published an anonymous review of the second edition of the Doctrine of Right, where he discusses both Kant's private reaction and the arguments in the Appendix to the *Doctrine of Right* and reiterates his criticism (Schütz 1799). On Bouterwek's and Schütz's initial criticism and Kant's response, see Robert Louden's paper in this volume and chapter 4 in Brecher 2023.

his readers with a proper explanation as to why he regards sexual enjoyment as *prima facie* objectifying. But we can draw on other sources to fill in the picture.

(1) In the *Anthropology*, Kant uses "enjoyment" ("*Genuß*") to designate that kind of "sensuous pleasure in the sensation of an object" that is generated immediately "through sense" (Anth 7:230). This also holds for sexual enjoyment. In the *Doctrine of Virtue* Kant characterizes sexual pleasure as a specifically "sensuous pleasure" (*Sinnenlust*) and sets it apart from "merely *sensible* pleasure [*sinnliche Lust*], as in objects that are pleasing in mere reflection on them (the receptivity for which is called taste)" (TL § 7, 6:426; translation modified): While we can experience aesthetic pleasure by just entertaining in thought the representation of an object of taste, sexual pleasure is generated by direct sensual stimulation (hence, sexual gratification is one kind of what Kant calls the agreeable [*das Angenehme*]; cf. KU § 3, 5:205–207).

By defining the "use that one sex makes of the other's sexual organs" as "*enjoyment*" (6:278), Kant claims that sex *qua* type of action is defined by the seeking of sensuous pleasure through the use of another's body. In a letter to Christian Gottfried Schütz, Kant explains that in the characterization of sex as a use of the body in which one sexual partner takes enjoyment from the other, one may readily replace 'enjoyment' "by the notion of the *use* of an immediately (that is, through sense, which here is a from all others specifically different sense) I say *of an immediately gratifying* thing" (Br 12:182; translation modified).[14]

(2) From his more elaborate discussion of sex in his lectures, we can draw the further conclusion that Kant regards the attainment of this pleasure as the *natural object of sexual desire:* "There is no case where a human being would already be determined by nature to be the object of another's enjoyment, save this, of which sexual inclination is the basis" (Mo-Collins, 27:385; cf. Mo-Kaehler, 298). Here Kant makes clear that he regards sexual desire as the source of the problem of sexual objectification: "there lies in this inclination a degradation of man" (Mo-Collins, 27:384; cf. Mo-Kaehler, 298).

The problem of objectification arises because in acting from sexual desire – which is, as we have seen, the natural determining ground of sexual action – we focus only on the attainment of sensual pleasure, disregarding that the object of that desire is a person, thereby equating her with a thing: "In loving from sexual inclination, they make the person into an object of their appetite." But "as soon as anyone becomes an object of another's appetite, all motives of moral relationship

---

14 Cf. in the Preparatory Notes for the Appendix: "Now if the manner of use which a human being makes of another's sexual organs *immediately for his pleasure* (not for other ends) is called enjoyment, then that is exactly the expression proper to the action and to the object itself" (VARL 20:464).

fall away; as object of the other's appetite, that person is in fact a thing, whereby the other's appetite is sated" (Mo-Collins, 27:384 f.; cf. Mo-Kaehler, 297 f.).

Kant argues that this desire involves a consumptive attitude towards its object: sexual desire makes us focus only on the attainment of sexual satisfaction, irrespective of our partner's personality. Kant argues that while sexual desire can go together with a benevolent interest in the other person, taken in itself sexual desire is an appetite, a mere desire for sensuous pleasure: "The sexual impulse can admittedly be combined with human affection, and then it also carries with it the aims of the latter, but if it is taken in and by itself, it is nothing more than appetite" (Mo-Collins, 27:384; cf. Mo-Kaehler, 297). This can be seen, Kant submits, in that an agent who desires another person merely sexually takes no interest in this person's well-being and is willing to accept harmful consequences:

> it is plain that those who merely have sexual inclination love the person from none of the foregoing motives of true human affection, are quite unconcerned for their happiness, and will even plunge them into the greatest unhappiness, simply to satisfy their own inclination and appetite (Mo-Collins, 27:384; cf. Mo-Kaehler, 297)

Once the desire is satisfied, the appetite satiated, all interest in the other person cedes and she (or he) is discarded:

> If they love from sexual inclination only, they make the person into the object of their appetite; as soon as they have enjoyed the other person, and have sated their appetite, they throw her away, just as one throws away a lemon after sucking the juice from it. (Mo-Collins, 27:384; cf. Mo-Kaehler, 297 f.)

The image of throwing away the other person like a squashed lemon is meant to indicate that no value is attached the other person beyond the pleasure they offer to deliver; in Kant's view, sexual desire regards its objects as disposable, exchangeable, consumable.[15]

In the Appendix to the *Doctrine of Right*, Kant in the same way argues that outside of marriage "carnal enjoyment is *cannibalistic* in principle (even if not always in its effect)" (6:359):

> Whether something is *consumed* by mouth and teeth, or whether the woman is consumed by pregnancy and the perhaps fatal delivery resulting from it, or the man by exhaustion from the woman's frequent demands upon his sexual capacity, the difference is merely in the manner of enjoyment. In this sort of use by each of the sexual organs of the other, each is actually

---

15 Lemons were being traded throughout Europe and were a common and rather inexpensive good. Cf. the entry "Citrone" in Krünitz' *Oeconomische Encyclopädie*, vol. 7 (1776), 153.

a *consumable* thing *(res fungibilis)* with respect to the other (RL, Appendix, 6:359 f.; translation modified).

It is important to note that in pointing out the medical risks of sex, Kant's argument is not that sex is inherently problematic because it in fact carries these risks (cf. Br 12:182; MS-Vigilantius, 27:637 f.). This would make marital sex just as problematic. Rather, Kant is making a claim about the attitude that agents take towards each other if they desire each other sexually. The problem is the "principle" that governs the agents' sexual behaviour, i. e., the fact that they regard each other as consumable insofar as they easily accept the risks associated with sex in order to satisfy their 'appetite'. In other passages in which Kant compares sexual intercourse with cannibalism we can see that it is the underlying principle and attitude of sexual desire which warrants the comparison with cannibalism: In his reply to Schütz he writes that "[a]n enjoyment of this sort involves at once the thought of her [sc. the other person] as merely *consumable*". Therefore, "the appetite of a cannibal differs only as regards the outer form [*nur der Förmlichkeit nach*] from that of a sexual libertine" (Br 12:182; translation modified). In a note, Kant claims that "[s]uch an enjoyment is thus one and utterly the same with cannibalism in accordance with the *spirit* of the proscriptive law" (VARL 23:358; Kant's emphasis).

Both the libertine and the cannibal want to "enjoy" another person, that is, they want to use her body to experience pleasure from the direct stimulation of their senses. In their longing both the cannibal and the libertine ignore her well-being and her personhood and readily accept negative consequences for her health and life (the detriment of her health and life being a necessary consequence in the case of the cannibal, while being merely possible in the case of sexual enjoyment[16]). In both cases, if an agent agrees to her body being used for enjoyment, she acts in violation of the dignity of her humanity.

(3) Beside libertine behaviour, Kant points to another phenomenon which in his eyes indicates that sexual action is by its nature problematic: the feeling of shame, which according to Kant reacts to degradations of our humanity:

> Now if the act of intercourse were permissible, in and for itself, there would be no explaining the shame; and it rests on nothing else but this, that in presenting ourselves to the other as an

---

16 Cf. Refl. 7662, AA 19:481: "There are only two kinds of enjoyment that one human being can take of another (of his flesh): cannibalistic and lust enjoyment. The latter leaves the person alive." (My translation. The German text reads: "Wir haben nur zweyerley Genuß eines Menschen von dem andern (des fleisches): der cannibalische oder der wollüstige Genuß. Der letztere läßt die Persohn übrig.")

object of enjoyment we feel that we are demeaning humanity in our own person and making ourselves similar to the beasts. (MS-Vigilantius, 27:638)[17]

This also holds for sex in marriage for, as Kant says in the *Doctrine of Virtue*, "even [when] the permitted bodily union of the sexes in marriage (a union which is in itself merely an animal union) is to be mentioned in polite society, this occasions and requires much delicacy to throw a veil over it" (TL 6:425). And as he says in the lecture notes, "we are ashamed of possessing such an impulse" because through sexual desire we are "determined by nature [!] to be the object of another's enjoyment" (Mo-Collins, 27:385; cf. Mo-Kaehler, 298).[18]

Kant believes that the feeling of shame is not culturally acquired, but a genuine reaction to the morally problematic character of sex. As any sexual relationship which "aim[s] merely at a satisfying of the natural impulse" constitutes a transgression of the moral law ("runs counter to all morality"), "no other assumption can be made, therefore, but that modesty [*Schamhaftigkeit*] is not a mere natural instinct, but in truth an idea founded upon morality" (MS-Vigilantius, 27:639).[19] Here, again, shame reacts to an immoral act that involves "a beast-like condition" (*ibid.*). And, as Kant points out, it is an ubiquitous, almost universal reaction: "even rude peoples possess it, and we find but few, and those in the rawest state of nature, who have paid no regard to it, or could do so" (*ibid.*).[20]

It is also important to note that Kant does not refer to the feeling of shame only with respect to sexuality. In the *Doctrine of Virtue*, Kant points to "disgraceful punishments that dishonor humanity itself (such as quartering a man, having him torn by dogs, cutting off his nose and ears)". Such kinds of punishment not only strip away honour and respect from the person being punished but they "also make a spectator blush with shame at belonging to a species that can be treated that way" (TL § 39, 6:463). Here, as in the case of sexuality, the feeling of shame indicates that a person is being treated in a way that is below her dignity as a being endowed with humanity, that is, as a rational being. In the *Pedagogy*, Kant ascribes

---

17 See also PP-Powalski, 27:216. In the *Religion*, in a note added to the second edition, Kant argues that "we look upon it [*sc.* natural generation by intercourse] as something to *be ashamed* of" because it involves sensual pleasure (*Sinnenlust*) and because it "seems to relate us to the mating of animals generally far too closely (for human dignity)" (RGV 6:80 n.).

18 Cf. also Refl. 7879 where Kant argues that it is appropriate to be shameful with respect to sexuality because here "the human being becomes by his nature the object of others' desires" (AA 19:543; my translation).

19 In fact, Kant in the 1760s apparently held the view, rejected in this quotation, that "genuine shame is an instinct, which has indeed no rational cause" (*ist doch eine wirkliche Scham Instinkt, der zwar keine Vernunftursache hat* [...]) (PP-Herder, 27:49).

20 A parallel passage can be found in Kant's notes at AA 23:106.

another function to the feeling (or sense) of shame with respect to morality, namely, that a person "betrays himself as soon as he lies" (Päd 9:478). Again, Kant regards this as a natural trait of human psychology.

(4) Finally, Kant ascribes the problematic characteristics of sexual desire and action to the fact that sex is part of our *animal nature:* "If the human being becomes the enjoyment of another, this lies indeed in animality but not in humanity." (PP-Powalski, 27:216; my translation) To desire another person "in order to *enjoy* her" consists in the desire "to take immediate satisfaction in merely animal intercourse with her" (RL, Appendix, 6:359). Kant's talk of "animal intercourse" not only refers to the fact that sex consists in bodily, genital interaction (and that this "is a phenomenon in man that is entirely similar in function to that of animals": MS-Vigilantius, 27:638). Rather, Kant regards our sexual *desire* as a form of animal desire. The "sexual drive" is part of "the predisposition to animality in the human being" (RGV 6:26) which is – beside the predispositions to humanity and to personality – one of our *"original"* predispositions that "belong to the possibility of human nature" (RGV 6:28). The desires that are part of the predisposition to animality aim at the fulfilment of very basic requirements (self-preservation, preservation of the species, community with other human beings) and are distinguished from other desires in that they operate by "physical or merely *mechanical* self-love, i.e. a love for which reason is not required" (RGV 6:26).[21]

While Kant admits that proper love for the other sex can develop out of the merely animal sexual drive,[22] he believes that sexual desire, and thereby sexual intercourse, remains animal in essence: The "bodily union of the sexes" is "a union which is in itself merely an animal union" (TL § 7, 6:425). Sex remains at its core 'animal': "But as long as it is brutal[23] and aims merely at enjoyment, it is only animal instinct" (Anth-Mrongovius, 25:1361). In sex outside of marriage, the partners "both renounc[e] their personalities (in carnal or bestial cohabitation)" (RL Appendix, 6:359), all non-marital types of sexual relationships or interactions fall under the heading of "sexual union" which "takes place [...] in accordance with mere animal *nature*" (RL § 24, 6:277).

---

21 As Kant points out, the predisposition to animality "does not have reason at its *root* at all" (RGV 6:28; Kant's emphasis). Hence, reason may still be employed instrumentally in leading to the satisfaction of our animal desires (think of a *libertine* who devises ways to seduce the 'object' of his interest).

22 Namely, once it is conjoined with benevolence and consideration of the other person's happiness (Anth-Mrongovius, 25:1360 f.; Mo-Collins, 27:384 f.).

23 Note that 'brutal' here does not denote physical violence of one person against another, but means 'animal', 'beastly'.

As several passages indicate, Kant further explains the problematic character of sexual desire by its function, namely to work towards the preservation of the species. In Kant's eyes, the natural function explains the intensity of sexual desire: the two drives love of life and sexual love are "[t]he strongest impulses of nature", which represent "the invisible reason (of the ruler of the world)", in order to guarantee the survival of the individual and the species "by means of a power higher than human reason, without human reason having to work toward it" (Anth 7:276). The species is "nature's dearest pledge" (Anth 7:306). To this importance Kant also ascribes the fact that sexual desire for another person is not only independent of a regard for her well-being but indeed often in conflict with it:

> God gave us an appetite for sex which is not always love but is often entirely at odds with aiming at the happiness of the other sex. God thus based the most urgent end, one that allows no respite, namely the maintenance of the species, on an unsurmountable drive [*unüberwindlichen Trieb*]. (Refl. 7599, AA 19:466; translation modified)

Hence, the problematic tendencies that in the ethics lecture notes get associated with libertine behaviour are in Kant's eyes a feature of natural sexual desire.

In addition, on Kant's view sexual pleasure does not function merely as an end by which nature slyly motivates us to create offspring; rather, in line with medical opinion of his time,[24] Kant regards the experience of pleasure on the part of both partners to be a prerequisite for the conception of offspring: "natural generation cannot take place without sensual pleasure on both sides", which for Kant has the unfortunate consequence of bringing us close to the "mating of animals" (*Religion*, 6:80 n.).[25] So despite all the other aspects that can go into the full-fledged love for another person, in Kant's eyes sex at its core necessarily involves this kind of (desire for) sensual enjoyment which is part of our animal set-up.[26]

---

24 For instance, Laqueur (1986, 1) points out that the view that conception depends on the orgasm of the female partner came into dispute only at the end of the eighteenth century.

25 This is also why in his discussion of cases of intercourse that do not lead to procreation Kant mentions, besides sterility and times of pregnancy, the case that the female partner "finds no stimulus within her" (TL 6:426; translation Grenberg/Timmermann). On this issue, see Brecher 2018b, section III.

26 Arroyo is correct in accentuating the importance of Kant's anthropology of sex for understanding his views about objectification (Arroyo 2017, 48). He is also correct in reconstructing Kant's conception of gender relations found in the anthropological writings as a relationship of mutual dominance and dependence shaped by of our unsocial sociability (cf. Arroyo 2017, chapter 5.1). However, Kant does not draw on these observations in his diagnosis of the problem of sexual objectification. As the textual evidence presented above shows, the problem of sexual objectification has its roots in the animal core of sexual desire. In contrast to this, our passion for domination springs from our predisposition to humanity which involves self-love in comparison with others (RGV 6:27; cf.

2.3 Avoiding Objectification through Marriage

In the preceding section, I have elaborated on Kant's conception of sexual objectification. As we have seen, Kant regards sexual desire as inherently problematic: sexual desire aims at attaining pleasure through sensual stimulation in direct bodily, genital interaction; this is the natural object of sexual desire; sexual desire is part of our animality; this means it operates without reason; as such it only aims at sensual gratification. Sexual desire is the natural determining ground of sexual action; it impresses its character upon sexual action; it is this feature that constitutes the specific difference of sexual action from other types of using a person's body. The moral problem is that in sex we allow to be used in a way that is determined by this animal desire. Outside of marriage, Kant claims, this implies that we become a mere means for satisfying this desire and therefore a thing. Allowing another person to use oneself in this way is a degradation of one's person, a violation of one's humanity.

Kant argues that marriage is "the only condition" under which it is possible to have sex without violating humanity in one's own person (RL § 25, 6:278). Agents who want engage in sexual intercourse, that is, who want "to enjoy each other's sexual attributes", "*must* necessarily marry, and this is necessary in accordance with pure reason's laws of right" (RL 6:278). Many natural law theories in the late German enlightenment considered marriage a matter of contractual agreement only where the duration of the marriage and the number of persons involved are up to the parties, so that both polygamous as well as temporary marriage be compatible with natural law.[27] Kant, however, holds that only a persistent and monogamous relationship – "the union of two persons [...] for lifelong possession of each other's sexual attributes" (RL 6:277) – qualifies as legitimate marriage: "the marriage contract is not up to [the partners'] discretion but is a contract that is necessary by the law of humanity" (RL 6:277).[28]

H. Wilson 2006, 76–80). This does not rule out domination and dependence from playing an important role in Kant's overall account of sexual morality; but the diagnosis of objectification is independent of and prior to such considerations.

27 See, for instance, Achenwall, *Ius naturae*, pars posterior, § 46. In general, see the entry "Ehe (nach dem Naturrecht)" in volume 7 (1783) of the *Deutsche Encyclopädie*.

28 Cf. the *Feyerabend* notes from Kant's natural law lecture: "But is the *pactum* into which one enters with the other sex completely arbitrary? The jurists consider it as completely arbitrary". Kant's answer is No. Rather, "*Matrimonium* is *contractus commercii sexualis continui et mutui*", that is, a contract for a continuing and mutual (i.e., reciprocal, non-polygamous) sexual union (NR-Feyerabend, 27:1379; translation modified).

It is important to see that, according to Kant, marriage does not change the natural characteristics of sexual action; rather, it provides a formal condition for sexual action by which its moral implications can be averted. By establishing an exclusive lifelong bond between the spouses, marriage counteracts the arbitrariness of sexual desire and prevents the partners from being exchangeable objects of enjoyment. This is why according to Kant marriage has to be monogamous and lifelong. This is also why in Kantian marriage the partners reciprocally *possess* each other in the form of a right to a person akin to rights to things: for such a right – insofar as it specifically includes the authority to "bring[] [one's] partner back under [one's] control, just as [one] is justified in retrieving a thing" (RL § 25, 6:278) – has as its function the exclusivity of the relation (cf. RL Appendix, 6:358 f.).[29] Marriage is thus one specific condition for sex being in conformity with the dignity of humanity in one's own person.

3 The Problem of 'Unnatural' Sex and the 'Natural End' of Procreation

Considered thus far, Kant's account of sex and marriage could, as many interpreters argue,[30] apply to couples of any their sexual orientation. Indeed, as I have already indicated, Kant does not justify his concept of marriage with respect to procreation. On the contrary, he explicitly criticizes accounts, such as in traditional natural law, that predicate marriage on the "end of begetting and bringing up children". Against such accounts, Kant holds that "it is not *requisite* for human beings who marry to make this their end in order for their union to be compatible with rights" (RL § 24, 6:277).[31] However, Kant still includes in the definition of marriage – specifically, in the definition that comprises those aspects that make marriage the only sexual union "in accordance with *law*" – as one aspect that it is a "union of two persons of *different* sexes" (6:277; emphasis added). For Kant, marriage has to be a "natural sexual union" (*ibid.*) in order to qualify as a legitimate sexual relationship. The reason for this is that, according to Kant, in order to avoid

---

29 I develop a detailed account of Kant's marriage right in Brecher 2023, chapter 6. For a critical approach to Kant's marriage right, see Robert Louden's paper in this volume.

30 See the references given in the introduction of this paper.

31 In fact, Kant argues that making procreation a legal requirement of marriage would undermine its very function of solving the problem of objectification. For this function depends on the fact that marriage consists in a lifelong union, but if the pursuit of procreation were legally required by marriage then "marriage would be dissolved when procreation ceases" (RL 6:277; cf. MS-Vigilantius, 27:639).

violating one's humanity, sexual action must conform with the 'natural end' of procreation.

As I shall argue in this part of my paper, Kant draws this requirement, too, from his notion of human sexual desire and its morally problematic nature as a part of our animality. Hence, just as legal marriage is a necessary condition for sexual intercourse to be formally in accordance with humanity in our own person, so too does Kant regard the conformity with the natural end of procreation a precondition for making sexual action, which by its nature arises from animal sexual desire, formally accord with humanity.

3.1 Kant on 'Unnatural Carnal Vices'

In the *Doctrine of Right*, Kant begins the section on marriage right with the concept of "sexual union" (*commercium sexuale*) which he explicates as the reciprocal use of one's "sexual organs and capacities" (RL § 24, 6:277). In a first step, Kant then distinguishes "*natural*" and "*unnatural*" sexual use; natural sexual use is that "by which procreation of a being of the same kind is possible" (*ibid.*). As cases of "*unnatural* use" Kant names intercourse "with a person of the same sex" or "with an animal of a nonhuman species" (*ibid.*), that is, homosexual and zoophilic sexual acts. In the *Doctrine of Virtue*, Kant discusses masturbation ('defiling oneself') as the third case of "an unnatural use (and so misuse) of one's sexual attribute" (TL § 7, 6:425).

All three types of sexual acts, Kant argues, constitute a violation of humanity in one's own person (RL 6:277; TL 6:424 f.). In line with the school tradition, Kant calls these acts "unnatural vices" (*unnatürliche Laster*, 6:277, cf. 6:425), "*crimina carnis contra naturam*" (6:277, literally 'vices of the flesh contrary to nature'), and sets them apart from "*crimina carnis secundum naturam*", that is, from impermissible cases of the 'natural' use of one's sexual organs (which on Kant's account includes any non-marital sex).[32] Both kinds of sexual vice involve a violation of humanity in

---

32 See Refl. 7594, AA 19:464, and Mo-Collins, 27:390. Baumgarten, *Ethica*, § 275, distinguishes between "crimina carnis" "naturalia" and "contra naturam". In this context the term 'crimen' is not used in a specific juridical sense, but in the broad sense of impermissible, forbidden action, or of a vice, and Kant accordingly uses the German term *Laster* (cf. RL § 24, 6:277; MS-Vigilantius, 27:632). Kant does not in general regard illicit sexual acts as being subject to criminal justice, with the exception of rape, pederasty, and bestiality (RL Appendix, 6:363). A different stance is taken by Dieter Hüning who argues that Kant, by considering the *crimina carnis* a violation of the inner duty of right, intends to designate all illicit sexual acts as punishable crimes in the legal sense (see Hüning 2017).

our own person. In the case of "unnatural" sexual acts, the violation of humanity that leads to their impermissibility arises from their 'unnaturalness', that is, from the fact that procreation is not possible.

In the *Doctrine of Right*, Kant does not furnish a justification for this claim with respect to same-sex and different-species sexual acts. He merely asserts that they constitute a "wrong to humanity in our own person" (RL 6:277).[33] However, in the *Doctrine of Virtue*, Kant puts forward a "rational proof" (*Vernunftbeweis*) to show "that unnatural, and even merely unpurposive, use of one's sexual attribute is inadmissible as being a violation of duty to oneself" (6:425): "The *ground of proof* is, indeed, that by it man surrenders his personality (throwing it away), since he uses himself merely as a means to satisfy an animal impulse" (*ibid.*). Thus, like the problem of objectification, the moral problem of 'unnatural' sex, too, arises from the character of sexual desire as a desire that is rooted in our animal nature.[34]

As we have seen in section 2, sexual action, the use of our sexual attributes, has sexual desire as its natural determining ground, that is, the desire for a specific kind of pleasure generated by immediate sensuous stimulation. Kant holds that by nature sexual desire, and hence sexual action, has as its end the creation of offspring and thereby the preservation of the species: "Just as love of life is destined by nature to preserve the *person*, so sexual love [*die Liebe zum Geschlecht*] is destined by it to preserve the *species*" (TL § 7, 6:424); to this end nature has "implanted the inclinations of the sexes for each other" (RL § 24, 6:277). A sexual action is 'unnatural' if the use of the agent's sexual attributes is not in line with this end. Thus, in the case of masturbation, as Kant describes it, one's desire is "aroused [...] not by a real object" (that is, a person of the other sex), but by an object of the imagination (TL § 7, 6:424 f.). Since the desire is not directed towards its proper object and does not lead to intercourse from which offspring may result, it runs "contrary to nature's end", and the "lust" (*Wollust*) that is involved in masturbation is "unnatural" (*ibid.*). Thus, masturbation, as the action that follows from such desire,

---

33 With reference to this passage Reinhard Brandt argues that Kant apparently reverts to views from Wolffian natural teleology (Brandt 2004, 209, 212). I shall present a different take on this below.

34 With respect to TL § 7, some interpreters have argued that Kant saw the health-risks which were associated with masturbation by widespread opinion at his time (see Hull 1996, 258 ff.) as the reason for regarding it a violation of a duty to oneself (Gregor 1963, 129 f., 139–142; Kerstein 2008, 212–215; Timmons 2013, 241 f.). However, neither in the *Doctrine of Virtue*, nor in the lecture notes or the extant reflections does Kant does allude to medical aspects when discussing masturbation. Moreover, while medical risks are mentioned in the *Pedagogy*, they are there not glossed as morally problematic. What is pointed out as morally problematic is, rather, that "one transgresses the boundaries of nature, and inclination rages without arrest" (9:497 f.).

constitutes an "unnatural [...] use of one's sexual attributes" (TL 6:425). The same applies to same-sex and zoophilic intercourse: in both cases one's desire is directed towards a being intercourse with which will not lead to "procreation of a being of the same kind" (RL § 24, 6:277). In these cases, too, there is a "contravention against the end of nature" (MS-Vigilantius, 27:641).

As we have already seen, Kant's answer to the question, posed at the beginning of TL § 7, whether the human being "is authorized to direct the use of his sexual attributes to mere animal pleasure, without intending that end" (TL 6:424; translation modified), is negative: by such acts we violate a duty to ourselves. Using one's genitalia in acts that as such can only serve the satisfaction of animal sexual desire, but cannot attain the end that nature has connected with this desire and this type of act, amounts to self-instrumentalization (TL 6:425). Now, while Kant provides this argument within the context of his discussion of masturbation, it holds for his claims about the two other *crimina carnis contra naturam* as well. In fact, Kant in the argument does not only talk about the 'unnatural' use of one's genitalia in general – rather than masturbation in particular –, but he moreover includes besides the "unnatural" use also the "unpurposive" use of one's genitalia: his argument intends to show "that unnatural, and even merely unpurposive, use of one's sexual attribute is inadmissible" (TL 6:425). By the 'unpurposive' use of one's sexual attributes Kant means 'natural', but non-procreative intercourse, that is, heterosexual sex which cannot lead to procreation. In particular, Kant has in mind such cases as sex during pregnancy or when one partner or both partners are sterile (TL 6:426). Such cases are not contrary to nature's end, because the formal or relational character of the act corresponds to the natural 'setup' of our sexuality. However, insofar as in these cases the partners engage in sex "without taking this end into consideration" [*ohne auf diesen Rücksicht zu nehmen*] (TL 6:426; emphasis removed), according to Kant they, too, use themselves as mere means for satisfying their animal desire (TL 6:425; cf. Brake 2005, 76 f., and Brecher 2018a). What is important in the present context is that this shows that Kant's 'proof' not only concerns the 'unnatural' use of one's genitalia in masturbation, but applies to the other *crimina carnis contra naturam* as well.

3.2 The End of Nature and the Demands of Morality

According to Kant, sexual acts have to be in accordance with the natural end of procreation: "Nature's end in the cohabitation of the sexes is procreation, that is, the preservation of the species. Hence one may not [...] act contrary to that end" (TL 6:426). It is important to see that this requirement to adhere to the natural end of procreation, as Kant sees it, is only a negative criterion, i.e., one that agents must not act against. Kant does not hold the view that we are morally bound to actively pursue the end of procreation. Indeed, he rejects it and positions himself against traditional approaches who consider it a moral obligation of agents to contribute to the propagation of the species. Thus, Pufendorf and Wolff, for instance, argue that we are obliged to form a marital relationship to conceive offspring. Pufendorf derives this obligation from the premise that the mutual attraction of the sexes is intended to lead to procreation (Pufendorf, *De officio*, II 2 §§ 2–3). Wolff argues that because our genitals enable us to propagate the species and we have a drive to use our genitals in a way that leads to the creation of offspring, we are therefore not merely required to engage in sex *only* for procreation, but according to Wolff, we are actually under a principal *obligation to* propagate the species (Wolff, *Institutiones/Grundsätze*, § 854). Kant discusses this position in one of the notes in his copy of Achenwall's *Ius Naturae:*

> If the Divine end always had to be our end as well, then we would not only be obliged when we marry to observe this end, which God has had with our inclination, as the ground of the authorization; but we would also be obliged to marry for the sake of our organization, for God has also given us this [organization] for that end. (Refl. 7598, AA 19:466; my translation)

As the way in which Kant formulates the position indicates, he rejects the idea that we are obligated to marry for the sake of procreation, and as we have already seen, Kant explicitly rejects the view that it is a requirement for the legal validity of marriage that the spouses pursue "the begetting and raising of offspring" (RL § 24, 6:277; cf. Refl. 7580, AA 19:461).

In contrast to the natural law tradition, for Kant the end of procreation is not an end that we have to set ourselves to pursue actively, it is not the object of a positive duty. Rather, if we want to engage in sex, we have to do so in a way that is in accordance with the natural purposiveness of our sexual capacities. The duty to adhere to the end of procreation is merely conditional and negative. Against the backdrop of Kant's anthropological claims about the nature of sexual action being determined by an animal desire for sensuous pleasure and his moral claims that acting on as well as becoming an object of animal desire, it becomes apparent that Kant regards this requirement as a condition that enables us to act from sexual desire without thereby degrading humanity in our own person – just as marriage is a conditional requirement or giving oneself to another person for sexual enjoyment. For Kant, it is not the fact as such that 'unnatural' sex does not lead to procreation that makes it inadmissible in his eyes, but the fact that it only serves the gratification of animal pleasure. In contrast, the property of being purposive with respect to procreation makes a sexual act *pro tanto* be in accordance with humanity in our own person (*pro tanto*, since of course further conditions have to be fulfilled).[35]

However, how can the correspondence of an action to an end of nature be morally relevant? How can it licence (at least *pro tanto*) acting on an animal inclination? As I have pointed out at the beginning of the paper, interpreters argue that considerations of what is natural or unnatural should apparently have no place in an *a priori* moral philosophy grounded on pure practical reason. Hence, Kant's appeal to natural ends appears both normatively and methodologically problematic. However, while we may disagree with Kant's normative conclusions, I think that Kant's argument can be construed in a way that it is methodologically in line with his theory of natural teleology. In what follows, I shall outline how Kant's idea that the adherence to the end of procreation can be a licencing reason for engaging in (as such animalistic) sexual action may be construed as warranted given both the specific content of teleological judgments about organisms the methodological and character of teleological judgment.

Kant claims that procreation is the purpose of sexual desire ("inclinations of the sexes" [*Geschlechtsneigung*]: RL 6:277; "sexual love" [*Liebe zum Geschlecht*]: TL 6:424) and hence of "the cohabitation of the sexes", that is, of sexual action (6:426). More specifically, he characterizes the connection between sex and procreation as an instance of natural purposiveness: procreation, or the preservation of the species, is "an end of nature" (RL 6:277), "nature's end" (TL 6:425) (*Zweck der Natur* both times), "a natural end" [*Naturzweck*] (6:426). As the use of these terms indicates, Kant's characterization of this purposiveness makes use of teleological judgment about nature as expounded in the second part of the *Critique of the Power of Judgment*. The connection to the third *Critique* is made very explicit at the opening of TL § 7:

> Just as love of life is destined by nature to preserve the person, so sexual love is destined by it to preserve the species; in other words, each of these is a *natural end*, by which is understood that connection of a cause with an effect in which, although no understanding is ascribed to the cause, it is still thought by analogy with an intelligent cause, and so as if it produced men on purpose. (TL 6:424)

---

35 Thus, in one of his notes relating to Bouterwek's 1797 review of the *Doctrine or Right*, Kant argues that while "by this giving of his body to use as a thing the human being always does something which must shame him, because it is actually in itself beneath the dignity of humanity, though due to natural need it has become a permissive law to leave human kind and the propagation of the species not to choice by reason but instead to entrust them to the animal instinct" (AA 20:463 f.; translation modified).

To regard sexuality as purposive is to consider it in analogy with intentional causality, hence *as if* nature intended to bring about offspring by means of sexual desire (and action). This corresponds precisely to Kant's explanation of teleological judgment in the *Critique of the Power of Judgment*. By judging an object teleologically, "we represent the possibility of the object in accordance with the analogy of such a causality (like the kind we encounter in ourselves)", that is, "in *analogy* with causality according to ends" (KU § 61, 5:360).

One important application of teleological judgment is to organisms. In the third *Critique*, Kant argues that we can only make sense of the natural processes of growth, reproduction and regeneration, which are the defining marks of organisms, by considering them teleologically as internally purposive (KU § 64, 5:370 f.). An object exists as a natural end if the being "is cause and effect of itself" (KU 5:370; emphasis removed). In reproduction, an organism generates another organism of the same species. It thereby "generates itself as far as the *species* is concerned" and can be considered cause and effect of itself: within the species, the organism, "on one side as effect, on the other as cause, unceasingly produces itself, and likewise, often producing itself, continuously preserves itself, as species" (KU 5:370). In regarding an organism as a natural end, the causal relations of growth, reproduction and regeneration are considered such that they are directed towards the whole organism as their end; the different parts of an organism exist for the sake of the whole organism (KU § 65, 5:372–374).[36]

Through reproduction an organism is the cause of itself (if only in kind), the reproductive process, thus, has the organism itself (in kind) as an end. Applied to Kant's theory of sexuality, sexual desire leads us to bring about other beings of the same kind through our desire for the pleasure generated through the use of one's genitalia; through sexual intercourse the human being is the cause of itself in kind. Judging human sexual desire and action teleologically involves the claim that the animal desire constitutive of this action has as its end the human being. Now, since the defining mark of the human being is humanity, we can say that through its natural purposiveness sexuality has humanity as its end. This, I suggest, is the reason why Kant thinks that acting in accordance with this purposiveness is a necessary condition of preserving the dignity of humanity in sexual action.

---

36 In the case of reproduction, the purposive relation of parts as means to the whole as end applies to the directedness of the two sexes towards each other, too. As Kant argues, in "the organization of the two sexes in relation to one another for the propagation of their kind", we find the only "external purposiveness that is connected with the internal purposiveness of organization": The pair of the two sexes "first constitutes an *organizing* whole, although not one that is organized in a single body" (KU § 82, 5:425).

Kant's recourse to natural ends in his sexual morals is criticized by interpreters because Kant regards teleological judgment as merely regulative, ascribing to it a heuristic function, and not as being constitutive of experience, which is the domain of mechanical causal explanation (e.g., Guyer 2005).[37] However, I think such concerns can be dispelled. First, within Kant's anthropology teleological judgment finds wide application, indeed what sets anthropology "apart from any other empirical science, in general, is its teleological nature" (H. Wilson 2006, 36), and this seems unproblematic insofar as anthropology is at bottom concerned with human agency which of course is defined by its teleological structure. Secondly, the fact that Kant holds that, properly speaking, there *are* no ends *in nature*, that is, that the principle of teleological judgment "lies only in the idea of the one who judges and never in any efficient cause" (KU § 66, 5:376), does not speak against Kant's recourse to teleological judgment in case of sexual action. One may argue that, on the contrary, the 'as if' character of teleological judgment is what warrants its employment for construing the nature of sexual action: for on Kant's view it is not nature that prescribes ends to us, but it is reason itself that, occasioned by experience (5:376), ascribes ends to nature. Finally, we should consider Kant's employment of teleology as an attempt to find conditions under which animal sexual desire can be said to have humanity in our own person as its end. Given the (as Kant sees it) problematic nature of sexual desire and given that "man, after all, possesses this impulse by nature" (Mo-Collins, 27:385), we need to identify conditions under which acting on this impulse is in accordance with our dignity as rational moral beings (*ibid.*). While we may disagree with Kant's normative conclusion, in his view the teleological consideration of our sexuality provides us with one such condition required for aligning our sexual desire, springing from our animality, with our rational nature.

4 Conclusion

I have argued that for Kant the fundamental problem of sexual morals lies in, or stems from, the nature of sexual desire. He regards sexual desire as a form of animal desire that seeks enjoyment, immediate sensuous gratification of a specific

---

37 Teleological judgment "belongs to the reflecting, not to the determining power of judgment" (*ibid.*): its function is not to determine a particular object by subsuming it under a given universal concept, but to find a universal to a given particular (KU, Introduction, 5:179). As an exercise of our reflecting power of judgment, teleological judgment has a merely heuristic function for our research into nature by bringing objects in nature, namely organisms, "under principles of observation and research" (KU § 61, 5:360).

kind. This desire for sexual enjoyment is the natural determining ground of sexual action, it thus specifically differentiates this type of action from other forms of the use of one's body. Making oneself an object of this impulse, Kant argues, contradicts our status as autonomous beings with dignity. As he argues in his ethics lecture from the mid-1770s, the problem pertains to the act itself. However, "conditions must be possible, under which alone the use of the *facultates sexuales* is compatible with morality" (Mo-Collins, 27:386). The task of sexual morals is to specify these conditions. These conditions have to address two questions: "To what extent is anyone entitled to make use of their sexual impulse, without impairing their humanity? How far can a person allow another person of the opposite sex to satisfy his or her inclination upon them?" (Mo-Collins, 27:386).[38]

Kant's answer to the second question is marriage: within the context of a life-long and exclusive sexual relationship, in which the partners reciprocally possess each other by right, they can surrender themselves to each other for sexual enjoyment without becoming mere means for the satisfaction of the other's animal desire. Kant's answer to the first question is that the sexual act must conform to the natural purposiveness of our sexuality, that is, it must conform to the end of procreation; this conformity ensures – *pro tanto* – that the sexual use does not only serve sensuous gratification, but that it can be judged to have at the same time the human being, hence humanity, as its end.

Both of Kant's criteria, marriage and the 'naturalness' criterion, respond to the specific characteristic of sexual desire. One cannot, therefore, retain Kant's claims about sexual objectification, while eschewing his arguments about 'unnatural' sex. Both turn on the same anthropological view of sexual desire and action. If one's aim is to develop a contemporary conception of marriage on the basis of Kant's account of marriage, one either has to replace Kant's notion of sexual objectification and with it his anthropology of sexual desire with a different notion of human sexuality, or – if the aim is to keep Kant's overall theory of sexuality – one has to revise Kant's claims about what the natural end of sex actually is. This seems to be the only way to accommodate same-sex marriage within Kant's own framework.

One way to revise Kant's notion of the natural end of sex is to ascribe one or more further natural ends (such that the human being can be judged to be the end of the action) to the use of one's sexual capacities. Some interpreters (e.g. Denis 1999, 237) point out that Kant assigns a second end of nature to the female sex: the culturalization of the male sex. Through man's desire for woman, man can

---

38 In TL § 7 Kant, in part implicitly, names the same two questions: while "[i]n the Doctrine of Right it was shown that man cannot make use of another person to get this pleasure apart from a special limitation" (namely marriage), "the question here is whether man is subject to a duty to himself with regard to this enjoyment" (TL 6:424).

be "led by her, if not to morality itself, to that which is its cloak, moral decency, which is the preparation for morality and its recommendation" (Anth 7:306). While this shows that Kant does have a nuanced (albeit debatable) overall picture of human sexuality, it does not provide us with a way to revise Kant's views regarding the natural end of the use of the sexual faculties as such. As I understand Kant, the nature-instilled social dynamics of the sexes that he envisages work apart from (and indeed in opposition to) sexual action as such. Apart from being premised on a problematic conception of heterosexual gender relations, the purpose of prompting the development of finer feelings in man, thereby making him more susceptible to morality, does not change the morally problematic nature of the sexual act itself.

If we want to revise Kant's distinction of 'natural' and 'unnatural' sex, we would have to identify a natural function related to sexual intercourse itself, because this act, insofar as it results from an animal desire, is what is problematic. Now, as we have seen above, for Kant the experience of 'animal' sexual pleasure is an essential part of, and even required for, conception. An alternative natural end that could serve as a surrogate for the end of procreation in a revised account would have to be just as closely tied to sexual desire and action. Maybe the emotional attachment to one's partner, which is enhanced by sexual enjoyment, could serve as such an end. First, it is part of the natural workings of our 'animal' sexuality and is involved in the sexual act itself. Secondly, it can be judged purposively with respect to our rational nature since it counteracts the 'disregarding' tendencies of our volatile sexual interest in the other person which Kant points out. If revised in this way, Kant's account of 'natural' sex could include same-sex sex as well.

However, I should like to end by pointing out that even with such a revision, retaining Kant's anthropology of sex means retaining, at least *prima facie*, his problematic concept of marriage as a monogamous, lifelong relationship marked by rights of possession: for this concept is justified by Kant with respect to the problem of sexual objectification. If one's aim is to justify marriage based on Kant's reasoning about sexual objectification, one in principle not only has to retain his overall notion of sexuality, but also his particular concept of marriage as the solution to that problem which he identifies on the basis of his anthropology of sex. One cannot have both, Kant's particular views about the problematic nature of sex on the one hand and on the other a modern sexual morality with a modern concept of marriage that allows for same-sex marriage as well as for amicable divorce and open marriages (as e.g., Varden 2017, 351, suggests). Thus it may make more sense, in the end, to think about the moral implications that our sexuality has with respect to our rational nature as autonomous agents not so much along the lines of Kant's own account, and thus within the confines of it, but in an overall more critical engagement with Kant's sexual morals and its different elements.

References

Achenwall, Gottfried, 1763, *Ius Naturae*, 5th edition, 2 vols., Göttingen.

Altman, Matthew C., 2010, "Kant on Sex and Marriage: The Implications for the Same-Sex Marriage Debate", *Kant-Studien*, 101, 309–330.

Altman, Matthew C., 2011, *Kant and Applied Ethics. The Uses and Limits of Kant's Practical Philosophy*, Malden, MA: Wiley-Blackwell.

Arroyo, Christopher, 2017, *Kant's Ethics and the Same-Sex Marriage Debate. An Introduction*, Cham: Springer.

Baumgarten, Alexander Gottlieb, 1751/1763, *Ethica philosophica*, 2nd and 3rd editions, Halle: Hemmerde [The text of both editions is reprinted in vol. 27 of the Academy edition of Kant's writings.]

Bouterwek, Friedrich, 1797, Review of Kant's *Metaphysische Anfangsgründe der Rechtslehre. Göttingische Anzeigen von gelehrten Sachen*, No 28 (18 February 1797), 265–276. Reprinted in AA 20:445–453.

Bouterwek, Friedrich, 1799, Review of Kant's "Erläuternde Anmerkungen zu den *Metaphysischen Anfangsgründen der Rechtslehre*". *Göttingische Anzeigen von gelehrten Sachen*, No. 120 (29 July 1799), 1197–1200.

Bouterwek, Friedrich, 2014, "Friedrich Bouterwek's reviews of Kant's *Metaphysical Foundations of the Doctrine of Right*", translated by Kenneth R. Westphal, *Kant Studies Online*, 2014, 240–261. Available online at https://kantstudiesonline.net/uploads/files/BouterwekWestphal02214.pdf [last accessed 15 June 2023].

Brake, Elizabeth, 2005, "Justice and Virtue in Kant's Account of Marriage", *Kantian Review*, 9, 58–94.

Brake, Elizabeth, 2012, *Minimizing Marriage. Marriage, Morality, and the Law*, New York: Oxford University Press.

Brandt, Reinhard, 2004, "Kants Ehe- und Kindesrecht", *Deutsche Zeitschrift für Philosophie*, 52, 199–219.

Brecher, Martin, 2018a, "Ehelicher Geschlechtsgebrauch und Fortpflanzungszweck in § 7 der *Tugendlehre*", in: Violetta L. Waibel, Margit Ruffing, and David Wagner (eds.), *Natur und Freiheit. Akten des 12. Internationalen Kant-Kongresses*. Berlin/Boston: de Gruyter, 1761–1768.

Brecher, Martin, 2018b, "Ein Zwangsrecht auf Geschlechtsverkehr? Das kantische Vernunftrecht und die 'eheliche Pflicht'", *Aufklärung. Interdisziplinäres Jahrbuch zur Erforschung des 18. Jahrhunderts und seiner Wirkungsgeschichte*, 30, 93–118.

Brecher, Martin, 2023, *Vernunftrecht und Verdinglichung. Eine Rekonstruktion von Kants Eherecht*. Berlin/Boston: de Gruyter.

Crusius, Christian August, 1744, *Anweisung vernünfftig zu leben*, 1st edition, Leipzig. Reprinted in: Christian August Crusius. *Die philosophischen Hauptwerke*, ed. Giorgio Tonelli, vol. 1, Hildesheim: Olms 1969.

Denis, Lara, 1999, "Kant on the Wrongness of 'Unnatural' Sex", *History of Philosophy Quarterly*, 16, 225–248.

Deutsche Encyclopädie oder Allgemeines Real-Wörterbuch aller Künste und Wissenschaften, eds. Heinrich Martin Gottfried Köster and Johann Friedrich Roos, 23 vols. (unfinished), Frankfurt a. M. 1788–1804.

Gregor, Mary, 1963, *Laws of Freedom: A Study of Kant's Method of Applying the Categorical Imperative in the "Metaphysik der Sitten"*, New York: Barnes & Noble.

Guyer, Paul, 2005, "Ends of Reason and Ends of Nature: The Place of Teleology in Kant's Ethics", in: Paul Guyer, *Kant's System of Nature and Freedom. Selected Essays*, Oxford: Oxford University Press, 169–197.

Halwani, Raja, 2010, Love, Sex, and Marriage, New York: Routledge.

Herman, Barbara, 1993, "Could It Be Worth Thinking About Kant on Sex and Marriage?", in: Louise M. Antony and Charlotte Witt (eds.), *A Mind of One's Own: Feminist Essays on Reason and Objectivity*. Boulder, CO: Westview Press, 49–68.

Hull, Isabel V., 1996, *Sexuality, State, and Civil Society in Germany, 1700–1815*, Ithaca/London: Cornell University Press.

Hüning, Dieter, 2017, "Kant und die crimina carnis. Zur Anwendungsproblematik der inneren Rechtspflichten". in: Bernd Dörflinger, Dieter Hüning, and Günter Kruck (eds.), *Das Verhältnis von Recht und Ethik in Kants praktischer Philosophie*, Hildesheim/Zürich/New York: Olms, 257–288.

Kerstein, Samuel J., 2008, "Treating Oneself Merely as Means", in: Monika Betzler (ed.), *Kant's Ethics of Virtue*, Berlin/New York, 201–218.

Krünitz, Johann Georg (founding editor), 1773–1858, *Oeconomische Encyclopädie, oder allgemeines System der Land- Haus- und Staats-Wirthschaft*, 242 vols., Berlin.

Laqueur, Thomas, 1986, "Orgasm, Generation, and the Politics of Reproductive Biology", *Representations*, 14, 1–41.

Nussbaum, Martha C., 1999, "Objectification", in: Martha C. Nussbaum, *Sex and Social Justice*, Oxford: Oxford University Press, 213–239.

Pufendorf, Samuel, 1673, *De officio hominis et civis juxta legem naturalem libri duo*, Lund. English translation: *The Whole Duty of Man. According to the Law of Nature*, translated by Andrew Tooke [1691], edited by Ian Hunter and David Saunders, Indianapolis: Liberty Fund 2003.

Rinne, Pärttyli, 2018, *Kant on Love*, Berlin/Boston: de Gruyter.

Sadler, Brook J., 2013, "Marriage: A Matter of Right or of Virtue? Kant and the Contemporary Debate", *Journal of Social Philosophy*, 44, 213–232.

Schaff, Kory, 2001, "Kant, Political Liberalism, and the Ethics of Same-Sex Relations", *Journal of Social Philosophy*, 32, 446–462.

Schütz, Friedrich Karl Julius, 1834, *Christian Gottfried Schütz. Darstellung seines Lebens, Charakters und Verdienstes; nebst einer Auswahl aus seinem litterarischen Briefwechsel mit den berühmtesten Gelehrten und Dichtern seiner Zeit*, 2 vols., Halle.

Soble, Alan, 1998, *The Philosophy of Sex and Love. An Introduction*, St. Paul, MN: Paragon House.

Timmons, Mark, 2013, "The Perfect Duty to Oneself as an Animal Being (TL 6:421–428)", in: Andreas Trampota, Oliver Sensen, and Jens Timmermann (eds.), *Kant's "Tugendlehre"*, Berlin/Boston: de Gruyter, 221–243.

Varden, Helga, 2017, "Kant and Sexuality", in: Matthew C. Altman (ed.), *The Palgrave Kant Handbook*, London: Palgrave Macmillan, 331–353.

Varden, Helga, 2020, *Sex, Love, and Gender. A Kantian Theory*, Oxford: Oxford University Press.

Wilson, Donald, 2004, "Kant and the Marriage Right", in: *Pacific Philosophical Quarterly* 85, 103–123.

Wilson, Holly L., 2006, *Kant's Pragmatic Anthropology. Its Origin, Meaning, And Critical Significance*, Albany: SUNY Press.

Wolff, Christian, 1736, *Vernünfftige Gedancken von dem gesellschaftlichen Leben der Menschen und insonderheit dem gemeinen Wesen zur Beförderung der Glückseligkeit des menschlichen Geschlechts [Deutsche Politik]*, 4th edition, Frankfurt/Leipzig.

Wolff, Christian, 1750/1754, *Institutiones juris naturae et gentium*, Halle 1750. German translation: *Grundsätze des Natur- und Völckerrechts.* Halle 1754.

Melissa Seymour Fahmy
How to Have Good Kantian Sex

Abstract: Most regard Kant's views on sex as unacceptable. Contemporary Kantians stand in need of a more plausible, and yet still Kantian, moral theory of human sexual relations. This paper aims to provide such an account. Good Kantian sex is sex that is compatible with all of our moral obligations. I argue that while obtaining valid consent may be sufficient to avoid using our partners merely as means, it is not sufficient for either permissible or morally worthy sex according to Kantian standards. We must additionally avoid acting on impermissible maxims and give careful consideration to the happiness and well-being of our sexual partners. Adopting the obligatory end *others' happiness* as our own requires that we care about whether our interest in sex is compatible with our partner's. This in turn entails obligations related to practices of self-reflection and transparency.

1 Kant on Sex

Kant's views about sex are fairly notorious. According to Kant, sexual desire for other persons necessarily involves objectifying them and frequently entails dishonoring their humanity. Consider the following passages from the *Lectures on Ethics.*

> In loving from sexual inclination, they make the person into an object of their appetite. As soon as the person is possessed, and the appetite sated, they are thrown away, as one throws away a lemon after sucking the juice from it. (Mo-Collins 27:384)

> Since the sexual impulse is not an inclination that one human has for another, qua human, but an inclination for their sex, it is therefore a *principium* of the debasement of humanity, a source for the preference of one sex over the other, and the dishonouring of that sex by satisfying the inclination. (Mo-Collins 27:385)

> So if a man wishes to satisfy his inclination, and a woman hers, they each attract the other's inclination to themselves, and both urges impinge on one another, and are directed, not to humanity at all, but to sex, and each partner dishonours the humanity of the other. (Mo-Collins 27:384)[1]

---

[1] All volume and page numbers refer to the Prussian Academy editions of Kant's *gesammelte Schriften*. Citations refer to the following English translations of Kant's work: *Lectures on Ethics* (Mo-Collins, MS-Vigilantius), translated by Peter Heath; *Religion within the Boundaries of Mere Reason* (RGV), translated by Allen Wood and George Di Giovanni; *Groundwork of the Metaphysics of Morals* (GMS) and *The Metaphysics of Morals* (MS), both translated by Mary Gregor.

https://doi.org/10.1515/9783111291130-005

Given such unrestrained condemnation, one might expect Kant to advocate total celibacy, but this is not the case. Kant understands the human sex drive to be part of our predisposition to animality, which he identifies as one of three predispositions to the *good* in human nature (RGV 6:26). The human sex drive is a predisposition to the good insofar as it serves the end of the propagation of the species.[2] This leaves Kant endorsing seemingly contradictory views. Sexual appetite or impulse is part of our predisposition to the good and yet, according to Kant, there is something *contemptible* about human sexual activity (Mo-Collins 27:386). As one might expect, Kant is no romantic. Love and affection are not the answer to the inherently morally problematic nature of sex. Rather, the solution, according to Kant, is the rightful reciprocal acquisition of one another through the legal institution of marriage. As he explains it,

> The sole condition, under which there is freedom to make use of one's sexual impulse, is based upon the right to dispose over the whole person. This right to dispose over the other's whole person relates to the total state of happiness, and to all circumstances bearing upon that person. But this right that I have, so to dispose, and thus also to employ the *organa sexualia* to satisfy sexual impulse – how do I obtain it? In that I give the other person such a right over my whole person, and this happens only in marriage. *Matrimonium* signifies a contract between two persons, in which they mutually accord equal rights to one another, and submit to the condition that each transfers his whole person. (Mo-Collins 27:388)[3]

I am by no means the first to observe that there is much to find objectionable in Kant's account of human sexuality.[4] The view that human sexual desire and sexual activity *necessarily* entail objectification of our partners runs contrary to the experience of many. Granted, it is not difficult to find examples of sexual desire and gratification that *do* involve objectification of another; however, this is far from sufficient for concluding that sexual desire must *necessarily* take this form. To my way of thinking, Kant's account is just too simple. Human sexuality is more complex than Kant recognizes or is willing to acknowledge. This is perhaps understandable given the rules of sexual propriety characteristic of 18th century Prussia. But if we examine how, when, and why human beings engage in sex when they are (more or less) free to do so, we quickly see that talk of biological appetite and its satisfaction is woefully under-descriptive.

---

2 See also MS 6:426 and MS-Vigilantius 27:638.

3 See also MS-Vigilantius 27:638 f. and MS 6:277–280. Notably, even in the context of marriage, a sexual partner "is acquired by the other *as if it were a thing*" (MS 6:278).

4 See Herman (1993), Denis (1999), and Varden (2007, 2020) for critiques. See Soble (2017) for an attempt to render consistent Kant's thoughts on sex and marriage.

And even if we were inclined to accept that sex necessarily entailed objectification, the idea that marriage could be the solution to this problem seems highly implausible. As Barbara Herman describes it, Kant's account of marriage "is a mess in Kant's own terms". It is a mess because

> it does not [...] make sense to 'grant reciprocal rights' over a self when one's self is not the sort of thing over which there can be rights. Nor is there any need for marriage as a public institution, because the granting of reciprocal rights, if one had them, would be a matter of free contract.[5]

If Kant's own views on sex are not ones contemporary Kantians can endorse, then we must construct a more plausible, and yet still Kantian, moral theory of human sexual relations.[6]

Alan Wertheimer has described the work such a theory should do in the following terms:

> A full moral theory of sexual relations would answer at least three questions: (1) when are sexual relations morally *unworthy*, or *bad?* (2) when are sexual relations morally *impermissible* or *wrong?* (3) when should sexual relations be *illegal* or *criminal?*[7]

These three questions suggest three distinct yet related standards for evaluating human sexual relations. Presumably, sexual relations that are criminal are also impermissible and unworthy, though not all instances of impermissible sex are (or should be) criminal. We could represent the ways sexual relations fall below some ideal moral standard as a set of concentric circles. Criminal sexual activity would be the smallest circle contained within the circle representing morally impermissible sexual activity, which itself would be contained within the largest circle representing morally unworthy sexual relations. While Kant's practical philosophy contains resources for answering all three of Wertheimer's questions, my

---

5 Herman (1993, 61).

6 Helga Varden's recent book, *Sex, Love, and Gender: A Kantian Theory* (2020), constructs and defends a more complete and inclusive philosophical theory of sex, love, and gender grounded in Kant's practical philosophy and theory of human nature. My focus in this paper is on what Varden calls "morally justifiable" sexual engagement. I develop an account of the obligatory ends that is more nuanced and demanding than Varden and other commentators have recognized, and demonstrate how it is applicable to a moral theory of human sexual relations.

7 Wertheimer (2003, 5). In addition to Wertheimer's three questions, which focus on ways sexual relations can be morally deficient, a full moral theory of sexual relations should also answer the question *when are sexual relations conducive to living a virtuous and fully flourishing human life?* This question, like Wertheimer's third question, is beyond the scope of this paper. See Denis (2007) and Varden (2020) for Kantian responses to this additional question.

interest in this paper lies with the two larger circles, those corresponding to morally unworthy and morally impermissible sexual relations.[8] I will use the phrase *good Kantian sex*, to describe sex that it not merely permissible, but also not morally unworthy or bad.[9]

Good Kantian sex is sex that is fully compatible with all our moral requirements, both strict requirements, like the prohibition against using persons merely as means, as well as wide or imperfect ones, like the duty to make others' happiness one's end. In the following section, I use Kant's formula of humanity as an initial point of departure. Very generally, good Kantian sex must be compatible with treating oneself and one's partner as ends in themselves.[10] To treat persons as ends requires, first and foremost, not using them merely as means. I concur with those who have argued that to avoid using others merely as means in sexual relations (as well as other contexts) we must obtain their valid consent.[11] In sections two and three, I consider the conditions that must be satisfied for consent to be valid or normatively transformative. Some of these conditions have been well-explored in literature on consent (e. g. the absence of deception and coercion), while others are distinctly Kantian (e. g. not lying beyond the limits of one's normative authority). In section three, I consider whether the more robust standard of *informed* consent, one comparable to what we find in the practice of medicine, is the appropriate standard for valid consent to sexual relations. I argue it is not.

While obtaining valid consent may be sufficient to avoid using our partners merely as means, it is not a sufficient condition for permissible sex, at least not according to Kantian standards. I argue that valid consent cannot be sufficient insofar as one can act on an impermissible maxim while engaging in consensual sexual relations.[12] More importantly, good Kantian sex is morally better than merely permissible sex. In section four, I demonstrate how the duties of virtue Kant describes in his later work provide additional moral guidance for how we ought to engage in sexual relations with others. I argue that obligatory ends give rise to both negative and positive obligations, and that acting in a manner consistent

---

8 Wertheimer, in contrast, focuses on morally impermissible and criminal sexual relations. See Varden (2007, 2020) for explorations of the Kantian juridical standard for rightful sexual relations.
9 I acknowledge that the phrase 'not bad Kantian sex' might be a better choice in terms of accuracy; however, I suspect the reader will agree that 'not bad Kantian sex' sounds far less attractive than 'good Kantian sex'.
10 For the purposes of this paper, I intend to ignore masturbation and bestiality, as well as sexual activity involving minors or incompetent adults. All references to *sexual relations* should thus be understood as activity that involves two or more competent adults including prostitution.
11 See O'Neill (1985), Wertheimer (2003), Dougherty (2013), Mappes (2017), Kleingeld (2020).
12 This point has been made previously. See Morgan (2017).

with the obligatory end *others' happiness* requires that we care about whether our interest in sex is compatible with our partner's. This in turn entails obligations related to practices of self-reflection and transparency. From the Kantian perspective, sex can be morally deficient even when it is both consensual and permissible. The conclusion I draw is that the more robust standard of informed consent is the standard we should endeavor to satisfy as a condition for engaging in sex that is morally better than merely permissible.

Though it was not my intention, what I find myself doing in this paper is vindicating Kant's view that there is something *morally precarious* about human sexual relations. I draw on Onora O'Neill's work to make the case that there are some formidable obstacles to obtaining informed consent to sexual relations, obstacles that are not well-captured by the familiar concern to avoid deception and coercion. Though I disagree with Kant's descriptions of the nature of sexual desire and gratification, I am sympathetic to his view that the arena of human sexual relations is fraught with the danger of mistreating others and allowing ourselves to be used in morally problematic ways. Because my interest lies in articulating what is required to satisfy the highest of the three moral standards identified by Wertheimer (not morally unworthy rather than merely permissible or non-criminal), the analysis I offer will be more applicable to sex education curricula than criminal law.

2 The Normative Significance of Consent

Kant provides three distinct formulations of the categorical imperative in his *Groundwork of the Metaphysics of Morals*. The first commands agents to act only on maxims they can will as universal laws (GMS 4:421). The second formulation, commonly referred to as the formula of humanity, commands agents to "act so that you use humanity, whether in your own person or in the person of any other, always at the same time as an end, never merely as a means" (GMS 4:429). One significant interpretive challenge this formulation of the categorical imperative presents is articulating plausible criteria for distinguishing *permissible* cases of using others – that is using others in ways consistent with regarding them as ends in themselves – from *impermissible* cases of using others. Consent has arguably been one of the most important concepts in meeting this challenge.[13] By way of example, in his book, *How to Treat Persons*, Samuel Kerstein develops and defends three distinct sufficient conditions for using another merely as means,

---

13 See O'Neill (1985), Korsgaard (1986), Parfit (2011), Kerstein (2013), Formosa (2014), and Kleingeld (2020).

as well as one necessary condition, and two sufficient conditions for *not* using another merely as means. All six of these accounts reference the presence, absence, or possibility of consent.

To understand why consent is so important we must look to what Kant calls the *ground* of the formula of humanity, the idea that rational nature exists as an end in itself (GMS 4:428 f.). Persons are ends in themselves in virtue of their rational nature or moral personality (GMS 4:435). Rational nature, Kant tells us, "is the supreme limiting condition of the freedom of action of every human being" (GMS 4:431). Notably, Kant contends that humanity (i.e. rational nature) is also the source of the one innate right we may all claim, the right to freedom, which Kant describes as "independence from being constrained by another's choice insofar as it can coexist with the freedom of every other in accordance with universal law" (MS 6:237).[14] Treating persons as ends in themselves calls for the recognition of their unique status, as well as the authority it entails. By making consent a condition of our acting, we acknowledge and respect others' moral and juridical authority – authority over their bodies, their property, their labor, etc. As Arthur Ripstein describes it,

> [...] consent is important against the background of a more general idea that private persons are free and equal to each other in the sense that each is entitled to pursue whatever purposes he or she might have, provided that this can be done in a way that is consistent with a like freedom for others to pursue their purposes [...] Consent is fundamental to this picture, because it enables people to modify the boundaries that make their equal freedom with others possible [...] That is why consent serves as a defense. It enables one person to permit another to do what would otherwise be forbidden.[15]

Demarcating the precise boundaries of our moral and juridical authority is not a simple matter, but the point remains that respect demands that we ought not cross these boundaries without permission or a truly compelling moral reason. The body, one's physical person, marks one such significant and relatively uncontroversial boundary, and it is this boundary that is most relevant to the ethics of human sexual relations.

---

14 See Pallikkathayil (2010) for an excellent discussion of the relationship between Kant's political philosophy and the formula of humanity.
15 Ripstein (2009: 133 f.).

2.1 Freedom from Deception and Coercion

Rape and assault are reprehensible insofar as they involve crossing important physical boundaries without permission, that is, in the absence of consent. Consent, however, can do the normative work of transforming an impermissible act into a permissible one only if it satisfies certain conditions. Some of these conditions have been well-explored in the literature. There is wide consensus that for consent to be normatively transformative, the consenting agent must not be deceived or coerced. Deception precludes the possibility of valid consent insofar as the deceived agent is misled regarding some fundamental aspect of the proposed action.[16] What the deceived agent consents to is not how the deceiver intends to use her. This is how Kant explains why false promising is incompatible with treating persons as ends in themselves. The victim of a false promise "cannot possibly agree to my way of behaving toward him" and thus we must conclude that the false promiser intends to use the other merely as means (GMS 4:429 f.). When we intentionally mislead others to get them to cooperate with us, we fail to respect their authority, and we act as if securing our discretionary ends were more important than respecting their rational nature. Notably, if we include lies of omission within the scope of deception, and I think we should, then avoiding deception will require more than refraining from making false claims with the intent to deceive. To secure valid consent, I will be obliged to refrain from misleading and to correct misperceptions should they occur.[17]

Coercion presents a problem that is more difficult to articulate. Technically, the one being coerced knows what is going on and is provided an opportunity to make a choice and withhold her cooperation; however, the coercer arranges things such that withholding cooperation comes at an unreasonably high cost. The paradigmatic example is the gunman who threatens to shoot you if you do not hand over your wallet. The gunman's threats are morally problematic insofar as he threatens to do what he has no right to do. Once the gunman has uttered his credible threat, he has rendered the victim unable to provide valid consent. This is to say that the victim's cooperation or even explicit permission cannot make it permissible for the gunman to take the victim's wallet or anything else. Contemporary scholarship

---

16 See O'Neill (1985), Korsgaard (1986), Wertheimer (2003), Dougherty (2013), Mappes (2017), and Kleingeld (2020).

17 According to Mappes, "If A has good reason to believe that B would refuse to consent to sexual interaction should B become aware of certain factual information, and A withholds disclosure of this information in order to enhance the possibility of gaining B's consent, then, if B does consent, A sexually uses B [merely as means] via deception" (2017: 278). I think this view is correct. See also Dougherty (2013).

on coercion has explored when costs imposed on others for refusing their cooperation are unreasonable or morally problematic.[18] I will not attempt to work out a theory of coercion here. For the purposes of the paper, it is sufficient to note that many forms of coercion have the effect of making valid consent impossible.

2.2 Intoxication

Can intoxicated persons give valid consent? Drugs and alcohol impair our judgment and our ability to communicate. The relationship between valid consent and intoxication, however, is complicated by the fact that intoxication occurs in varying degrees. At one end of the spectrum are persons who are so intoxicated that they are deemed to be "incapacitated". Those who are incapacitated from drugs or alcohol cannot give valid consent insofar as their incapacitation renders them unable to clearly express or token consent.[19] On the other end of the spectrum are persons who experience mild effects from the minimal consumption of intoxicating substances. They may feel more relaxed or experience reduced social inhibitions, but such persons are still fully capable of expressing themselves. And then there is everything in between. How many drinks is too many for valid consent? Surely there is a point prior to becoming unconscious or even incapacitated where an agent has lost her ability to provide valid consent. We could specify a particular blood alcohol level where one loses the ability to give valid consent, but this would be of little practical use given that most do not have access to a breathalyzer. It would seem the best practical guidance would be to err on the side of caution and refrain from engaging in sexual activity with persons who exhibit signs of intoxication (e.g. slurred speech).

If an intoxicated person cannot provide valid consent, this would make it morally impermissible for someone to engage in sex with the intoxicated person. Whether we should regard sex with intoxicated persons as criminal behavior is another question. It is worth noting that the same point could be made about deception and sex. If someone agrees to sex as the result of a deception, then her consent is not valid, and the sex is impermissible. There may nonetheless be good reasons not to criminalize this sort of behavior, immoral as it may be, evidential problems being one such reason.

---

18 See Wertheimer (2003), Miller and Wertheimer (2010), Pallikkathayail (2011), and Dougherty (2021).

19 The same is even more obviously true for persons who are unconscious.

Regarding drunken sex as morally impermissible may strike some as objectionably restrictive or excessively moralistic. If two otherwise competent adults desire to engage in drunken sex, what is the harm in this?[20] From the Kantian perspective, there is reason to find fault with the drunkenness itself. As Kant puts it, "A human being who is drunk is like a mere animal, not to be treated as a human being" (MS 6:427). When Kant says that a drunk person is "not to be treated as a human being" we should not understand him as saying that we are authorized to treat drunk persons as if they were things. Rather, I take Kant's meaning to be that a drunk person is temporarily alienated from his moral personality, and we should treat him accordingly.[21] We should not enter into contracts with drunk persons, we should not take their promises seriously, and we should not regard their consent as normatively transformative. In a state of intoxication persons are temporarily alienated from their moral powers.[22]

---

20 When one party is intoxicated and the other is not, there is a legitimate concern that the sober party has taken advantage of the other's inebriation. When both parties are intoxicated, this concern is no longer relevant, and this might support the intuition that mutually drunken sex is morally innocent. I do not think this intuition holds up to scrutiny. If an intoxicated person cannot give valid consent to a sober sex partner, I see no reason to think that she can give valid consent to an intoxicated partner.

21 This reading is supported by the following passage: "[...] if I have drunk too much today, I am incapable of making use of my freedom and my powers" (Mo-Collins 27:346). See also Mo-Collins 27:288–291.

22 My purposes in this paper do not require me to take a position on whether or to what extent intoxicated persons are rightly held accountable for their actions. According to Kant, "The drunkard cannot, indeed, be held accountable for his actions, but he certainly can, when sober, for the drunkenness itself" (Mo-Collins 27:288). See Chapter 11 of Wertheimer (2003) for a discussion of the relationship between the view that intoxication makes valid consent impossible and the view that intoxicated persons are responsible for their intoxicated behavior. Even if we accept that intoxicated persons cannot give valid consent, one might wonder whether sober adults can give *ex ante* consent to drunken sex in the future. In my opinion, the answer to this is no. Consent must be given at the time of sexual engagement and may be withdrawn at any time thereafter. The skeptic might respond by observing that it is common practice to give *ex ante* consent to be anesthetized prior to surgery. Under general anesthesia we are at least as alienated from our moral powers as we are when we are seriously intoxicated. If one can give *ex ante* consent to be anesthetized for surgery, why can one not give *ex ante* consent to drunken sex? The difference, I believe, lies in the fact that surgery is frequently (though not always) performed in service of moral ends including self-preservation (MS 6:421), self-perfection via the alleviation of pain (MS 6:388) or the restoration of our powers of the body (MS 6:445).

2.3 Not Beyond the Limits of One's Normative Authority

Many recognize the absence of deception and coercion to be necessary conditions for valid consent. Other conditions are more distinctly Kantian. For instance, the Kantian perspective recognizes limits on the normative power of consent that at least some libertarian views do not. An additional condition that must be met for consent to be valid, according to the Kantian standard, is that the treatment an agent is consenting to does not lie beyond the limits of her normative authority. Slavery contracts are one prominent example. In the *Doctrine of Right*, Kant explains that "a contract by which one party would completely renounce its freedom for the other's advantage would be self-contradictory, that is, null and void, since by it one party would cease to be a person and so would have no duty to keep the contract but would recognize only force" (MS 6:283).

The party contracting away her freedom would not actually cease to be a person. What she would be contracting away would be her rightful claim to equal freedom, what Ripstein calls her legal personality. But once she has renounced her legal personality she cannot be bound by the contract.[23] Thus Kant concludes that a slavery contract is self-contradictory. I find this explanation to be somewhat unsatisfying, as well as more complicated than needed. A simpler explanation is readily available. In the section of the *Doctrine of Right* devoted to property right (which is just prior to the section on contract right just quoted), Kant asserts that "someone can be his own master (*sui iuris*) but cannot be the owner of himself (*sui dominus*) (cannot dispose of himself as he pleases) – still less can he dispose of others as he please – since he is accountable to the humanity in his own person" (MS 6:270). One can only dispose over property to which one has a rightful claim. Persons are not property, not even their own, thus we lack the authority to dispose of ourselves.

Slave contracts are not legitimate because individuals lack the normative authority to alienate themselves from their moral and legal personality. Notably, this is the same reason Kant provides for why suicide (at least in many cases) is impermissible:

> A human being cannot renounce his personality as long as he is a subject of duty, hence as long as he lives [...] disposing oneself as a mere means to some discretionary end is debasing humanity in one's person (*homo noumenon*), to which man (*homo phenomenon*) was nevertheless entrusted for preservation. (MS 6:422 f.)

---

23 See Ripstein (2009, 133–140).

While we retain the normative authority to waive certain rights, it is beyond an agent's authority to renounce her personality altogether. Thus, while someone may token consent to be a slave or to be killed, this consent lacks normatively transformative power; it does not render the killing or enslavement rightful or permissible. Some of what Kant says about sex between consenting adults suggests that he regards sexual intercourse as akin to suicide and slavery.

> Man cannot *dispose over himself*, because he is not a thing. He is not his own property – that would be a contradiction [...] But now if a person allows himself to be used, for profit, as an object to satisfy the sexual impulse of another, if he makes himself the object of another's desire, then he is *disposing over himself*, as if over a thing, and thereby makes himself into a thing by which the other satisfies his appetite, just as his hunger is satisfied on a roast of pork. (Mo-Collins 27:386; emphasis mine)

Kant does not restrict this view of sex to prostitution. According to Kant, "those who give themselves to another person, merely to satisfy inclination, still continue to let their person be used as a thing; for the impulse is still always directed to sex, merely, and not to humanity" (Mo-Collins 27:387).

Kant uses remarkably similar language when discussing slavery contracts, suicide, and sexual intercourse, but, surely, one of these things is not like the others. It is highly implausible to think that engaging in sex – even casual sex outside of marriage – entails disposing over oneself or a renouncement of one's personality comparable to what we find in suicide or slavery. To the contrary, voluntary sex entails neither the destruction of nor the alienation from one's autonomy. Thus, the more truly Kantian position (as opposed to Kant's own position) is that consent can be normatively transformative where human sexual activity is concerned, provided it meets the appropriate conditions.

A distinctly Kantian condition for normatively transformative consent is that the treatment one consents to does not lie beyond what one has the authority to sanction. I have argued that sex *per se*, unlike slavery, does not lie beyond the agent's power to authorize or normatively transform with her consent. However, this does not preclude there being certain forms of sex that do. Treating another *as a thing* is inherently morally objectionable and forbidden by the formula of humanity. Sexual relations which treat another as a thing, or endeavor to do so, cannot be made permissible by consent.[24]

---

24 It is beyond the scope of this paper to investigate when sexual relations fit this description; however, Rae Langton's account of sexual sadism appears to be one such example. See Langton (2009, 325–342).

3 Informed Consent and Mere Means Treatment

To avoid treating persons merely as means in sexual relations we must obtain their valid consent. In the previous section, I endorsed the view that for consent to be valid it must be given by an appropriately capable being (one who is sufficiently mature and of sound mind) in the absence of deception, coercion, and intoxication, and the treatment one consents to must not lie beyond one's authority to sanction. In this section, I want to consider whether the appropriate standard for valid consent to sexual relations demands even more than this. In the context of the practice of medicine and research involving human subjects, the standard that has been embraced since the end of the 20th century is the standard of *informed* consent. This is to say that researchers or medical practitioners act in permissible ways only if they obtain the informed consent of their subjects or patients (who capable of giving such consent) prior to acting.[25] This is a more demanding standard than what we find in other contexts. A waiter, for instance is not expected or required to inform me of any health risks I undertake when I order a cheeseburger and an extra-large milkshake. The Latin phrase, caveat emptor, "let the buyer beware", expresses the view that it is the buyer's responsibility to do her due diligence, not the seller's responsibility to inform.

What might account for this difference in standards? There are at least three features, which might explain why the more demanding standard is appropriate in the context of medicine and research. First, medical procedures often involve crossing *physical* boundaries. Surgery is an extreme example of this, but even an examination involves putting hands on another, crossing a threshold into another's personal space. Second, we might expect a more demanding standard in a context in which individuals are exposed to greater risks. Allowing others to cross a threshold into our personal space or into our very bodies makes us especially vulnerable to physical risks such as infection or injury. Medical practitioners gain intimate knowledge of our bodies during examination and treatment and thus our privacy is at risk as well. And, finally, the practice of medicine and medical research is rife with current and historical examples of abuse. Indeed, it was in response to such abuses that the standard of informed consent was conceived and adopted.[26]

---

25 It should be noted that the standard of informed consent is neither simple nor uniformly understood. There is debate, for instance, regarding what is required to meet this standard: (1) patient understanding, (2) mere disclosure of information, or even (3) the mere opportunity to be informed which one might decline. See Beauchamp and Childress (2019) and Dougherty (2020).
26 See Beauchamp and Childress (2019).

These three features, which justify the more demanding standard for normatively transformative consent in the practice of medicine, are also salient in human sexual relations. Sex entails crossing physical boundaries. The physical intimacy of sexual relations exposes us to new physical risks (e. g. sexually transmitted diseases, pregnancy), as well as risks to our privacy. The physical intimacy of sexual relations may also render us more emotionally vulnerable. The potential physical and psychological costs associated with sex are higher than the potential costs associated with playing tennis or dancing. And like medicine, the history of human sexual activity is rife with abuse. Many cultures continue to stigmatize certain forms of sex, disproportionately penalize women for sexual activity, and fail to take seriously abuses of power. These shared features with the practice of medicine suggest that the higher standard of *informed* consent is the appropriate standard for human sexual relations.

While I think the above observations are correct and worth bearing in mind, the analogy between sex and medicine is far from perfect. There are important differences between the physician-patient relationship, and the relationship between sex partners or potential sex partners. Most notably, the physician or researcher is acting in a professional role and is bound by professional obligations.[27] The physician is not merely a moral agent, she is also part of an institution of medicine or research with professional codes of conduct aimed at protecting, among other things, the institution itself. The relationship between physician and patient is not a symmetrical relationship where each party as identical reciprocal rights and duties. The physician has more stringent duties to act in the interest of her patient. The standard of informed consent serves this duty by giving the physician reason to believe that the patient regards the intervention as one that serves her ends.

In my opinion, the similarity between biomedical practices and sexual relations is not strong enough to warrant endorsing the higher standard of informed consent as the appropriate standard for valid consent to sex.[28] Provided I obtain undeceived, uncoerced, and unintoxicated consent from my competent, adult partner, and the way I treat her is not inherently morally objectionable, I will not have

---

27 I am open to the possibility that sex workers can also act in a professional capacity and may be subject to more stringent professional obligations.

28 Thomas Mappes (2017) has endorsed the view that voluntary, *informed* consent is required to avoid using persons merely as means in the context of sexual relations, and perhaps all other contexts as well. However, Mappes appears to understand voluntary, informed consent as consent that is given by a competent adult in the absence of deception and coercion. Though he uses the phrase *informed consent*, there is little else to indicate that Mappes believes sex partners have obligations to inform comparable to those attributed to researchers and medical partitioners.

used her merely as means. However, while obtaining valid consent from one's partner is sufficient to avoid treating your partner merely as a means, it is not sufficient to render sex permissible, at least not according to the Kantian standard. In addition to obtaining valid consent from one's partner, for sex to be permissible an agent must not be acting on an impermissible maxim.[29] I will return to this point in the final section of the paper.

4 Obligatory Ends

In the previous section, I defended an account of the conditions that must be met if we are to avoid treating our sex partners merely as means, which itself is a necessary condition for morally permissible sex. I now want to consider what more is required if we are to engage in what I am calling *good Kantian* sex. To reiterate, good Kantian sex is sex that is compatible with *all* of our moral requirements. In the remainder of the paper, I attempt to ascertain what one must do, in addition to securing valid consent, to satisfy the higher moral standard. I argue that a compelling case can be made for thinking that informed consent is the appropriate moral standard we should be aiming at if we wish to engage in sex that is morally better than merely permissible.

In the *Groundwork*, Kant maintains that treating persons as ends in themselves requires more than not using them merely as means. One additional requirement is a concern for the happiness of others. According to Kant,

> [...] humanity might indeed subsist if no one contributed to the happiness of others but yet did not intentionally withdraw anything from it; but there is still only a negative and not a positive agreement with humanity as an end in itself unless everyone tries, as far as he can, to further the ends of others (GMS 4:430).

In the *Doctrine of Virtue*, published more than a decade later, Kant retains the notion that beneficence is a duty, but reconceives the duty in a novel manner. In this later work, Kant introduces the concept of an obligatory end or *an end that is also*

---

29 Seiriol Morgan has defended this view employing characters from the novel *Les Liaison Dangereuse* to serve as a counterexample to the view that universal participant consent is sufficient for the moral permissibility of any sex act. While Alan Soble is correct to point out that the consent condition has not been satisfied in Morgan's example given that Madame de Tourvel has been deceived, this is not a devasting critique. We can easily imagine the story differently, where the Vicomte reveals himself to Madame de Tourvel and she consents to consummate their relationship despite this information. Sex in this case would still be impermissible for precisely the reason Morgan identifies, the Vicomte is pursuing a malicious end.

a duty. These are ends that reason represents as objectively necessary (MS 6:380 f.). Kant explicitly identifies two such ends: one's own perfection and the happiness of others (MS 6:385). Human beings are morally obligated to make others' happiness their end, but what does this entail? First, and most obviously, the obligatory end entails the positive duty of beneficence, which Kant describes as a duty "to promote according to one's means the happiness of others in need, without hoping for something in return" (MS 6:453). This duty of love is wide and imperfect meaning that it allows for latitude or choice in deciding how, when, and to what extent one promotes others' happiness.[30] That said, if an agent never or rarely attempted to contribute to the happiness of others despite opportunities to do so, this would be evidence that others' happiness is not one of her ends.

Others have argued that the obligatory end also requires us to cultivate certain kinds of dispositions.[31] Here I want to go further and suggest that obligatory ends entail both positive and negative obligation.[32] This follows from the logic of ends. If something is your end, then you have reason to perform actions that are conducive to achieving or securing your end, but you also have reason to refrain from doing things that will hinder or undermine your success, and these reasons are equally rationally compelling. For instance, if my end is to achieve a personal best time in an upcoming race, I have reason to train, but also reason to avoid over-training, which may cause injury. Similarly, my end gives me reason to consume certain kinds of food and drink (e.g. ample amounts of water), but also reason to avoid consuming others (e.g. ample amounts of alcohol). When it comes to the rational pursuit of ends, what we refrain from doing can be as important as what we do.

The same logic applies to obligatory ends.[33] If others' happiness is our end, then we have reason to avoid doing things that will cause unhappiness *even when doing such things would not be morally impermissible.* In many situations, these moral reasons to refrain from doing things we anticipate will be detrimental to the well-being of others will not be decisive by themselves owing to the wide

---

30 See MS 6:390; 6:393; 6:450.

31 See Denis (2007), and Fahmy (2010).

32 Kant mentions a more restricted version of this negative obligation in the following passage: "The happiness of others also includes their *moral well-being* (*salubritas moralis*) and we have a duty, but only a negative one, to promote this" (MS 6:394). I defend the broader position that the obligatory end, *others' happiness* (which includes, but is not restricted to others' moral well-being) entails both positive and negative obligations.

33 This point is perhaps most obvious when thinking about the self-regarding obligatory end. Pursuing the end of our own moral perfection clearly entails that we refrain from doing that which is impermissible in addition to doing that which is obligatory and cultivating a virtuous disposition.

and imperfect nature of the duty.[34] Knowing that if I win a race my competitors will be disappointed is not by itself a compelling reason to deliberately slow my pace, for doing so would undermine the integrity of the competitive activity.

The obligatory end establishes that the well-being and happiness of others is always a deliberately salient consideration. As I pursue my own ends, including my own happiness, I must be mindful of how my actions impact the well-being of others. It might make me happy to greet each day by singing loudly from my back porch at sunrise, but I should consider the impact this practice has on my neighbors. There are not precise rules for how to do this, but the general point remains that the obligatory end gives us reason to promote others' happiness, as well as reason to avoiding doing things when we foresee that they would diminish others' well-being, though these reasons will not always be decisive.

What does this entail in the context of sexual relations? Several things. First, the obligatory end gives me reason to *care* about whether engaging in sexual relations with me would be detrimental to my partner's well-being, just as I have reason to care about whether my morning singing might be problematic for my neighbors. Second, if I care about whether sexual relations with me is detrimental to my partner's well-being, then I have reason to seek out relevant information, to investigate. If I cannot be bothered to investigate the efficacy of different means of bringing about some state of affairs, if I am indifferent regarding whether my behavior will be conducive or detrimental to an end, this is evidence that I do not regard the end as very important. And third, the obligatory end gives me moral reason to refrain from sexual relations when I have reason to believe that such relations would likely diminish the happiness or well-being of my partner, *even if sexual relations would not be morally impermissible.* In the following section, I argue that acknowledging the negative and positive obligations that follow from the Kantian obligatory end supports the conclusion that the standard of *informed consent* is the appropriate moral standard to strive for in the context of human sexual relations.

---

34 Moral reasons to promote the happiness of particular others in particular ways will often not be decisive either. See Fahmy (2019).

5 How to Have Good Kantian Sex

5.1 Transparency

It is not consistent with holding others' happiness as my end, as well as an end I recognize as objectively necessary, to be content with a state of ignorance or to make assumptions regarding how my actions are likely to impact others when it is within my power to become better informed. It follows that the obligatory end, *others' happiness*, gives me moral reason to care about whether sexual relations with me would be detrimental to my partner's well-being. Putting aside cases of clearly morally impermissible sex (e. g. assault, coercion), when might sexual relations be detrimental to my partner's well-being? Very generally, sexual relations might be detrimental to my partner's well-being when we have mutually incompatible interests in sex. If sex partners desire a sexual relationship (or even a mere encounter) for very different reasons, this will likely result in frustration, disappointment, regret, and possibly even humiliation. The trouble is that human beings pursue sexual relationships and encounters for a wide variety of reasons.

As I indicated at the beginning of the paper, one of the defects of Kant's account of human sexuality is its simplicity. Kant describes sex in terms of a desire that is simply an appetite for another's body. But human sexual activity is not simply a matter of acting on a natural, biological impulse. Human beings engage in sex for a multitude of reasons and can imbue sex acts and sexual relationships with a multitude of meanings. This is what makes human sexual activity distinctly *human.* Sex can be as Kant describes; one could have sex for the sake of pleasure or to satisfy an appetite; but it could also be quite different.

Sex could be a form of revenge. One could act on the maxim of sleeping with his former partner's best friend to incite jealousy. Alternatively, sex could be a form of distraction. One might engage in sexual relations to avoid dealing with problems that overwhelm and appear intractable. Sex could be about ridding oneself of one's virginity. In such a case, it matters not whether the sex is pleasurable or gratifying; what matters is that once it is done one will no longer bear the stigma of being a virgin. Sex could be a means to getting something else. The cliché example is sleeping with the director to secure a part in a film. A recently published article reported that in economically hard times, women will remain in a sexual relationship because it provides them with a safe, comfortable place to live.[35] Sex could be about status or identity. In some cultures, having sex with many partners is correlated to a masculine identity. Sex could be about reclaiming one's youth or bolstering one's self-esteem. Sex could be about proving something: "I'll have sex with this person in order to prove that I no longer have feelings for my former lover." Sex could be an act of beneficence or even pity. Sex could be about procreation or earning a living. Sex could be about power and domination, or it could be imbued with romantic meaning. The list could go on.[36]

Humans clearly can and do engage in sexual activity for a plethora of reasons that are not always clear even to ourselves. In her 1985 paper, "Between Consenting Adults", Onora O'Neill describes the problem of the opacity of intentionality:

> When we consent to another's proposals, we consent [...] only to some specific formulation of what the other has it in mind to do. We may remain ignorant of further, perhaps equally pertinent, accounts of what is proposed, including some to which we would not consent.[37]

Another way to talk about the opacity of intentionality is to say that maxims are not transparent. A maxim, according to Kant, is a subjective principle of volition (GMS 4:401). A maxim describes what we intend to do and why. Maxims, at least sometimes, are transparent neither to the agent who acts on the maxim nor to the agent who agrees to be used in a particular way.

If I am to make some judgement about whether our interests in sex are compatible, and I am arguing that the obligatory end requires this, I must have some understanding of what our respective interests are. If my intentions and reasons are opaque to me, then I cannot communicate them to my potential sex partner; they must remain opaque for her as well. The problem of the opacity of intentionality may be especially severe in the context of sexual relations where our fundamental reasons for acting are obscured by excitement, hormones, complicated feelings, and social expectations. Moreover, in light of the features sexual activity shares with the practice of medicine – the crossing of physical barriers, increased

---

35 See West (2017) for presentation of numerous reasons a woman might consent to sex she does not desire.

36 We observe something similar regarding the consumption of food, at least in contexts where food is abundant and relatively cheap. Humans eat when we are hungry to satisfy a natural impulse, but we also eat for many other reasons. We eat when we are bored or nervous. We eat to be polite or for the sake of cultural rituals. We eat for novelty and pleasure. And we are not always consciously aware of our reason for eating. My examples above suggest that sexual desire may not be the primary motivation for sexual activity, but even when it is, sexual desire is not a simple, uniform thing. For a deeper look into the diversity of human sexual desire and its moral implications see Morgan (2017).

37 O'Neill (1985, 256).

vulnerability and exposure to risk, and a history rife with abuse – there is reason to believe that the opacity of intentionality is a more pernicious problem in this context. These attributes contribute to what I am calling the morally precarious nature of human sexual relations.

The solution, of course, is transparency. Given that we cannot be transparent with our partners if we are unknown to ourselves, the first step must be to identify what lies behind our interest in sex with another.[38] This will require being very honest with ourselves about what we *are* after, as well as what we are *not*, resisting the temptation to engage in self-deception. Once we have identified our feelings and intentions, we should make them clear to our partner or potential partner. By informing my partner of my intentions, I allow her to assess whether a sexual encounter or relationship with me is compatible with her pursuit of her own happiness as she understands it. And by asking my partner about her interests or intentions, I can make this sort of assessment myself. In short, the honest dialogue allows us to determine whether our ends are compatible. This kind of open disclosure reflects the attitude that the other's happiness matters to me, that I am not willing to pursue my own happiness at the expense of hers. It also guards against the danger of objectifying a sex partner.[39] To be concerned about the compatibility of my ends and those of my partner necessitates that I view her as someone *with ends*, that is, a person. Of course, there is a real danger that one might not have epistemic access to certain forms of self-knowledge until *after* one has engaged in sexual relations with particular others and so cannot disclose these facts in advance.[40] I think this too is part of the unavoidably precarious nature of human sexual relations.

If I have reason to believe that our ends are not compatible and that a sexual relationship with me might cause my partner more harm than benefit, then I have moral reason to decline to engage in (or to continue to engage in) a sexual relationship with her, even if she has given valid, informed consent to such a relationship. To be clear, according to the account I am defending, if I were to pursue sexual interactions where I have obtained my partner's valid consent, I would *not* be using my partner merely as a means. Nevertheless, if I were to pursue sexual re-

---

38 A point emphasized by Robin West is that persons, especially heterosexual women, often consent to have sex in the absence of a desire for sex. See West (2017). One's willingness to have sex in response to someone else's desire is not really an "interest in sex", however, I am using the phrase broadly to capture an agent's intentions, motivations, and interests related to a sexual encounter or relationship.

39 See "Sexual Solipsism" in Langton (2009) for a discussion of objectification in sexual relations.

40 Relatedly, one's interest in sex could be primarily epistemic. One might engage in sexual relations to satisfy a curiosity or in the hope of figuring something out.

lations where I had reason to believe that this was contrary to the happiness and well-being of my partner, *despite her consent*, this would be an instance of what Wertheimer calls morally unworthy sex, though not impermissible.

5.2 Impermissible Maxims

Even if one were to satisfy the standard of transparency, concerns might rightly linger regarding some of the reasons for engaging in sexual relations I identify above. A reason like revenge seems clearly morally objectionable by Kantian standards, given the malicious intentions. Acting for the sake of bringing about a third-party's suffering is incompatible with holding others' happiness as one's end, even if I am transparent with my partner and obtain her informed consent. Likewise, insofar as a macho attitude is inherently disrespectful to persons, having sex for the sake of affirming this identity is inconsistent with the end of our own moral perfection.[41] According to the Kantian standard, it seems that we ought not engage in sex for these reasons, even if we are appropriately transparent with our partners and obtain their valid, informed consent. Moreover, it seems equally true that we should not engage in sex with those who are motivated by these reasons – not because we risk treating them or ourselves merely as means, but rather for the sake of refraining from "doing anything that, considering the nature of a human being, could tempt him to do something for which his conscience could afterwards pain him" (MS 6:394). Simply put, we ought not facilitate others acting on impermissible maxims.

6 Conclusion

Social expectations regarding sexual propriety have changed significantly since Kant's day. Much of this change has been for the better, especially for women and sexual minorities. In the 21st century, we have seen technology transform how individuals locate and engage with sex partners. The proliferation of mobile phones and social network apps like Tinder have made it easier than ever for large numbers of people to solicit sexual relations and share sexually explicit content. These technologies are neither good nor bad in themselves, however they present new opportunities to behave in morally problematic ways. Human sexual activity remains morally precarious.

---

41 Morgan (2017) has made a similar point regarding arrogant motivations.

In this paper I have tried to provide an account of how we can navigate these waters, that is, how we can engage with others sexually without transgressing Kantian moral ideals. While consent is undoubtably important, I have argued that valid consent is not sufficient for even merely permissible sexual relations. Obtaining our partner's valid consent will not resolve the problem of a morally objectionable maxim. More importantly, I have argued that if we are going to engage in sexual relations with others, we should be aiming for a higher standard than merely permissible. And when we educate our children about sex, it is this higher standard of conduct that should be emphasized. According to the account I have offered, to engage in good Kantian sex we must do a lot more than refrain from deception and coercion. We must also be attentive to the happiness and well-being of our partners. To this end, we should identify the nature of our interest in sex and be transparent with our partners, and we should expect our partners to do the same.

References

Beauchamp, Tom and Childress, James F., 2019, *Principles of Biomedical Ethics*, 8th ed., New York: Oxford University Press.

Denis, Lara, 1999, "Kant on the Wrongness of 'Unnatural' Sex", *History of Philosophy Quarterly*, 16, 225–248.

Denis, Lara, 2007, "Sex and the Virtuous Kantian Agent", in Raja Halwani (ed.), *Sex and Ethics: Essays on Sexuality, Virtue, and the Good Life.* London: Palgrave, 37–48.

Dougherty, Tom, 2013, "Sex, Lies, and Consent", *Ethics*, 123/4, 716–744.

Dougherty, Tom, 2020, "Informed Consent, Disclosure, and Understanding", *Philosophy and Public Affairs*, 48/2, 119–150.

Dougherty, Tom, 2021, "Why Does Duress Undermine Consent?", *Noûs*, 55/2, 317–333.

Fahmy, Melissa S., 2010, "Kantian Practical Love", *Pacific Philosophical Quarterly*, 91/3, 313–331.

Fahmy, Melissa S. 2019, "On Virtues of Love and Wide Ethical Duties", *Kantian Review*, 24/3, 415–437.

Formosa, Paul, 2014, "Dignity and Respect: How to Apply Kant's Formula of Humanity", *The Philosophical Forum*, 45/1, 49–68.

Herman, Barbara, 1993, "Could It Be Worth Thinking About Kant on Sex and Marriage?", in Louise Antony and Charlotte Witt (eds.), *A Mind of One's Own: Feminist Essays on Reason and Objectivity*, Boulder, CO: Westview Press, 49–67.

Kant, Immanuel, *Lectures on Ethics*, translated by Peter Heath, Cambridge: Cambridge University Press 1997.

Kant, Immanuel, *Religion within the Boundaries of Mere Reason*, translated by Allen Wood and George Di Giovanni, Cambridge: Cambridge University Press 1998.

Kant, Immanuel, *Groundwork of the Metaphysics of Morals*, translated by Mary Gregor, Cambridge: Cambridge University Press 1997.

Kant, Immanuel, *The Metaphysics of Morals*, translated by. Mary Gregor, Cambridge: Cambridge University Press 1996.

Kerstein, Samuel, 2013, *How to Treat Persons*, New York: Oxford University Press.

Kleingeld, Pauline, 2020, "How to Use Someone 'Merely as a Means'", *Kantian Review*, 25/3, 389–414.

Korsgaard, Christine, 1986, "The Right to Lie: Kant on Dealing with Evil", *Philosophy and Public Affairs*, 15/4, 325–349.

Langton, Rae, 2009, *Sexual Solipsism*. Oxford: Oxford University Press.

Mappes, Thomas, 2017, "Sexual Morality and the Concept of Using Another Person", in Alan Soble (ed.), *The Philosophy of Sex: Contemporary Readings*, 7th edition, Lanham: Rowman & Littlefield, 207–223.

Miller, Franklin/Wertheimer, Alan, 2010, *The Ethics of Consent: Theory and Practice*, New York: Oxford University Press.

Morgan, Seiriol, 2017, "Dark Desires", in: Alan Soble (ed.), *The Philosophy of Sex: Contemporary Readings*, 7th edition, Lanham: Rowman & Littlefield, 349–369.

O'Neill, Onora, 1985, "Between Consenting Adults", *Philosophy and Public Affairs*, 14/3, 252–277.

Pallikkathayil, Japa, 2010, "Deriving Morality from Politics", *Ethics*, 121, 116–147.

Pallikkathayil, Japa, 2011, "The Possibility of Choice: Three Accounts of the Problem of Coercion", *Philosopher's Imprint*, 11/16, 1–20.

Parfit, Derek, 2011, *On What Matters*, vol. 1, Oxford: Oxford University Press.

Primoratz, Igor, 2001, "Sexual Morality: Is Consent Enough?", *Ethical Theory and Moral Practice*, 4, 201–218.

Ripstein, Arthur, 2009, *Force and Freedom: Kant's Legal and Political Philosophy*, Cambridge, MA: Harvard University Press.

Soble, Alan, 2017, "Sexual Use", in: Alan Soble (ed.), *The Philosophy of Sex: Contemporary Readings*, 7th edition, Lanham: Rowman & Littlefield), 293–320.

Varden, Helga, 2007, "A Kantian Conception of Rightful Sexual Relations: Sex, Gay Marriage, and Prostitution", *Social Philosophy Today*, 22, 199–218.

Varden, Helga, 2020, *Sex, Love, and Gender: A Kantian Theory*, New York: Oxford University Press.

Wertheimer, Alan, 2003, *Consent to Sexual Relations*, Cambridge: Cambridge University Press.

West, Robin, 2017, "The Harms of Consensual Sex", in: Alan Soble (ed.), *The Philosophy of Sex: Contemporary Readings*, 7th edition, Lanham: Rowman & Littlefield, 371–377.

Jeanine Grenberg

Kant and Austen on Free Love

Abstract: Successful fulfillment of duties of love—including those duties of love pointed toward that other who is, or is potentially, one's romantic partner—requires that one acquire a high level of freedom: successful loving requires that one express one's basic capacity for free choice *in* one's will and character, through the accomplishment of what Kant calls "inner freedom" or "autocracy." The composed person of inner freedom—that person who not only respects others but who has also gotten a hold of herself and is thus not ruled by her affects and passions—is best situated to fulfill the other-centered requirements of love: maintaining attentiveness to and loving concern for the situation of the other. I conclude by illustrating this idea in an analysis of the characters of Mary and Anne Eliot in Jane Austen's *Persuasion.*

Introduction

In this paper, I argue that successful fulfillment of duties of love – including those duties of love pointed toward that other who is, or is potentially, one's romantic partner – requires that one obtain a particularly high level of freedom. More precisely, successful loving requires that one express one's basic capacity for free action in one's choice, will and character, through the accomplishment of what Kant variously calls "inner freedom" or "autocracy". To explore this idea, I first reflect upon this notion of "inner freedom", then turn to consideration of duties of love, focusing upon Kant's claim that inner freedom – and especially that self-mastery of one's affects, inclinations and passions characteristic of the person of inner freedom – is a condition for the possibility of fulfilling duties of love. In so doing, I consider what is and is not required of a free person moral psychologically in order to love another person in the sense of making that person's ends one's own. As Melissa Fahmy has argued, respect for a person is necessary in order to love a person properly. But respect – even when matched with a clear understanding of the Categorical Imperative – is insufficient. It is the composed person of inner freedom – that person who has gotten a hold of herself and is thus not ruled by her affects and passions – who is best situated to fulfill the other-centered requirements of love: maintaining attentiveness to and loving concern for the situation of the other. Feeling sympathy for the other, though also within the scope of capacities of the person of inner freedom, is only a helpful tool, but not a strictly necessary requirement of, successful loving of others. I conclude by illustrating

https://doi.org/10.1515/9783111291130-006

this idea that inner freedom is necessary for successful respectful and attentive fulfillment of duties of love in an analysis of the characters of Mary and Anne Eliot in Jane Austen's *Persuasion.*

I Inner Freedom/Autocracy

What is a Free Person?

What does it mean to be "free" for Kant? I realize I am heading into deep waters here, so let me clarify exactly what I am asking. I am asking this question from a moral psychological perspective, not a strictly metaphysical one. I'm not asking, for example, whether Kant can affirm freedom in the face of thorough-going causal determinism. Rather, I want to understand the quality and character of a person whom we consider to have *become* free. One could instead speak of freedom in the sense of *existing* as a free, autonomous being. Unlike other sorts of beings – a cat, a platypus, a petunia – we humans have a particular *capacity* for free and autonomous choice. Whenever we choose – that is, whenever we incorporate or reject incorporation of an inclination or other incentive – we do so under the auspices of a rational capacity to view that incentive vis a vis a standard that goes *beyond* desire and inclination. That is just what it is to be an autonomous, rational being, and it is this capacity – well or poorly used – that affirms the imputability of our choices. But I am asking how it is that this bare capacity for freedom becomes an acquired free disposition. How is it that a person with a *capacity* for freedom becomes a free *person*, one who *characteristically* chooses in accordance with her capacity for autonomy?

To answer this, we need to consider how one's "[law-giving reason] constitutes itself an authority *executing* the law" (TL 6:405). 'Law-giving reason,' already the source of our autonomous self-*legislation*, must, in other words, also assert itself as an *executive* authority through what Kant calls the moral self-constraint of virtue. Importantly for our purposes, though, such *virtue* is, only "possible in accordance with the laws of inner *freedom*" (TL 6:405, emphases added). Simply put, *virtue*, or self-constraint, is a state of *freedom*, more specifically, "*inner* freedom", which is the successful *execution* of that very same law which I have already *legislated* to myself. To see what a free person looks like, we thus need to investigate that person who has accomplished this virtuous constraint of herself in accordance with laws of inner freedom.

Inner freedom as Autocracy

So, to begin: although Stephen Engstrom speaks of this strength of virtue as "inner freedom" whereas Anne Margaret Baxley speaks of it as "autocracy",[1] these two terms are essentially identical: inner freedom is that autocratic state in which we claim mastery over our affects, inclinations and passions. There is, however, something helpfully *descriptive* about calling this state an "autocracy". In so doing, we continue the governmental metaphor begun with the assertion of the moral law being legislated and executed. We now understand such execution as achieving autocratic governance of one's person.

We tend to look negatively at autocratic governments. Autocracy is, after all, "(a system of) government by *one* person with *absolute* power"[2], and therefore conflicts with democracy. Kant's point, though, is that proper rule of oneself is *not* a democracy. We should not allow *all* parts of ourselves equal say in what we cultivate or constrain in ourselves. The common rabble of our inclinations do not possess legitimate authority in running the state of the person; so do not allow the *rabble* of your soul to *rule* your soul! Instead, proper self-governance requires rule by *one* person with *absolute* power. But my legislating autonomous self is the only part of me that is both authorized to provide and capable of this absolute rule. Inner freedom is thus the constraint, control, or even the proper encouragement and guiding *of* our inclinations by the only autocratic authority justified to engage in such control.[3]

Kant later expands on this claim: "[T]wo things are required for inner freedom: being one's own master in a given case (*animus sui compos*) and ruling oneself (*imperium in semetipsum*), that is, subduing one's affects and governing one's passions." (TL 6:407) We are still in the realm of controlling inclination here, but now with a bit more psychological precision. An affect is previous to and more fleeting than an inclination, whereas a passion establishes an already existing inclination as a principle. An affect "belong[s] to feeling" and "precede[s] reflection", making such reflection "impossible or more difficult" (TL 6:407). It comes upon a person unexpectedly, confusing her reflection, but then departs, "a tempest [that] quickly subsides" (TL 6:408). A passion, however, is "a *lasting* inclination" (TL

---

1 See Baxley 2010 and Engstrom 2002. My work here doesn't challenge, but rather seeks to illustrate and explore what the person of inner freedom (as Engstrom calls her) or the person of "autocracy" (as Baxley calls her) accomplishes in her person.

2 *Oxford English Dictionary Online*, s.v. 'autocracy', 2.b., emphasis added.

3 Baxley does some particularly nice work to emphasize this idea that autocracy is not just about constraint but also cultivation. See Baxley 2010, 61–73 and ch. 4.

6:408, emphasis added), one which *does* "permit reflection", and even "allow[s] [...] the mind to form principles upon it" (TL 6:408).

The difference in these psychological states helps clarify what exact autocratic control is required to achieve inner freedom. With an affect, one loses one's *composure*; the autocratic *goal* is thus to *regain* composure, precisely what is suggested in Kant's parenthetical Latin gloss, 'animus sui *compos*'. But does being composed mean that one has affects but is able to keep them in their place, or that one simply is no longer subject to affects?

Textually, things are ambiguous on this point. In the *Anthropology*, Kant explicitly *defines* an affect *as* a *loss* of composure[4], suggesting that one cannot be composed when experiencing an affect. And yet, surely, if one had the mastery of inner freedom, one would be *better* at managing these surprises when they show up. As such, it seems best to define composure as *both* the *infrequency* of surprise affects but also as the ability to manage unexpected affects. For the composed person experiencing an affect, "reason says, through the concept of virtue, that one should *get hold of* oneself" (TL 6:408) while the flutter of the affect passes. Jeeves, from P.G. Wodehouse's *Jeeves and Wooster*, is perhaps the paradigmatic example of a person of composure. Jeeves experiences very strong affects when he observes various indiscretions in his lord, Bertie. But the only evidence we observe of those affects is the slightest raising of an eyebrow followed by a clever plan for extricating Bertie from his troubles.[5]

Passions, however, because they are more firmly entrenched than affects, require more stern autocratic control: one must *"govern* passions" (TL 6:407, emphasis added). Such governance is glossed in Latin as an *'imperium in semetipsum'* (TL 6:407), an *absolute* power over oneself. Indeed, the Latin phrase 'imperium' referred, in ancient Rome, to "the supreme power, held esp by consuls or emperors, to command and administer in military [...] affairs".[6] When passions are around, we need to get more stern about controlling ourselves precisely because the passion threatens a quasi-rational mutiny of the true autocratic ruler. Passions "permit [...] reflection" and "allow the mind to form principles upon [one's inclinations]" (TL 6:407). They thus encourage us to reason in ways "contrary to the law" (TL 6:407). Such rational passions become something "to brood upon", or "to get [...] rooted deeply" (TL 6:407) in one's mind. Mutinous passions must therefore be defeated by reason much as a seditious plotter would be defeated.

---

4 "Affect is surprise through sensation, by means of which the mind's composure (animus sui compos) is suspended" (Anth 7:252).

5 Wodehouse 1991.

6 *Collins English Dictionary*, s.v. 'imperium', www.collinsdictionary.com/dictionary/english/imperium – last accessed April 17, 2023.

Autocracy is thus the execution of the moral law whereby one's affects, inclinations and passions are brought under the absolute, singular rule of that law. The result of this autocratic work of inner freedom is what Kant calls a free "aptitude" (TL 6:407), which he describes as both "a facility in acting" and "a subjective perfection of the faculty of choice [*Willkür*]" (TL 6:407). Through my chosen constraint of my affects, inclinations and passions, I acquire an alacrity and ease in the exercise of my free choice, one which constitutes the most perfect realization of what that capacity for choice should be.

There is complexity here, however. An aptitude is a facility in the operation of one's faculty for choice (*Willkür*), but we need to trace this facility back to one's legislating will (*Wille*) which is really what is doing this work of controlling affects, inclinations and passions. It is tempting to think one's faculty of choice is doing all the work here. This is, after all, the capacity at work in any act of incorporation: when I incorporate, or reject incorporating, an inclination, I am *choosing* to do so. Crucially, though, this ease in choosing, to be truly an inner expression *of freedom*, needs to issue from the very depths of one's legislating self. After all, it would be possible to establish an *ease* or facility in choosing that had very little to do with *freedom* of choice. The more that I let my husband make me martinis, the *easier* it is for me to choose every evening to have a martini before dinner. It used to be *hard* for me to decide whether to have so strong a drink as a martini, but there is now an *ease* or facility in making this choice that wasn't there before. I have, in other words, developed an *aptitude* for choosing martinis. A *free and autonomous* aptitude, however, needs to be more than this. As Kant argues:

> [N]ot every such facility [i.e., aptitude] is a free aptitude [...]; for if it is a habit [...], that is, a uniformity in action that has become a necessity through frequent repetition, it is not one that proceeds from freedom, and therefore not a moral aptitude. Hence virtue cannot be defined as an aptitude for free action in conformity with law unless there is added 'to determine oneself to act through the thought of the law', *and then this aptitude is not a property of choice but of the will, which is a faculty of desire that, in adopting a rule, also gives it as a universal law.* Only such an aptitude can be counted as virtue. (TL 6:407, last emphasis added)

Kant's point here is not immediately clear. When he says that an 'aptitude is not a property of choice but of the will', he must surely mean that an aptitude is not *merely* a property of choice but is *also* simultaneously a property of the will. After all, Kant has already told us that an aptitude is 'a facility in acting' and "a subjective perfection of the *faculty of choice* [*Willkür*]" (TL 6:407, emphasis added). It thus makes no sense to say that 'this aptitude is *not* a property of choice': if an aptitude were not a *property* of our faculty of choice, it could not be a *perfection* of our faculty of choice! Kant's point here is thus that, when one acquires an aptitude, one's faculty for choice so perfectly takes on the laws of one's will that it is as if one's *Willkür* simply has become one's *Wille*. A free aptitude is the perfect expression in one's choices of the constraints of law legislated by one's will; or, as Kant puts the point, to say that a free aptitude is a property of the will is to say that it is a property of the 'faculty of desire that, in adopting a rule, also gives it as a universal law'. In short, when one has a free aptitude, one's *Willkür* is perfectly in line with the universally legislating *Wille*. And this aptitude of the *Wille/Willkür* simply is the inner freedom of the *Wille/Willkür*. When, via a thorough constraint of one's affects, inclinations and passions, the moral law perfectly pervades one's capacity for choice, one's *Willkür* becomes an expression of that freedom and autonomy legislated by one's will.

Kant speaks in strikingly strong language about what the process of choice is like for this person of inner freedom. This person not only has the capacity to choose autonomously (all rational persons have that); beyond that, the person of inner freedom has an *ease* or *facility* in so choosing. He is "in possession of himself" (TL 6:405) and therefore reliably and unchangingly chooses in line with moral demands. Kant even says that the person of inner freedom "cannot lose his virtue" (TL 6:405). For such a person, it is not so much "as if a human being possesses virtue but rather as if virtue possesses him; for in the former case it would look as if he still had a choice (for which he would need yet another virtue" (TL 6:406). This is a particularly strong reading of what happens when choice perfectly aligns with one's autonomous will. It is as if one no longer chooses among options because, for such a faculty of choice, the only real option is clear. We are now seeing what choice is like for the person of inner freedom who is in control of her affects, inclinations and passions.

II Free Love

Love, the Intimacy of End-Setting and Other-Centeredness

The executive, autocratic authority of inner freedom thus *constitutes* virtue as strength. Further, Kant insists: "inner freedom must [...] [also] be treated [...] as the *condition* of *all* duties of virtue" (TL 6:407, first emphasis added). One must thus acquire inner freedom to fulfill *any* of the duties to self or others catalogued in the *Doctrine of Virtue*. As such, inner freedom is clearly also a 'condition' for the fulfillment of duties of *love:* the only *real* love is a *free* love. Let's explore this new territory.

Although this doesn't do full justice to Kant's account of love, I focus here on the idea that a duty of love involves making another's end of happiness one's own end. This connection of love to ends is, perhaps, disappointing to the romantics among us: love is not a *feeling*-centered, but rather an *action*-centered state.[7] Love is a *"practical"* maxim of *action* centered on accomplishing something for the beloved.[8] Further, calling love "practical" emphasizes what love is amongst those beings capable of *practical reason*. The distinctive capacity of such beings is to set *ends*.[9] As such, practical *love* (a realization of one's practical, end-setting capacity directed toward *other* rational beings) is just that love through which I promote the *happiness* of others by promoting their *ends*.

Reflection on end-setting can further inform our understanding of duties of love. End-setting, the ultimate act of freedom, is something one can only do for oneself: "another can indeed *coerce* me to do something that is not my end [...], but not to *make this my end*; [...] I can have no end without making it an end for myself" (TL 6:381). One can even thus say that end-setting is a particularly *intimate* act. When I set an end, *I* identify a particular matter of choice as *my own*. I look at all the world, and make a decision, based on reasons (including reasons related to my personal history and my hopes for my future), that I want to accomplish *that*. The choice of an end is, furthermore, not a singular time-limited thing, but something I pursue throughout my life.

Given Kant's concern to respect the free end-setting of other persons, and given also how very personal this end-setting is, it is thus interesting that loving others involves claiming their *ends* as one's own. That is: loving another involves *barging in* on this intimate, free end-setting process! I don't merely get out of others' way to promote their happiness, but must also enter into their projects of end-setting. Describing love in just this way brings me, finally, to the central question that needs exploration. When I contribute to another's pursuit of ends, I need, simultaneously, to respect the other but also to understand and promote what it is that they are seeking to accomplish. To fulfill a duty of love, then, I need to enter an "other-centered" state, a state in which I have both a deep respect for and an

---

7 "[L]ove is not to be understood as feeling, that is, as pleasure in the perfection of others; love is not to be understood as delight in them (since others cannot put one under obligation to have feelings)." (TL 6:449) If it is any consolation to the romantics, Kant does admit that the feeling of love can *"accompany* the carrying out of these duties" of love (TL 6:448, emphasis added).

8 "Since the love of human beings (philanthropy) we are thinking of here is practical love, not the love that is delight in them, it must be taken as active benevolence and so as having to do with the maxim of actions." (TL 6:450)

9 As Kant puts it, when he is distinguishing us from animals, it is our existence as practically rational members of the realm of "humanity by which [one] alone is capable of setting himself ends" (TL 6:387).

intimate appreciation of the other's needs, hopes and desires. Here, then, is my question: what is *necessary* to assure this other-centeredness?

This question has not been ignored in recent literature. Melissa Fahmy (2015), for example, argues convincingly that taking another's ends as one's own requires that we respect that other's free capacity for choice in a very particular way. The way to respect another's ends while assisting with them is insistently to remember that I (the helper) am not simply trying to bring about another's end but, rather, am seeking to facilitate the process by which the other person brings about her end. Even as I respect another as a being capable of and responsible for her own choices, I thus also promote her successful realization of her set ends.

It might seem odd to think of respect and love as working side-by-side here like this; but, once you think about it, this is the only way one free, autonomous being *could* love another free, autonomous being: if you have an end, I cannot take on that end for you. Neither can you obligate me to claim your end. The only way to respect autonomy while loving others is for the person to be loved already to have claimed an end for herself and then for the person loving also to promote that other person's end without overtaking that end as her own. I see the end that another has set, and decide freely to contribute *my* efforts toward *her* realization of that end. As Kant puts it, when we love others, we are "*mak[ing]* ourselves an end *for* others" (TL 6:393, emphases added).

But is respect enough? To be other-centered, do I need nothing more than to be respectful of that person? One might be tempted, for example, to think that being sympathetic is also necessary. Feeling sympathy might help me enter into the situation of that other person: I could feel the way she is feeling and therefore be that much more able to understand her feelings, needs and challenges as she pursues her ends.

I am sympathetic to this suggestion, at least in general terms. I do not worry that sympathy, or feelings generally, are destructive of or unregulatable by reason. Active sympathy can, as Kant argues, even enhance our ability to see another's ends. Further, the ideal for taking another's ends as one's own should involve the expression of sympathy. Nonetheless, I find it too strong a claim to say that it would be *impossible* to take another's end as one's own without feeling sympathy, or to suggest that true other-centeredness *requires* feeling sympathy for the other. Indeed, to say this is to miss the point about what it is in one's moral psychological state that most often *prevents* other-centeredness. We thus need a fuller story of what is necessary to take another's ends as my own.

In short, my claim is this: end-taking – and any feeling of sympathy attached to it – need to have, as a condition for their possibility, not just respect for the other, or even simply the general guidance of reason (basically, assessing one's maxims and sympathies via the Categorical Imperative), but also the composure of inner freedom. That composure allows me to get a hold of those excessively self-centered feelings, ends and obsessions which would prevent me from understanding another's ends properly. Once we have this composure, although sympathy is an important further moral accomplishment, it is not strictly required for taking another's ends as one's own. Let's explore these ideas more.

Making Another's End My Own: Other-Centeredness vs. Self-Centeredness

First: in what exactly does the other-centeredness implicit in taking another's ends as one's own consist? The first requirement of other-centeredness is to *know* the chosen end of another. We can appreciate how difficult this is by thinking about how easily it goes wrong. A parent might, for example, think she understands what her college-age child has chosen for her career. But she might unwittingly have let her fears about her child not getting a well-paying job inform that confident (but mistaken) belief that her child has chosen to give up her passion for philosophy to become a doctor. Remember, no one – not even your mother – can force you to acquire an end. But that doesn't stop some people – especially your mother – (with the best of intentions) from trying!

It is thus all too easy to assume one understands another person's ends when, in fact, one is only viewing them through one's own fears, prejudices, hopes or desires. Psychologists have a word for this: transference. Something in my mind clouds the space between me and you such that, when I look at you, I can only see a version of you most agreeable to me. To be able even to accomplish this first step of *understanding* your end, I thus need to overcome that self-centeredness perhaps particularly characteristic of a nervous parent but, in the end, typical for all human beings.

There are other, more egregious, forms of self-centeredness which involve seeing all too *clearly* what another's ends are and especially seeing how much more *successful* others are than I in realizing them. Just because I *see* another person's end *clearly* does not promise that I will promote that end *lovingly.* Kant explores this territory when he reflects on *failures* of loving. Every one of these failures – envy, ingratitude, schadenfreude – reduces to some misguided, excessive involvement of the dear self. Consider, for example, envy. Envy is "a propensity to view the well-being of others with distress", and to allow this propensity to "break [...] forth into action (to diminish [others'] well-being)" (TL 6:458). The envious person may *recognize* the ends of others perfectly clearly; but instead of being *drawn* to promote them, she finds them *distressing.*

How to explain such a reaction to others' ends? Why do some of us look at another's ends and want immediately to help, but others look at them and want to thwart that person's efforts? Such a reaction is rooted in obsessive self-centeredness: I am envious when I look at others through the lens of myself (as with the nervous mother), but now not through my fears *for* that *other* but instead through fears about *my* self-worth: "the standard [the envious person] use[s] to see how well off [she] is not the intrinsic worth of [her] own well-being but [rather] how it compares with that of others" (TL 6:458 f.). Failing to value herself properly as having intrinsic worth, the envious person instead judges her worth in comparison with others. That is why the success of others is distressing to her: if I compare myself to you, and you are high, then I am distressingly low. The envious person thus has an interest in assuring that others are brought low, that is, an interest in acting enviously to 'diminish their well-being'.[10] If love is the *other*-centered interest in *another* person's end, its opposite, envy, is a *self*-centered interest in *another* person's ends, that is, an interest in seeing those ends thwarted so as to raise one's own self-assessment.

These *failures* of love put a finer point upon just exactly what *true love* is. We fail at love when we look at others' ends only through the lens of our own self-related fears. True love thus occurs only when:

1) We view another's ends clearly (not via some veiled self-interest). I would call this being *attentive* to the other.

2) We take a *positive interest* in that other person's end *for her* and *in itself* (not only in comparison to my successes or failures). I would call this *loving concern* for the other.

3) We understand that person and her end so well that we know what to do on her behalf to promote that end without undermining her autonomous pursuit of it. I would call this attentive, loving *action*.

What we discover in the progress of these steps is the establishment of an attitude of *other-centeredness*. I must accomplish these three things in order truly to take another's end as my own, and thus to become a true help-mate to that person in the pursuit her ends.

---

10 It is thus only because I fail in that duty to myself to value myself by the proper standard of my intrinsic worth that I also fail in my duty to be loving to others. Kant thus calls this envious state a "sullen and *self*-torturous state" (TL 6:459). The concerns of the envious person are, that is, entirely *self*-centered, even (or perhaps especially) as she looks out at other people. This is why Kant insists that envy "is therefore contrary to one's duty to *oneself* as well as to others" (TL 6:459, emphasis added).

Conditions for the Possibility of Other-Centeredness

Our claim is that it is only the composed, autocratic person who could accomplish these demands of other-centeredness. But why?

First, think about someone trying to be attentive to another's ends, but who then experiences a surprise affect. This person therefore *turns in on herself* to figure out what the heck is going on. One who lacked the composure to get a hold of her affects would thus be a very self-focused person. She would be incapable of seeing another's ends because her view would be clouded by her own confusing, internally-focused experience of affects. This is what is going on for our nervous mother: she experiences understandable affects but is not able to 'get a hold of herself.' Instead, her affects make her think more about herself than her child, and lead her to her false beliefs about her child's ends. She is, literally, self-centered, and cannot be attentive. Attentiveness thus requires the composure of inner freedom: if I lack that control of my affects defined by composure, I lack attentiveness.

What, then, of the second step, viz., assuring that I react lovingly, not enviously, to another's ends? Because envy is a lasting passion, not a surprising affect, the envious person is not made self-centered by a surprise. But she ends up being even *more* self-centered than the person who cannot control her surprise affects. The envious person forms lasting, self-centered principles based on her inclinations of jealousy so as to thwart the ends of the person she envies. Bringing others down is the envious person's, reflective, "principled" way of focusing intensely on herself and her self-worth.

The composure of autocracy helps here by giving a person governing control over her passions. Indeed, a truly composed, autocratic person most likely would never even *form* these passions. Inner freedom, being a condition for the possibility of all duties of virtue, is also a condition for fulfilling the duty to avoid servility, i. e., the duty to respect oneself properly. The autocratic person *qua autocratic* thus has clear access to the true standard by which to affirm her self-worth (viz., the absolute value of all rational beings grounded in our capacity for autonomous choice). She thus avoids the false valuing of self that would ground a passionate pursuit of envious actions. The person of inner freedom is thus in a better position both to prevent the establishment of envious passions and to restrain one if it threatens to develop. Even if she has moments of self-doubt when she is tempted to cause injury to others in the name of upholding her sense of self-worth, she gets a hold of herself: she reminds herself of the true basis of her worth, and refuses to succumb to such temptations.

So, the moral of the story? Inner freedom is a condition for the possibility of loving others because it is a state whereby one gets a hold of oneself. The composed person has control of those affects and passions that threaten to infect loving other-centered attentiveness with excessive self-centeredness (in either a passing, confusing affect or a stubborn, established passion). Seeing another's end clearly and reacting lovingly to it require that we remove the static of excessive self-centeredness.[11]

We should thus reject the idea that we cannot take others' ends as our own unless we sympathize with them. Although sympathy is not necessarily at odds with making another's end my own, I needn't feel sympathy as such to accomplish that other-centeredness required for loving. Rather, attentiveness guided by that control of affects and passions found in the composure of inner freedom is sufficient. Our nervous mother, once she identified and controlled her fears, would quickly see her daughter more clearly. It is not that sympathy for her daughter's pursuit of philosophy couldn't be integrated into her frame of mind; indeed, in the ideal virtuous person, sympathy corresponding to the permissible ends of others would be an emerging feature of one's character developed through the continual exercise of one's autocratic composure.[12] But feeling sympathy is not at the *heart* of what allows her to see her daughter's end; attentiveness – a setting aside of one's affects and passions so as to gain a clearer view of others – is more basic. Composure and attentiveness are thus prerequisites for any morally-guided sympathy. And yet, one *can* be successful in making another person's end one's own *without* feeling sympathy as such. All that is required is the composure and attentiveness inspired by inner freedom. As long as our nervous mother gets a hold of her fears, she can take her daughter's end as her own. She can pay her tuition, maybe even pick up a copy of Kant's *Groundwork* to try to figure out what the big deal is about this philosophy thing. She can act in these ways to promote her daughter's end without feeling sympathy toward her. She might even feel some pain ("Eek! My daughter is becoming a philosopher!"). But as long as she controls those affects, they will not prevent her from seeing her daughter's end clearly and then acting so as to promote it.[13]

---

11 One mustn't under-estimate how frequently affects and passions are found in our relationships with others. *Whenever* we deal with other people, we must expect *lots* of surprise affects and deep-seated passions. Mother-child relations are one obvious example, but romantic love relationships are another. If one tries to be loving toward others without the tool of composure, one simply is not going to be in a frame of mind that allows you to see, clearly and lovingly, the ends of others.
12 "[B]e *beneficent* to your fellow human being, and being beneficent will then effect in you love of humanity (as an aptitude of the inclination to beneficence generally)" (TL 6:402).
13 The friend of humanity in *Groundwork I* is an example of just this sort of capacity for taking another's ends as one's own without feeling sympathy. This man, accustomed to acting out of sympathy, becomes "beclouded by his own grief" and loses all natural sympathy. When he still acts morally, "inclination no longer stimulates him", yet he is able "to tear himself out of this deadly

Taking another's ends as one's own thus requires not just respect for others and not just a clear understanding of the formulations of the Categorical Imperative. Beyond all this, one also needs that self-control and composure guaranteed by inner freedom. Without the attentiveness that results from a proper constraint of one's self-focused affects, inclinations and passions, respectful efforts to reason via the Categorical Imperative about another's ends would be so subject to self-deception – or at least to confusion – that we would rarely hit the mark of successful beneficence. To acquire that other-centeredness necessary for loving others, we must thus set ourselves – our affects, inclinations and passions – aside, and focus honestly, attentively and lovingly upon the needs of others.

III Austen: Composure, Usefulness and Self-Persuasion

Unfree, Discomposed, Self-Centered, Useless and Envious Mary

I want now to *illustrate* the impact that having – or not having – this state of inner freedom has upon the possibility of becoming a loving person. Mary and Anne Elliot, sisters in Jane Austen's *Persuasion*, are perfect examples, respectively, of unfree and free would-be lovers dealing with their affects and passions.

Let's start with the younger sister, Mary. Mary is very much caught up with her own affects and passions, and also has a strong tendency toward failures of love: she is both useless (she cannot identify and/or take others' ends as her own) and envious (by basing her self-worth in self-other comparison she is motivated to cause injury to others and their ends in the interests of calming her distress about her feared worthlessness).

In Anne's first visit to Mary, we are introduced to the most childish, self-centered, useless and spoiled person imaginable. She can do nothing but complain to Anne about how everyone is ignoring her; but then also complains about how awful everyone is anyway. Her own sons "are so unmanageable that they do me more harm than good", and the "Miss Musgroves" (two young aristocratic neighbors of a marriageable age) "never put themselves out of their way" to come

---

insensibility, and [...] do the action without any inclination, solely from duty" (GMS 4:398). He is thus acting for others without access to any feelings. At most, the indirect reference to acting 'from duty' might suggest he is feeling the moral feeling of respect.

visit Mary (*Persuasion*, 36). When Anne apologizes for not visiting Mary sooner because "I [...] have had so much to do that I could not very conveniently have left [their family estate] Kellynch sooner", Mary's immediate response is "Dear me! What can *you* possibly have to do?" (*Persuasion*, 37) You get the picture. Mary is a particularly self-centered person.

Being so self-centered, Mary is simply not capable of practical love. She cannot, that is, take others' ends as her own. In Austen's language, she is not "useful" to others. Her husband, Charles Musgrove, himself not a *very* useful person, is at least clear-headed enough to see that Mary is not useful or other-centered, especially in caring for their children. He complains to Anne, and she sympathizes. But Anne, "when listening in turn to Mary's reproach of 'Charles spoils the children so that I cannot get them into any order,' – she [Anne] never had the smallest temptation to say, 'Very true'" (*Persuasion*, 42). Anne is very aware that Charles is the better parent, and always sympathizes when he complains about Mary; but Anne would never agree with Mary when she complains about Charles. Mary just isn't good at seeing her children's true needs and therefore loving them. She is simply not useful.

Mary's self-centered uselessness is, in true Kantian fashion, tied both to her inability to control her affects and her failure to value herself properly. Let's consider each of these in turn. If the composed person is one who has gotten control of herself, the discomposed person is one whose affects have gotten control of her, and this is exactly Mary. One of the best places to see Mary's affects getting out of control is in a central scene of Volume I: a young, single aristocratic neighbor, Louisa Musgrove, while flirting with the very marriageable Captain Wentworth, gets a little too pleased with herself about jumping up and down on the rocks around the Cobb (the stone-lined seaside pathway/walk) in Lyme Regis, in part through Captain Wentworth's gentle flirtations with her. She slips in one jump, falls to the ground, and knocks herself unconscious. Let's join the scene at this point:

> Captain Wentworth, who had caught [Louisa] up, knelt with her in his arms, looking on her with a face as pallid as her own, in an agony of silence. 'She is dead! She is dead!' screamed Mary, catching hold of her husband, and contributing with his own horror to make him immovable. (*Persuasion*, 102)

This is quintessential Mary: immediate and uncontrolled sputtering of unreflective affects.

Mary is, furthermore, not loving, but instead that envious person of whom Kant spoke, the one who gets easily distressed by the well-being of others precisely because another's well-being only assures, in one's own mind one's own declining worth. The aftermath of Louisa's fall on the Cobb gives us the best sense of Mary's enviousness. Everyone is trying to figure out how best to care for Louisa at Lyme even as some in their party need to return home. Captain Wentworth realizes that "useful" (that is, practically loving) Anne is the clear choice to stay in Lyme and attend to Louisa: "'If one stays to assist [...], I think it need be only one. – [Mary] will, of course, wish to get back to her children; but, if Anne will stay [...] no one so proper, so capable as Anne!'" (*Persuasion*, 106)

Even such indirect preferencing of Anne over herself is not something Mary can tolerate. Even if she really isn't useful, Mary cannot bear anyone suggesting that she isn't:

> When the plan was made known to Mary [...] there was an end of all peace in it. She was so wretched, and so vehement, complained so much of injustice in being expected to go away, instead of Anne; – Anne, who was nothing to Louisa, while *she* was her sister[-in-law], and had the best *right* to stay [...]! Why was not *she* to be as useful as Anne? And to go home without Charles, too – without her husband! No, [...] it was too unkind! And, in short, she said more than her husband could long withstand; and as none of the *others* could oppose when *he* gave way, there was no help for it: the change of Mary for Anne was inevitable. (*Persuasion*, 106 f., emphases added)

What we are seeing here is the intense *jealousy* that Mary feels toward Anne for being recognized publically as being useful. Mary is evaluating Anne's usefulness through the lens of her own fears of worthlessness: if Anne is useful, Mary is useless. The affirmation of Anne is therefore, in Mary's eyes, an insult to Mary. And so, as with anyone who judges his or her worth comparatively, the only way Mary can react is enviously to swipe down Anne, to insist that she – Mary – could 'be as useful as Anne'. She must, that is, pull down this public affirmation of Anne so as to pull herself up. Mary is truly useless and Anne is the useful one. But it is the useless one who will stay on at Lyme pretending to be useful to Louisa.

One also gets the sense from this episode of how inadequate a romantic lover Mary is. Everyone can see here just how unfortunate a match her husband has made. Everyone rolls their eyes quietly, if sympathetically, as they watch Mary's self-centered petulance and Charles' relenting, just for the sake of family peace. The spouse of an envious person is not someone to be envied.

This, then, is Austen's particularly Kantian moral assessment of Mary Elliot. Mary fails to be loving in Kant's sense of practical love. In Austen's language, Mary fails to be useful and becomes envious instead, precisely because her affects and passions are not autocratically composed and because she judges her worth only in comparison to others. In short, Mary is not a *free person*. She *is* a person and so is free in that she could have done otherwise. But she is not the person of

inner freedom. She is instead the Unfree, Discomposed Queen of Envious Uselessness.

Free, Composed, Other-Centered, Useful and Loving Anne

If Mary is the Unfree, Discomposed Queen of Envious Uselessness, then her elder
sister Anne is the Free, Composed Queen of Other-Centered and Loving Usefulness.

First, Anne is *exceedingly* useful, with a particular flair for taking others' ends
as her own. We first see this in the loving, tolerant way she manages her petulant
sister. When she comes to visit Mary and finds her so out of sorts, Anne helps Mary
identify and reach an end that Mary herself didn't know she had. Anne knows that
if Mary would just stop focusing on her worries, she would get into a better mood.
She thus gently – lovingly – nudges Mary in that direction. While petulant Mary
continues in her litany of complaints, Anne's gentle, "cheerful" rejoinder is "'you
will soon be better now' [...] 'You know I always cure you when I come.'" (*Persuasion*, 36) And indeed, Anne is right; as the narrator confidently reports, "[a] little
farther perseverance in patience, and forced cheerfulness on Anne's side, pro-
duced nearly a cure on Mary's" (*Persuasion*, 38).

This cheerful, loving attitude, capable of melting even the most recalcitrant of
ill-tempered persons like Mary, is something Anne seems to carry with her regu-
larly, wherever she goes. Indeed, *everyone* seems to want Anne to help them
with something. Everyone recognizes her cheerful usefulness as well as her
good sense and judgment, especially as compared to her sister Mary:

> Known to have some influence with her sister, she was continually requested, or at least re-
> ceiving hints to exert it, beyond what was practicable. 'I wish you could persuade Mary not to
> be always fancying herself ill,' was Charles's language; and, in an unhappy mood, thus spoke
> Mary; – 'I do believe if Charles were to see me dying, he would not think there was any thing
> the matter with me. I am sure, Anne, if you would, you might persuade him that I really am
> very ill – a great deal worse than I ever own.' [...] [Even] Mrs. Musgrove [Charles' mother]
> took the first opportunity of being alone with Anne, to say, 'Oh! Miss Anne, I cannot help
> wishing Mrs. Charles [i. e., Mary] had a little of your method with those children. They are
> quite different creatures with you! [...] It is a pity you cannot put your sister in the way of
> managing them. (*Persuasion*, 42)

Poor Anne! So many people depend on her loving usefulness, and especially on her
ability to be gently *persuasive* toward those in need of improving their judgment
and character. And yet Anne does not take on this role reluctantly or with hesita-
tion. To the contrary, she fulfills it to the best of her ability and in a most exemplary manner.

Nowhere is Anne's capacity for usefulness so clearly on display as in that same Cobb scene wherein Mary collapsed into a blithering mess. While Mary is screaming "She's dead! She's dead!" and Captain Wentworth hears Mary's screams and sees the other Miss Musgrove, Henrietta, faint in response, here is Anne's response:

> 'Is there no one to help me?' were the first words which burst from Captain Wentworth, in a tone of despair, and as if all his own strength were gone. 'Go to him, go to him,' cried Anne [to Captain Benwick, Captain Wentworth's friend and colleague], 'for heaven's sake go to him. I can support [Henrietta] myself. Leave me, and go to him. Rub her hands, rub her temples; here are salts, – take them, take them.'" (*Persuasion*, 102)

Besides the fact that Anne is the sort always to carry smelling salts around with her, ready for any occasion, her calm, directive manner at a moment of extreme urgency is particularly telling of her character. One might call this "calm urgency": at exactly the moment when affects are flying high and causing everyone to be in disarray, Anne may experience the same affects but does not allow them to take over her judgment. Instead, that calm, composed, attentive judgment shines through even as affects fly about all around her. This is like Jeeve's raised eyebrow: even in the midst of high affect, Anne remains calm and is able to act in a way that is truly useful to others. Anne is as useful as she is – that is, can take another's ends as her own as well as she does – precisely because she is composed, and therefore attentively other-centered. Anne is, in other words, a free person. The contrast with her sister Mary's utter inability to acquire such control, composure, attentiveness and other-centeredness couldn't be more stark.

Anne's Unruly Affects and Bad Judgment

One might be surprised, then, to learn that Anne is not in control of all her affects. When her would-be love interest, Captain Wentworth, so publically proclaims her usefulness, Anne is internally shaken by unexpected strong affects. When he says there is "'no one so proper, so capable as Anne!" Austen tells us: "[Anne] paused a moment to recover from the emotion of hearing herself so spoken of". And after Captain Wentworth speaks to her "with a glow, and yet a gentleness which seemed almost restoring the past, [...] [Anne] colored deeply; and [Captain Wentworth] recollected himself, and moved away" (*Persuasion*, 106). I know this doesn't seem a huge discomposure, but keep in mind that this is Austen, and they are English! There had been no mention of even a flutter of emotion when Anne took charge of a potentially life-threatening situation. So when she has to pause and even blushes in response to Captain Wentworth's attentions to her, this is *high drama!*

Let's dwell for a moment on Anne's affects related to Captain Wentworth. A much younger – 19 year old – Anne had turned down Captain Wentworth's offer of marriage on the advice of her mother-figure and family friend, Lady Russell. Captain Wentworth then went off to become a wildly successful and wealthy navy captain. His return to England eight years later to a still single but now 27 year old Anne Elliot is the event that moves the whole novel forward. His return throws Anne into an emotional tizzy to which she is not accustomed. His return is thus a challenge to Anne to utilize her developed composure to take her inner freedom to the highest level. Can she attain even that level of inner freedom in which one is so much in control of one's affects and passions that one is even capable of composure and fulfillment of duties of love within the context of an affect-filled relationship of *romantic* love? Let's find out!

Remember, affects are surprises, and Anne *is* surprised when Captain Wentworth speaks so highly of her. In a way, she *shouldn't* be surprised. She has, since his return to England, been reigniting her love for him, and so should have started to *expect* such things. But she's not been honest with herself about her love; she just isn't able to admit to herself that she loves him nor that he has been acting in ways that suggest he still loves her. Indeed, Anne's been busy trying to convince herself that Captain Wentworth is in love with one of the Miss Musgroves; that would be so much safer. It is precisely because she is deceiving herself in this way that one of her affects gets under her otherwise very impressive radar detection system and unsettles her. She is genuinely surprised when Captain Wentworth is complimentary of her. She is expecting him to shower compliments on one of the Miss Musgroves.

Anne was, however, just previous to this Cobb incident, starting to admit to herself that she's not really been honest with herself about her feelings in relation to Captain Wentworth. In an interesting earlier interaction with Captain Benwick (a recently widowed navy captain who is still intensely grieving the loss of his wife), Anne earnestly recommends to him that he stop reading so much poetry since "the strong feelings which alone could estimate it *truly*, were the very feelings which ought to taste it but *sparingly*" (*Persuasion*, 94, emphases added). Anne goes on to recommend to Captain Benwick that he expand his reading list, that he consider "such collections of the finest letters, such memoirs of characters of worth and suffering, as occurred to her at the moment as calculated to rouse and fortify the mind by the highest precepts, and the strongest examples of moral and religious endurances" (*Persuasion*, 94). This all seems very good advice to a widower who might be using his love of poetry to languor in melancholic reminiscences about his lost wife: read things instead that will make you strong, not things that cause you to lose yourself in your sad feelings!

And yet Anne has enough composure, and also enough of a resulting self-knowledge, to realize her advice to Captain Benwick was really advice she needed to give herself. Anne hasn't been needing to dwell on *literal* feelings of grief; but the reappearance of Captain Wentworth, eight years after Anne had spurned his love, *has* been inspiring feelings of grief of a certain sort: she is feeling the grief of having been ill-persuaded to have made a bad decision in turning down Captain Wentworth's offer of marriage to her. Having Captain Wentworth back in her world is now only making her reflect with melancholy on all that could have been for them in their life together. She thus admits to herself:

> When the evening was over, Anne could not but be amused at the idea of her coming to Lyme, to preach patience and resignation to a young man whom she had never seen before; nor could she help fearing, on more serious reflection, that, like many other great moralists and preachers, she had been eloquent on a point in which her own conduct would ill bear examination. (*Persuasion*, 94)

Anne is thus indeed *struggling* with those affects related to the reentry of Captain Wentworth into her life. As her reflections on her interactions with Captain Benwick reveal, her first response to experiencing them is to *indulge* them instead of *control* them. One might even say that Anne is tempted toward establishing her regular flutters of romantic affects as established passions.

One result of this failure of control of her affects is that, whereas she has a particular capacity for attentiveness to most everyone else around her, her efforts to be attentive to Captain Wentworth sometimes get muddled. The continuation of the Cobb scene discussed above is a case in point. Anne is perplexed by Captain Wentworth's reaction upon learning that Mary, instead of Anne, will stay at Lyme. He only learns of this when it is Anne, instead of Mary, who climbs into his carriage to return home. Here is his reaction, and then Anne's reaction to him:

> [H]is evident surprise and vexation, at the substitution of one sister for the other – the change of his countenance – the astonishment – the expressions begun and suppressed, [...] made but a mortifying reception of Anne; *or must at least convince her that she was valued only as she could be useful to Louisa* [...] She endeavored to be composed and just [...] [S]he *would* have attended on Louisa with a zeal above the common claims of regard, for *his* sake; and she hoped *he* would not long be so unjust as to suppose *she* would shrink unnecessarily from the office of a friend. (*Persuasion*, 107 f., emphases added)

Anne is confused here: she mistakes Captain Wentworth's consternation at Mary for a judgment about *her* character. It is not. He is angry about Mary's childish envy, and about how everyone has given in to her instead of standing up to her. But Anne believes his consternation reveals that he cares for Anne only to the extent that she can be useful to Louisa, and that he does not care for Anne in herself.

Essentially, she still believes (self-deceptively) that Captain Wentworth's romantic interests are for Louisa, not her, and that his previous appreciation for her capabilities and usefulness were only active as long as Anne was focusing her concerns on Captain Wentworth's true love, Louisa. Nothing could be further from the truth; she entirely misreads Captain Wentworth's reactions and beliefs. Her affects thus lead her to a failure of attentiveness; her armor of inner freedom has a chink in it. Anne has not gotten a hold of herself here; rather, her affects have gotten a hold of her. As Kant reminds us, affects, "preceding reflection [...] make [such reflection] impossible or more difficult" (TL 6:407).

Reclaiming Proper Persuasion

In order to hope for true love with Captain Wentworth, Anne needs to learn to get a hold of her affects, and thereby become more attentive to him. She must, that is, improve her capacity to *love* him. Happily, even while Anne struggles with her affects, she also, at least intermittently, succeeds in being very attentive to Captain Wentworth, and this fact is indirect evidence that she has control over at least some of her affects in relationship to him. One good example of her attentiveness to his emotional state is when Mrs. Musgrove laments the death of her son, Richard, who had been a member of Captain Wentworth's crew during the war, but whom both Captain Wentworth and Anne know to have been a particularly difficult, inept and annoying person:

> 'Poor, dear, [Richard]!' continued Mrs. Musgrove; 'he was grown so steady, and such an excellent correspondent, while he was under your care! Ah! It would have been a happy thing, if he had never left you. I assure you, Captain Wentworth, we are very sorry he ever left you.' There was a momentary expression in Captain Wentworth's face at this speech, a certain glance of his bright eye, and curl of his handsome mouth, which convinced Anne, that instead of sharing in Mrs. Musgrove's kind wishes, as to her son, he had probably been at some pains to get rid of him; but it was too transient an indulgence of self-amusement to be detected by any who understood him less than herself; in another moment he was perfectly collected and serious; and almost instantly afterwards coming up to the sofa, on which [...] Mrs. Musgrove [was] sitting, took a place by [here], and entered into conversation with her, in a low voice, about her son, doing it with so much sympathy and natural grace, as shewed the kindest consideration for all that was real and unabsurd in the parent's feelings. (*Persuasion*, 63)

Similarly, Anne attentively observes CW's reaction to Mary when she makes an egregious complaint about her "lower" relations, the Hayters:

> Mary took the opportunity of looking scornfully around her, and saying to Captain Wentworth, 'It is very unpleasant, having such connexions! [i.e., the Hayters] But I assure you, I

have never been in *the*[ir] house above twice in my life.' She received no other answer, than an artificial, assenting smile, followed by a contemptuous glance, as he turned away, which Anne perfectly knew the meaning of. (*Persuasion*, 80)

Clearly, Anne is capable of being attentive to Captain Wentworth! Even as she struggles through the difficult emotional time of his return to England, Anne retains at least some of her characteristic underlying composure which assures a clear vision of others around her.

And I am happy to report that it is these attentive reflections that win the day: Anne's attentiveness to Captain Wentworth (and his capacity to reciprocate it) are the first steps in them being able to take each other's ends as their own, that is, in them being able to love each other.

Indeed, as Austen affirms, Anne was always much better at attentiveness than her mother-figure, Lady Russell: "There is a quickness of perception in some, a nicety in the discernment of character, a natural penetration [...] and Lady Russell had been less gifted in this part of understanding than her young friend." (*Persuasion*, 233) Anne has a 'quickness of perception' which allows 'discernment of character;' that is, she has an attentiveness to others that allows her to see others clearly. It is this persistent attentiveness, even in the face of the storm of social pressures and internal personal affects she had to weather in order to retain it, that insures Anne will love Captain Wentworth truly. It also explains her "usefulness" generally. Anne is so useful – so practically loving – precisely because she has this capacity for attentiveness. She does not allow self-centered concerns to get in the way of her perception of others. She is, therefore, able to take up those ends with a loving concern instead of a vengeful enviousness. This, then, is what the truly free person looks like: if her sister Mary is the Unfree, Discomposed Queen of Envious Uselessness, Anne is the Free, Composed Queen of Other-Centered and Loving Usefulness, even to the point of being truly other-oriented in that most fraught of love situations, romantic love.

Of course, in Austen's world, this means that she lives happily ever after: Anne and Captain Wentworth go swanning off into the sunset. Kant is, perhaps, less confident that everything will go well for a person just because she is so fully moral: the world will not always conform to even the most excellent good will. Nonetheless, even Kant would admit that Anne can at least hope for that steadiness of character that is virtue. Although one cannot be guaranteed to live *happily* ever after, one can live *freely* and *virtuously* ever after. As Kant says (with some gender modification to apply all this to Anne's situation): "Only in [virtue's] possession is [one] 'free,' 'healthy,' 'rich,' 'a [queen],' and so forth and can suffer no loss by chance or fate, since [she] is in possession of [herself] and the virtuous [woman] cannot lose

[her] virtue" (TL 6:405). May Anne and Captain Wentworth live *freely* and *virtuously* ever after!

References

Austen, Jane, *Persuasion*, London: Penguin Classics 2015.

Baxley, Anne Margaret, 2010, *Kant's Theory of Virtue: The Value of Autocracy.* Cambridge: Cambridge University Press.

Collins English Dictionary, online version, www.collinsdictionary.com/dictionary/english – last accesses April 17, 2023.

Engstrom, Stephen, 2002, "The Inner Freedom of Virtue", in: Mark Timmons (ed.), *Kant's Metaphysics of Morals: Interpretive Essays*, Oxford: Oxford University Press, 289–316.

Oxford English Dictionary Online, www.oed.com – last accessed April 17, 2023.

Wodehouse, P.G., 1991. Th*e Jeeves Omnibus*, London: Hutchinson Publishers.

Fahmy, Melissa S., 2016, "Love's Reasons", *Journal of Value Inquiry*, 50, 153–168.

Dieter Schönecker

Kant on *Menschenliebe* as a Moral Predisposition of the Mind

Abstract: I will first offer a brief interpretation of Kant's theory of "Aesthetic pre-concepts of the mind's receptivity to concepts of duty as such" (section XII of the "Introduction to the Doctrine of Virtue"). These moral predispositions (moral feeling, conscience, love of human beings, and self-respect), I argue, lie at the ground of morality inasmuch as they are the subjective conditions for being affected by concepts of duty to become aware of the necessitation that lies in the concept of duty and, hence, to be able to think of a duty and thus to be obligated at all. I shall then argue that the "love of human beings" as one of those four moral predispositions must be identified with "love that is delight (*amor complacentiae*); this *Menschenliebe* is not to be confused with "benevolence (*amor benevolentiae*)" nor is it the "dexterity of the inclination to beneficence in general".

In this paper, I shall try to achieve two things: First, I will offer a brief interpretation of how to understand Kant's theory of moral predispositions as he develops it in section XII of the "Introduction to the Doctrine of Virtue". Based on this understanding, I shall, secondly and primarily, address the question of how to understand the "Love of human beings" (TL 6:401)[1] that is one of those four moral predispositions "of receptiveness to the concept of duty" (TL 6:399); the other three of those four moral predispositions are moral feeling, conscience, and self-respect. My claim will be that the 'love of human beings' – I will refer to this love with the German term *Menschenliebe*[2] – must be identified with what Kant calls "love that is delight (*amor complacentiae*)" (TL 6:402), and *not*, as is often assumed, with "benevolence (*amor benevolentiae*)" (TL 6:401). My focus will be almost only on the *Doctrine of Virtue*.[3]

---

1 All translations are my own, based upon the translation by Mary Gregor. "TL" stands for Kant's "Metaphysische Anfangsgründe der Tugendlehre" (*Metaphysical First Principles of the Doctrine of Virtue*), the numbers in brackets refer to the pagination of the so-called *Akademie-Ausgabe* (AA). – Special thanks to Martin Brecher and Pärttyli Rinne for very helpful critique and observations on an earlier draft of the paper.

2 For a brief account of the historical and etymological perspective of the term "Menschenliebe" cf. Rinne (2018, 125).

3 This paper is based on Schönecker (2010) in which a comprehensive reception of the secondary literature was undertaken. Here, I will only discuss literature on *Menschenliebe* as a moral predis-

https://doi.org/10.1515/9783111291130-007

1 Kant's theory of moral predispositions

To begin with, let us quote the crucial, introductory passage in chapter XII of the "Introduction to the Doctrine of Virtue". (For short, I call this introductory passage *EXII*; the section on *Menschenliebe* in chapter XII [TL 6:401.23–402.26] I call *love-section*.)

> *Aesthetic preconcepts[4] of the mind's receptivity to concepts of duty as such*
>
> There are certain moral endowments [*Beschaffenheiten*] such that if one does not have them, there also can be no duty to acquire them. – They are moral feeling, conscience, love of one's neighbor, and respect for oneself (self-esteem), which there is no obligation to have: because they lie at the ground of morality, as subjective conditions of receptiveness to the concept of duty, not as objective conditions of morality. All of them are aesthetic and preceding, yet natural predispositions of the mind (*praedispositio*) for being affected by concepts of duty; to have these predispositions cannot be considered a duty, rather, every human being has them, and it is by virtue of them that he can be obligated. – Consciousness of them is not of empirical origin; rather, it can only follow upon that of a moral law as the effect thereof on the mind. (TL 6:399).[5]

Kant speaks both of 'moral endowments' and 'natural predispositions'. Since the German word *Beschaffenheiten* (endowments) is somewhat ambiguous, I shall

---

position published ever since. Many thanks to Pärttyli Rinne for some helpful references. – In that paper, I have also discussed several passages in other writings of Kant's on *amor complacentiae*, including the *Religionsschrift* and his *Lectures*. Here, I have no room for this, but note that one cannot simply assume that Kant holds the same position on *amor complacentiae* throughout his writings; cf. Rinne (2018, 124–129).

4 Guyer (2017, 247) translates "Ästhetische Vorbegriffe" (TL 6:399.2) with "preconditions", arguing that this is closer to Kant's talk of 'predispositions'; Deimling (2014, 122 fn. 4) and Rinne (2018, 124) follow Guyer's suggestion. However, not only is "preconditions" not a literal translation, but it misses the resemblance to the most important "V o r b e g r i f f e z u r M e t a p h y s i k d e r S i t t e n (*Philosophia practica universalis*)" (MS 6:221), and also to the "Vorbegriffe zur Eintheilung der Tugendlehre" (TL 6:410.2); in each case, "Vorbegriffe" certainly cannot be translated with "preconditions". (Note that "Vorbegriffe" is quite unusual in German as well.) On this, also cf. Goy (2013, 185 f.).

5 As I have tried to show in Schönecker (2010), this passage has gone almost completely unnoticed in the literature, and this is even true for some of the more recent literature: Sherman (2014, 31 fn. 13) quotes the crucial passage from *EXII* (TL 6:399), but she says very little about it and nothing about *Menschenliebe*. Baron (2014, 85 fn. 21) just sees "some relevance" in the moral predispositions and she, too, says very little about it (just as Deimling 2014). Grenberg (2014) emphasizes the importance of 'love' in a Kantian account of morality, but she does not mention *Menschenliebe* as a moral predisposition at all.

use the Latin term 'praedispositio' (predisposition) instead; this term I connect with the term 'moral', and so I will speak of *moral predispositions*.[6]

It is Kant's claim that these moral predispositions 'lie at the ground of morality'. As a matter of fact, in *EXII*, Kant uses three different formulations to express this thought. Slightly reconstructed, we have the following propositions:

(G1) The moral predispositions lie at the ground of morality as subjective conditions of receptiveness to the concept of duty.[7]

(G2) The moral predispositions are predispositions of the mind for being affected by concepts of duty.[8]

(G3) The moral predispositions are predispositions by virtue of which the human being can be obligated.[9]

In the subsection on moral feeling (TL 6:399.18–400.20), there is a fourth and very important formulation: "any consciousness of obligation depends upon moral feeling to become aware of the necessitation that lies in the concept of duty" (TL 6:399). On the assumption that we may apply this formulation to all four moral predispositions (I shall get back to this assumption in due course), we get:

(G4) Any consciousness of obligation depends upon moral predispositions to become aware of the necessitation that lies in the concept of duty.[10]

In the subsection on self-respect (TL 6:402.29–403.6) there is one sentence that includes two more formulations of the same basic idea. The feeling of self-respect, Kant says, is

> the ground of certain duties, that is, of certain actions that are consistent with his duty to himself. Not: he has a duty of respect towards himself, for he must have respect for the law within himself in order even to be able to think of a duty (TL 6:403).

---

6 A little later in the *Einleitung*, Kant speaks of an "aesthetic of morals" (TL 6:406) and of "feelings that accompany the constraining power of the moral law" (*ibid.*); here, I cannot discuss how this is related to the moral predispositions. – I can only mention in passing that there is a medical background here: In Kant's time, 'predisposition' is a term primarily used by physicians; furthermore, Brownianism plays an important role, and indeed Kant refers to the "language of physicians" (TL 6:400) in his analysis of the 'moral feeling' as one of the four moral predispositions. Thanks to Maja Schepelmann for discussions about this aspect.

7 Cf. TL 6:399.7–10.

8 Cf. TL 6:399.12.

9 Cf. TL 6:399.13 f.

10 Cf. TL 6:399.30 f.

This yields:

(G5) The moral predispositions are the ground of certain duties.[11]
(G6) The human being must have moral predispositions in order even to be able to think of a duty.[12]

So there can be no doubt whatsoever that the moral predispositions function as a 'ground' for morality. But how exactly? Let us make three preliminary and brief observations on this claim.

First, Kant speaks of the moral predispositions both with regard to the endowments as such as well as with regard to the actual feelings they enable us to have; in each case, there is a moral predisposition that is "affected" (TL 6:399.12), and this affection yields a 'feeling'.[13] So there is, for instance, *amor complacentiae* as a moral predisposition and *amor complacentiae* as a moral feeling grounded in this predisposition.

Second, Kant repeatedly claims in the entire chapter on moral predispositions (in *EXII*) *that there can be no duty to have them.* Whatever exactly it means that the moral predispositions 'lie at the ground of morality', it is not disputable that to have or acquire these moral predispositions is not obligatory *"because"* (TL 6:399.8, my emphasis) they 'lie at the ground of morality'. The argument is as simple as it is convincing: It obviously cannot be obligatory to have or acquire something that is already presupposed for obligation itself. Since the moral predispositions are already presupposed for obligation itself insasmuch they 'lie at the ground of morality', there can be no duty to have or acquire them.[14]

Third, Kant underlines that the moral predispositions are not '*objective* conditions of morality'. Thus, the question of what the moral norms *are* is not answered in reference to the moral predispositions (but in reference to some kind of test using a categorical imperative). In the *Preface* of the *Doctrine of Virtue*, Kant explic-

---

11 Cf. TL 6:403.2.
12 Cf. TL 6:403.5 f.
13 And there can be no doubt that Kant then speaks directly and indirectly of actual feelings with regard to each of the moral predispositions; cf., for instance, TL 6:399.25; 430.30; 402.25; 402.30.
14 Kant does say that there is a duty to "cultivate" (TL 6:399.33; 401.19) moral feeling and consicence. This, however, does not imply the danger of a circle in that we would be obliged to this cultivation and yet could not be obliged because obligation already presupposes cultivated predispositions (as Guyer, 2017, 249, claims): Kant is very strong in his claim that everyone has these dispositions and they as such, regardless of their cultivation, enable us to be at least minimally receptive to the claims of moral duty (TL 6:400.9–15; 401.31–33).

itly says that no moral feeling, not even the moral feeling understood as one of the moral predispositions, serves to "determine duties" (TL 6:377.1).

Now at first sight, the relation between formulations (G1), (G2), and (G3) seems fairly easy: The moral predispositions are subjective conditions of receptiveness to the concept of duty in that they enable us to be affected by concepts of duty; and since to be affected by concepts of duty is a necessary condition to be obligated, the moral predispositions are predispositions by virtue of which the human being can be obligated. Therefore, it is tempting to understand Kant's theory of moral predispositions *merely* as a theory of moral receptiveness and hence as a theory of moral motivation. On this reading, to be morally receptive is equivalent to be receptive to a motive that, *ceteris paribus*, brings about an action; as a matter of fact, Kant speaks of the moral feeling as one of the four moral predispositions as "a susceptibility of free choice to be moved by pure practical reason" (TL 6:400). I do not deny that this function to move us is essential to the moral predispositions.

However, I do not think that this is the whole story. Let me explain why and let us begin with (G4): 'Any consciousness of obligation', says Kant, 'depends upon moral predispositions to become aware of the necessitation that lies in the concept of duty'. It is striking that Kant here (with direct regard to the moral feeling: TL 6:399.29–31) does not claim that the moral predispositions motivate; rather, the claim is much stronger, to wit, that our very 'consciousness of obligation' depends on moral predispositions insofar as we cannot have a consciousness of the 'necessitation that lies in the concept of duty' without moral predispositions. However, since the 'necessitation that lies in the concept of duty' is exactly what makes the moral law a categorical *imperative*, (G4) implies that we cannot even have a consciousness of the categorical imperative without moral predispositions.

This stronger interpretation is also supported by (G6). With reference to moral self-esteem, but possibly in a generalizable manner, Kant claims that the human being must have moral predispositions in order 'even to be able to think of a duty'. A being that is unable to understand the necessitation involved in the categorical imperative does not understand this imperative at all. Such a being (say some kind of artificial intelligence) might be able to run some kind of test of universalisation in order to ask itself whether a given maxim can be a moral law; but it is unable to understand the normative force involved in a categorical imperative unless it has the appropriate moral feelings. Since this imperativeness of the categorical imperative – the imperative that I *ought* to do something or that I *ought* to refrain from doing something – is essential to the moral law as a categorical imperative, there is no understanding of the categorical imperative without moral predispositions; without them, the human being is unable, *sich nur eine Pflicht überhaupt denken zu können* (to 'even *think* of a duty').[15]

Thus we can distinguish three interpretations as regards the function of the four moral predispositions. According to a possible *weak* interpretation, they just have a supporting function; they might help us to do our duty from respect, but we can do without them. This interpretation, I submit, runs clearly contrary to what the text actually says. On a *modest* interpretation, the moral predispositions are necessary conditions for moral motivation, but our *understanding* of the categorical imperative does not depend on them. On a *strong* interpretation, the moral predispositions not only motivate us to act according to the moral law, and they not only make our actions moral actions; rather, they enable us to *understand* that there are certain actions that are commanded categorically. On the strong reading, Kant's claim is this:

(G) The moral predispositions lie at the ground of morality inasmuch as they are the subjective conditions for being affected by concepts of duty to become aware of the necessitation that lies in the concept of duty and, hence, to be able to think of a duty and thus to be obligated at all.

I have argued for this strong interpretation of moral predispositions. But the last sentence of *EXII* seems to contain a difficulty for this reading. Let us have a look again at the original formulation:

(C) Consciousness of them is not of empirical origin; rather, it can only follow upon that of a moral law as the effect thereof on the mind. (TL 6:399.14–16).

By virtue of some easy grammatical reconstructions and by eliminating, for now, the negative claim ('that the consciousness of the moral predispositions is not of empirical origin'), we get:

(C)* Consciousness of the moral predispositions can only follow upon the consciousness of a moral law as the effect thereof on the mind.

In German, there is quite a problem in (C) because of the reference both of 'thereof' (*desselben*) and of 'effect' (*Wirkung*). The 'effect' brought about we have already

---

15 Cf. Schönecker (2022). As I have claimed elsewhere (Schönecker 2013a, 2013b), this is also what Kant means by *Faktum der Vernunft*. The 'moral feeling' in *EXII*, I take it, is identical with what Kant calls elsewhere 'respect' (*Achtung*).

identified as the 'consciousness of the moral predispositions', although, as a matter of fact, there are, grammatically speaking, four possible reconstructions. For our purposes, I skip this tedious work[16] and simply refer 'thereof' to the moral law (and not to the 'consciousness of the moral law'). Also, we can replace '*a* moral law' by '*the* moral law', that is, by the categorical imperative, and thus we get:

(C)** Consciousness of the moral predispositions can only follow upon the consciousness of the categorical imperative as the effect of this categorical imperative on the mind (the consciousness of the moral predispositions being the effect).

I should mention in passing that Mary Gregor's translation here as almost everywhere is quite loose. For instance, she translates the German 'folgen ... *auf*' (follow ... *upon*) with 'follow ... *from*'; just ten lines later, in a similar passage, she translates 'folgen ... *auf*' with 'follow ... *upon*'. In any case, it is exactly this '*folgen ... auf*' that causes the difficulty mentioned above for the strong interpretation: If – as the strong interpretation claims – the moral predispositions allow us to have a consciousness of the categorical imperative, or *at least are part of what it means to be aware of the categorical imperative*, how then can it be true what Kant says in (C), to wit, that consciousness of the moral predispositions somehow '*follows upon*' the consciousness of the categorical imperative?

To answer this question, let us first ask what the 'consciousness of the moral predispositions' in (C) consists in. Kant certainly does not mean to say that we have a 'consciousness of the moral predispositions' in an abstract way, that is, in the way, for instance, that philosophers have a 'consciousness of the moral predispositions' when they discuss or analyze them. Call the latter the *non-manifest* 'consciousness of the moral predispositions'; by this I mean that there is no or very little phenomenal quality involved (no actual feeling). But Kant also can hardly mean that the 'consciousness of the moral predispositions' consists in being aware of the actual feelings we have in case a moral predisposition is affected. Why should Kant emphasize that we are aware of a moral feeling when we have it? The 'consciousness of the moral predispositions' is not simply something that we have in terms of the consciousness *of* an object. Rather, the 'consciousness of the moral predispositions' is something that we are *in* if a moral predisposition is affected. I propose to understand the 'consciousness of the moral predispositions' as a *genitivus definitivus:* it defines what *kind* of consciousness one has in reference to the moral predispositions. The affection of these predispositions

---

16 For a detailed analysis cf. Schönecker (2010).

brings about a certain consciousness; I call this the *manifest* 'consciousness of the moral predispositions'.

But what then about the term *folgen* ('follow')? Generally speaking, it certainly has a temporal meaning in terms of one event following another event. If we assume this meaning, however, we have the described conflict between claim (G) and claim (C). Now Kant is eager to point out – as he always does when it comes to genuine moral feelings – that the moral feelings that are grounded in the four moral predispositions do not *precede* the moral law. This is important, because those moral feelings that are grounded in the moral predispositions are "aesthetic" (TL 6:399.10)[17] and "natural" (TL 6:399.11), even in some sense "preceding" (TL 6:399.11), and that is why he says in (C) that nonetheless 'the consciousness of the moral predispositions is *not* of empirical origin'. In discussing 'moral feeling' as one of the four moral predispositions – a feeling which, I think, is what Kant elsewhere and mostly calls *respect* (*Achtung*) – Kant also says that this moral feeling "can only *follow* upon [the representation of the moral law]" (TL 6:399.27, my emphasis). At the same time, recall, Kant claims that "any consciousness of obligation depends upon moral feeling *to become aware* of the necessitation that lies in the concept of duty" (TL 6:399, my emphasis; cf. G4). Since our *manifest* consciousness of the moral law is a consciousness of the categorical imperative and therefore always also a consciousness of the imperativeness of this moral law, it is impossible to have *first* the manifest consciousness of the categorical imperative and *then* the moral feeling. Also, recall that the manifest consciousness of the categorical imperative is a *fact of reason* insofar as the imperativeness (obligatoriness) of the moral law is felt in the feeling of respect; it is a *felt* fact of reason.[18] In the *Critique of Practical Reason*, too, Kant puts emphasis on his claim that this feeling is brought about by the moral law and yet he does not mean that the feeling of respect *temporally* follows a manifest consciousness of the categorical imperative. Hence I would suggest that the term 'follow' does not have a strict temporal meaning here; rather, it must be understood both as a causal expression to refer to the origin of the 'consciousness of the moral predispositions' as well as a validity-

---

17 Cf. § 25 where Kant also says that *amor complacentiae* is "aesthetic" (TL 6:449.17). – Arroyo (2016, 10) construes an "interpretive dilemma" on the assumption that "the only kind of felt love Kant identifies is pathologically felt love". But where does Kant say that? What he actually says it that it is 'aesthetic' (TL 6:399.10; 449.17), but as Kant then says in the context of the moral feeling, the "a e s t h e t i c condition [Zustand] (of the affection of the inner sense) is either a pathological *or* moral feeling" (TL 6:399.24, my emphasis); cf. Schönecker (2010) and Rinne (2018, 129). Hence Filippaki (2012, 32) is wrong in saying that pathological love is "alternatively defined" as amor complacentiae.

18 Cf. Schönecker (2013a, 2013b).

claim, as it were, to express that the moral feelings have a non-empirical origin in that they are related to and dependent on the moral law. As I said above, the affection[19] of the moral predispositions brings about a certain consciousness; reason is the origin of this affection, and only in this sense 'follows' the 'consciousness of the moral predispositions' the 'consciousness of the moral law'.

Again, Kant begins that last sentence (C) with the *negative* claim that 'the consciousness of the moral predispositions is *not* of empirical *origin*'; in what follows, he formulates the *positive* claim that it has another 'origin', namely the moral law itself.[20] Thus we get:

(C)*** Consciousness of the moral predispositions is not of empirical origin; rather, consciousness of the moral predispositions has its origin in practical reason and its (reason's) categorical imperative that affects the moral predispositions and thus brings about a consciousness that is determined by the feelings that correspond to the moral predispositions.

As one can see, there is a certain ambiguity here. But in any case, the point is that the moral predispositions are necessary conditions in order to become aware of the necessitation of the categorical imperative and therefore are necessary conditions in order to grasp the moral law as a categorical imperative. Affected moral predispositions are part of what a manifest consciousness of the categorical imperative consists in.[21]

Let us now return to the assumption I made above (that what Kant says specifically about the moral predispositions as such, e.g., G 4, can be applied to all predispositions). This assumption could be doubted if one, quite plausibly, assumes that not all four moral predispositions become manifest in every instance of (not) following the moral law, but only in some. For it could very well be that Kant correlates the four moral predispositions to different duties: Moral feeling and conscience seem to be necessary for *all* duties; as a matter of fact, Kant explicitly refers in sec. XIV to EXII when he says that "conscience was treated earlier

---

19 Cf. TL 6:399.24

20 Note, by the way, that 'follow' can also be understood logically. As one can easily see, the proposition "S is in a state of having an affected moral predisposition" and "S has a consciousness of the categorical imperative" are logically equivalent, i.e., they imply each other, i.e., one *follows* from the other.

21 According to Guyer (2017, 248), Kant says that the moral presdispositions "are effected by the consciousness of the moral law". However, Guyer does not discuss the complications and implications of sentence (C). Fahmy (2010, 325) quite strongly formulates that "one becomes aware of these predispositions *only after* one is conscious of the moral law" (my emphasis).

[i. e., in *EXII*] as the condition of all duties as such" (TL 6:406 f.). *Menschenliebe*, however, could be particularly correlated to duties to others, and self-respect to duties to oneself.[22] And if this is correct, it could also be the case that the four moral predispositions – although all of them in some sense 'lie at the ground of morality' – have different functions. Thus it could be that (G4) – according to which any consciousness of obligation depends upon moral predispositions to become aware of the necessitation that lies in the concept of duty – is a rather strong epistemological claim in terms of (C), whereas the function of *Menschenliebe* could be motivational only. In other words, it could be that the weak or modest understanding of the moral predispositions makes sense with regard to *Menschenliebe*, but not as regards the other three predispositions. I shall leave this undecided here; in any event, (G1)–(G3) are claimed by Kant in reference to *all* moral predispositions, (G4) is true for all moral and immoral actions, and (G5) and (G6) only allow for a strong interpretation.[23]

Much more could be said about this. For the purposes of this paper, however, it is mainly important that the moral predispositions 'lie', in some sense anyway, 'at the ground of morality' and that one, therefore, cannot be obliged to have a moral disposition and the corresponding feeling. As we shall see, this is one important key to identify what Kant means by *Menschenliebe* as one of those four moral predispositions.

2 On *Menschenliebe* as one of the four moral predispositions

So how are we to understand this *Menschenliebe*? What exactly is it? To begin with, note that in the first paragraph of *EXII*, Kant does not speak of *Menschenliebe*, but of "love of one's neighbor" (*Liebe des Nächsten*, TL 6:399.6). This can be quite misleading,[24] since in the sections on *duties* of love (TL §§ 23–36), Kant always speaks of such a 'love of one's neighbor' as a duty; there is, he claims, a "*duty* of love of

---

22 Cf. TL 6:403.1–3, where Kant says that self-respect could be the "ground of *certain* duties" (my emphasis).

23 Note, by the way, that in (G1) Kant refers to '*the* concept of duty' in the singular ("*den* Pflichtbegriff", TL 6:399.9, my emphasis) as well as to morality as such ("*der* Moralität", TL 6:399.10, my emphasis).

24 Cf., however, Rinne (2018, 142 ff.) who offers a reading such that 'love of benevolence' and 'love of delight' both fall under 'love of one's neighbor'.

one's neighbor" (TL 6:450.3, my emphasis).[25] As we have seen, however, there can be no duty to have moral predispositions, neither as dispositions nor as manifest feelings. To 'have these predispositions', says Kant, 'cannot be considered a duty', because obligation itself is only possible on the *ground* of these very moral predispositions. But from this it follows that the kind of love that Kant in the *love-section* calls "*amor benevolentiae*" (TL 6:401.27) is *not* and *cannot* be the *Menschenliebe* as one of the four moral predispositions. For this "benevolence (*amor benevolentiae*), as conduct, can be subject to a law of duty" (TL 6:401.27); a bit later Kant repeats this claim by saying "to do good [...] is a duty" (TL 6:402.1), and then, in one sentence: "Beneficence is a duty" (TL 6:402.14).[26] And even if love that is benevolence is also a feeling, it is a feeling "which *at the same time* [zugleich] is a duty for us" (TL 401.32); but *Menschenliebe* as a moral predisposition can never be a duty.

Thus, it seems undeniable to me that the *Menschenliebe* that is one the four moral predispositions is *not* and *cannot* be *amor benevolentiae*. But there is another candidate that we need to discuss. 'Beneficence is a duty', Kant says, and then he continues:

> If someone practices it [i. e., beneficence] often and succeeds in realizing his beneficent intention, he eventually comes actually to love the person he has done good. So the saying 'you ought to love your neighbor as yourself' does not mean: you ought immeditaley (first) to love him and (afterwards) by means of this love do good to him, but: do good to your fellow human being, and this beneficence will effect love of human beings [*Menschenliebe*] in you (as a dexterity of the inclination to beneficence in general). (TL 6:402.14).

It is tempting to identify this '*dexterity*' [*Fertigkeit*] with the *Menschenliebe* that is a moral predisposition. But an easy consideration proves this wrong: Kant says very clearly that 'love of human beings' understood as a 'dexterity of the inclination to

---

25 Goy (2013, 190 f.) argues that *none* of the forms of love mentioned in the love-section (including *Menschenliebe* and *amor complacentiae*) is referred to as a predisposition. But in TL 6:399, Kant *clearly* identifies four moral predispositions, and then obviously discusses them consecutively in the following subsections a–d; it seems very arbitrary to assume that Kant does not mean the four moral predispositions in a–d. Note, by the way, that subsection (d) is titled "V o n d e r A c h - t u n g" whereas in that enumeration in TL 6:399, Kant speaks of "A c h t u n g für sich selbst (S e l b s t s c h ä t z u n g)" (TL 6:399.7).

26 The contrasting term of benevolence 'as a conduct' (*als ein Tun*) is not passive "benevolence" (TL 6:452.26), as it were, but *amor complacentiae*. Cf. § 26 where Kant distinguishes practical and non-practical (aesthetic) love of human beings such that the latter is *amor complacentiae* (not benevolence) and the former (practical love of human beings) is "active benevolence" (TL 6:450.18). The Latin term *amor complacentiae* is, by the way, grammatically speaking, a *genitivus definitivus:* it defines what *kind* of love one is referring to; hence the English translation 'love that is delight' is quite right.

beneficence in general' is an 'effect' of beneficence. Beneficence, however, is a duty: 'do good to your fellow human being', it says. But then the moral predispositions – and certainly *Menschenliebe* as one of them – must be presupposed already, since there can be no duty (and no duty of beneficence either) without moral predispositions. Hence love of human beings must already be presupposed if there is to be a duty of beneficence; and therefore love of human beings *understood as that 'dexterity'* cannot be the love of human beings that is a moral predisposition.[27]

Three further arguments speak against the identification of *Menschenliebe* with the 'dexterity of the inclination to beneficence in general': First, it is hard to see how such a 'dexterity' (*Fertigkeit*) could be a moral 'endowment' or 'predisposition', the more so as, in the *Doctrine of Virtue*, the concept of 'dexterity' is closely related to a "long-standing habit" (TL 6:383.34). But if one needs to "practice beneficence *often*" (TL 6:402.14, my emphasis) in order to "eventually" (TL 6:402.15) 'effect' *Menschenliebe*, how could this *Menschenliebe* be a fundamental moral presupposition required to apprehend duties in the first place? Second, note that Kant speaks of a 'dexterity of the *inclination* to beneficence in general'. Again, it is hard to see how such an 'inclination' could be a moral predisposition. If, thirdly and on the other hand, one understands 'dexterity' as a "facility in acting and a subjective perfection of choice" (TL 6:407.5) – that's Kant's definition in a remark on chapter XIV of the introduction to the *Doctrine of Virtue* – then one is talking already about duties and hence not about a moral predisposition.

---

27 A strong advocate of identifying *Menschenliebe* with that 'dexterity' is Arroyo: "In other words, doing good to others from a sense of moral duty has certain effects on our sensible natures, and there is a receptivity (*Empfänglichkeit*) to this on the part of our sensibility. In the case of beneficence, the result is a training of our pathological desires so as to produce a sensible inclination to do good to others, and this is what Kant calls *Menschenliebe*" (Arroyo 2016, 591). And while *amor complacentiae*, he continues, "is a pathological emotion that arises in us immediately as an affective response, the latter [*Menschenliebe* as a 'dexterity'] is a cultivated inclination that develops as a result of deliberative, rational choices" (*ibid.*). Another clear example for ignoring the problem with this interpretation is Goy (2013, 191); cf. Fahmy (2014, 325) who also seems to identify *Menschenliebe* with the 'dexterity of the inclination to beneficence in general'. Muchnik, too, clearly sees that this 'dexterity' "is based on duty" (Muchnik 2014, 233), but he does not draw the conclusion that, therefore, it cannot be love as a moral predisposition. It is hard to see what Baxley's final account of *Menschenliebe* is; but she also seems to identify *Menschenliebe* with 'dexterity' and then says that it "derives from practicing the particular duty of beneficence and is thus consequential on active benevolence" without recognizing the problem (Baxley 2010, 152). Korsgaard (2014, 54) quotes the passage on 'dexterity', but does not relate it to the moral predisposition nor to *amor complacentiae*. None of these interpreters takes into account that Kant says of *amor complacentiae* what he says of all moral predispositions – that to have it cannot be commanded.

Thus, *Menschenliebe* as a moral predisposition is not *amor benevolentiae* and it is not the 'dexterity of the inclination to beneficence in general'. But what then is it?[28] It is, I submit, *amor complacentiae*, that is, love that is delight. It is only in the very last paragraph of the *love-section* that Kant elucidates this love:

> Hence only the love that is delight (*amor complacentiae*) is direct. But to have a duty to this (which is a pleasure joined immediately to the representation of an object's existence), that is, to have to be necessitated to take pleasure in something, is a contradiction. (TL 6:402.22–26).

Here Kant says about *amor complacentiae* what he says all over the place with regard to all moral predispositions: that there is no duty to have them, and so there is no duty to have *amor complacentiae*. As a matter of fact, the *very first thing* Kant says about moral predispositions is that 'if one does not have them, there also can be no duty to acquire them'. To be more precise, Kant says (as quoted above already): 'There are *certain* moral endowments *such that* if one does not have them, there also can be no duty to acquire them.' Given that in *EXII* Kant says *three* times that there is no duty to have the moral predispositions, and given, furthermore, that in the following sections he makes the same point with regard to moral feeling, conscience, and respect *five* times, it seems very legitimate to assume that Kant by saying that there is no duty to have *amor complacentiae* is implying that this love of delight is one of the moral predispositions.[29] In *this* context,

---

28 How important it is to raise this question is demonstrated by Guyer (2017, 254) who understands Kant as claiming that "feelings of love towards (specific) others are [...] *not* an aesthetic precondition" (my emphasis); on Guyer's account, Kant only provides a "merely negative account" (Guyer 2017, 257) in *EXII*. This, however, makes no sense, since Kant explicitly states that *Menschenliebe is* one the four moral predispositions – why should he introduce it as such and then say nothing positively about it? Guyer identifies such an 'aesthetic precondition' only in the feelings accompanied with sympathy – which, again, amounts to saying that Kant does *not* introduce *Menschenliebe* as a moral predisposition, after all. *Amor complacentiae* plays no role whatsoever in Guyer's interpretation. Fahmy (2014, 325) writes that "Kant never tells us what *Menschenliebe* actually is"; rather, she claims, in the *love-section* Kant discusses *Menschenliebe* as a duty. It is striking that even in the more recent literature, many commentators do not take *amor complacentiae* into account *at all*; cf. Baron (2014), Deimling (2014), Guyer (2010), Korsgaard (2014), Fahmy (2010), Wiebing (2014). – Rinne (2018, 125) and Römer (2018, 177) adopt the main results of Schönecker (2010). Geiger (2011, 296) also concurs, I take it, with the proposal that *amor complacentiae* is *Menschenliebe* as a moral predisposition (though with another interpretation of how this love functions). In the papers edited by Failla and Madrid (2021), *Menschenliebe* is not discussed.

29 In *EXII*, Kant clearly makes the claim that 'one can have no duty to have such-and-such' with regard to the moral predispositions ("welche *Anlagen* zu haben nicht als Pflicht angesehen werden kann", TL 6:399.12 f., my emphasis). When it comes to *amor complacentiae*, however, this claim is made with regard to *amor complacentiae* as "pleasure" (TL 6:402.24), i.e., as a feeling. But this is no contradiction: There is neither a duty to have the moral predispositons as such nor is there a duty

that there is no obligation to have x is like a litmustest by which we recognize a moral predisposition: it is that thing which to have there is no duty.[30] Note, by the way, that the next section on self-respect begins with "again" (*eben sowohl*, TL 6:402.29), pointing out that there is no duty to have self-respect; this 'again' refers back directly to the preceding paragraph on *amor complacentiae*.

And there is further evidence. Recall that Kant says: 'Hence only the love that is delight (*amor complacentiae*) is *direct.*' Hereby, Kant discriminates *Menschenliebe* as *amor complacentiae* from *Menschenliebe* as the 'dexterity of the inclination to beneficence in general' (note the 'hence', *also*). Whereas the latter is 'effected' by some habit of beneficence, the former (*amor complacentiae*) is 'joined *immediately* to the representation of an object's existence'. Kant then continues with a 'But' (*aber*) at the beginning of the next sentence: '*But* to have a duty to *amor complacentiae* [...] is a contradiction.' Kant says 'but', because of the 'directness' of *amor complacentiae* which makes it that there is no duty to have it. *Amor complacentiae* is not an 'effect' of benevolence; rather, it 'lies at the ground' of this duty. And *amor complacentiae* 'alone' is direct; neither *amor benevolentiae* nor the 'dexterity of the inclination to beneficence in general' have this quality. Hence only *amor complacentiae* can be the moral disposition we are looking for, and I think Kant himself confirms this reading in § 26 of the *Doctrine of Virtue*. There he says:

> Since the love of human beings [*Menschenliebe*] (philanthropy) we are thinking of here is practical love, hence [*mithin*] not the love that is delight in them, it must be taken as active benevolence, and so as having to do with the maxim of actions (TL 6:450.16–19).

Note that Kant says that '*here*', that is, in the context of *duties* of love, *Menschenliebe* is understood as '*practical* love' *as opposed to* the 'love that is delight in them'. This clearly implies two things: First, there is a kind of *Menschenliebe* that is *not* practical, that is, something that is not a duty; second, this non-practical love is identified with *amor complacentiae* which not 'here' (TL 6:450.16), yet elsewhere (to wit, in *EXII*) has been discussed already. Third, the antonym to 'practical' (in 'practical love') is 'aesthetical'. And again, Kant himself says so, and again he relates this difference to *amor complacentiae*. In the preceding section of the *Doctrine of Virtue* (§ 25) Kant says:

---

to have the manifest feelings; and there is no duty to have the manifest feelings because there is no duty to have the predispositions that make them possible. – Many thanks to Pärttyli Rinne for pointing out this issue to me.

30 It is true that there is no duty to develop a 'dexterity of the inclination to beneficence in general'. However, unlike the moral predispositions, this 'dexterity' is wrought by following a duty.

> Here, however, love is not understood as feeling (aesthetic), that is, as pleasure in the perfec-
> tion of others, not as love that is delight (since others cannot put one under obligation to have
> feelings); it must rather be thought as the maxim of benevolence (as practical), which results
> in beneficence (TL 6:449.17–22)

Understood as a feeling, love is not a duty. This is exactly what Kant says in *EXII*
about the moral predispositions: They are "aesthetic" (TL 6:399.10), and they cannot
be commanded. Again, Kant distinguishes here between practical love and aesthetical love, and again he emphasizes that 'here' (TL 6:449.17) – that is, in the context
of duties of love – love is understood as 'practical', not 'aesthetical', and again he
identifies this aesthetical love with 'love that is as delight' (*amor complacentiae*).
What is more, Kant gives us a hint what we are to understand by this aesthetical
love, to wit, 'pleasure in the perfection of others'. Let us look at this more closely.

3 What is *amor complacentiae*?

Given that *amor complacentiae* is a feeling, and that 'feeling' is defined as the "capacity for having pleasure or displeasure in a representation" (TL 6:211.19), it is no
surprise that Kant understands *amor complacentiae* as 'pleasure'. Putting the last
paragraph of the *love-section* and the first paragraph of § 25 of the *Doctrine of Virtue* together, we get the following picture: *amor complacentiae* is a 'pleasure joined
immediately to the representation of an object's existence', and it is a 'pleasure in
the perfection of others' where these 'others' are other human beings. On the reasonable assumption that the 'object's existence' is the 'perfection of others',[31] *amor
complacentiae*, understood as a manifest predisposition, can be defined as follows:

(AC) *Amor complacentiae* is pleasure joined immediately to the representation of
the perfection of other human beings.

---

31 Goy (2013, 193) argues that "Existenz eines Gegenstandes" (TL 6:402.24) can only mean an empirical object; if this is true, *amor complacentiae* would be caused by an empirical object and
would, therefore, be empirical itself. However, I submit that in the *love-section*, Kant describes
amor complacentiae in a general way (as 'a pleasure joined immediately to the representation
of an object's existence'), and then only in § 25 it is specified as a moral predisposition, to wit,
as the 'pleasure in the perfection of others'. Others and their perfections (or striving for perfection)
exist; and 'existence' is a term that is certainly wide enough in Kant's usage to be used here as well
(recall that Kant in the *Groundwork*, 4:427 ff., for instance, speaks of the "existence" or rational beings as ends in themselves).

As we have seen, in the *Doctrine of Virtue* (as in his other published writings) Kant says very little about *amor complacentiae*. It is important to note, however, that this concept – *amor complacentia* resp. *love that is delight* – is still quite common in the philosophical and theological writings of Kant's time, and these writings confirm the interpretation of (AC).[32] The basic and original idea is that *amor complacentiae* is the love we feel for God's perfection. Walch (⁴1775, 2286), for instance, speaks of such love that is delight "wenn wir Gott wegen seiner Vollkommenheit, Vortrefflichkeit und Schönheit lieben" ('when we love God for his perfection, excellence and beauty'); Rambach (1744, 349) refers to *amor complacentiae* such that "wir an Gott und seinen Vollkommenheiten, an seinem Umgang und Wegen das innigste Vergügnen haben" ('we have the most intimate pleasure in God and his perfections, in his dealings and ways'). Christian Wolff in his *Grundsätze des Natur- und Völckerrechts*, among others, uses a wider concept of *amor complacentiae* by saying that "unter der Liebe des Wohlgefallens (*amor complacentiae*) versteht man diejenige, welche ganz allein in der Empfindung des Vergnügens des andern Vollkommenheit besteht" ('by the love of complacency (amor complacentiae) is meant that [love] which consists entirely in the feeling of the pleasure in the other's perfection', Wolff 1754, 106); and Benedict Stattler (Kant's notorious opponent) discusses "Liebe des Wohlgefallens an der persönlichen Vollkommenheit des Mitgatten" ('love of pleasure in the personal perfection of the spouse', Stattler 1789, 111). – Against this historical background (which Kant was certainly familiar with), let us try to spell out *amor complacentiae* a bit more on our own. Perfection (*Vollkommenheit*), that is, self-perfection, is an end that it also duty. Perfection can never be reached; hence perfection must be understood as "cultivating one's faculties" (TL 6:387.1). These faculties are natural faculties and moral faculties. Natural perfection refers to the development of one's powers of spirit, mind, and body. To develop these faculties is a "human being's duty to himself" (TL 6:444.18); therefore, this kind of perfection appears to be an object of *amor complacentiae* as well.[33]

But how are we to understand the actual affection of *amor complacentiae* as a moral disposition? To begin with, what is the actual object by which we are affected? *Prima facie*, there are three options: It could be (i) the "moral endowment" (TL

---

32 As Walschots (2017) points out, the distinction between *amor complacentiae* and amor benevolentiae can be clearly found in Hutcheson's *An Inquiry into the Original of Our Ideas of Beauty and Virtue* (1725); Kant was familiar with the German translation. How close Kant's interpretation of these terms is to that of Hutchseon I cannot deal with here.

33 Moral perfection is very hard to understand, mainly, because the most relevant sections (§§ 21 and 22) are almost impossible to decipher. What Kant says there about wide and narrow duties seems to contradict what he says elsewhere, esp. in the 'introduction'. I shall not get into this.

6:435.10) bestowed on every human being which brings about our delight, or (ii) the actual moral striving, (iii) something like the ideal of a morally striving human being. As regards (i), recall that our general moral endowment, our autonomy, is the object of *respect* (what Kant calls 'moral feeling' in *EXII*); Kant says so throughout his ethical writings. Hence it is standing to reason that it is *not* at the same time the object of *amor complacentiae*. What about the two other options (actual moral striving, the ideal of striving)? Let us look at a passage, again in § 26 of the *Doctrine of Virtue* which, I think, is enlightening. Here it is:

> But someone who avoids other human beings because he can find no *delight* in them, though he indeed *wishes all of them well* [*wohl will*], would be *shy of human beings* (an aesthetic misanthropist) and his turning away from them could be called anthropophobia. (TL 6:450.25).

This passage causes trouble: How is such an 'aesthetic misanthropist', who 'can find no delight in human beings' possible, if every human being possesses *amor complacentiae* as a moral predisposition which means that everyone *does* have delight in other human beings? And if to 'wish all human beings well' (benevolence) is a maxim that reflects a duty, and if to follow such a duty implies to have manifest moral predispositions, including *amor complacentiae*, how then could an 'aesthetic misanthropist' 'wish all human beings well' without finding delight in human beings?

The solution to this problem could be to understand *amor complacentiae* not only as the capacity to feel moral pleasure (delight) in other human beings, but also to feel *displeasure*, just as the 'moral feeling' proper (as one of the four moral predispositions) is the "susceptibility to feel pleasure *or* displeasure" (TL 6:399, my emphasis). The 'aesthetic misanthropist', one could propose, would feel *displeasure* about other human being's lack of perfection (or cultivation thereof) rather than pleasure. Yet it seems that the 'aesthetic misanthropist' can only feel this *displeasure* if *at the same time* she feels *pleasure* about moral perfection. Displeasure about a lack of perfection cannot be like a pain which one just has. One can only experience this moral displeasure *in distinction to* the pleasure that is the delight in the moral perfection of others. There must be something that the 'aesthetic misanthropist' finds delight in so she can experience the lack of it as displeasure; it is just because moral perfection pleases her that she painfully feels the lack of it. So it seems that the 'aesthetic misanthropist' does feel love that is delight, after all. But how?

In the *Critique of the Power of Judgment*, Kant says about the 'aesthetic misanthropist' that she, "as far as benevolence is concerned, is philanthropical enough, but still far removed from the delight in human beings through long and sad experience" (KU 5:276). To be more precise, who is shy of human beings is shy because the way most human beings act is "so contradictory to the *idea* of what men could be if they wanted to, and conflict so with the lively wish to see them better, that, in order not to hate them (since we cannot love them), the renunciation of all social joys seems but a small sacrifice" (KU 5:276, my emphasis). What human beings 'could be', what constitutes their 'idea' is the fact that they could be 'better' human beings which is to say: human beings that strive for perfection, and what the 'aesthetic misanthropist' sorely misses is exactly this pursuit of perfection. This lack of striving causes her displeasure which, however, she can only feel in distinction to the pleasure she feels in that 'idea' of morally striving human beings. Despite being an 'aesthetic misanthropist', she still has that 'lively wish to see them better' – a wish that can only be explained on account of her delight in the idea of perfection. The actual feeling of *amor complacentiae* might very well be caused in the real presence of a moral striving person, but it seems to be not only that individual person but he or she as a *representative* of humanity as a moral species.

Let us now address the question of whether *amor complacentiae* is directed only to other human beings or also to oneself. Three arguments speak against this idea that there could be such a thing as *self-love of delight:* First, Kant refers to *amor complacentiae* with the term *Menschenliebe*, but also with the term 'love of one's neigbor' (*Liebe des Nächsten*) which semantically does not fit in (well) with the idea of self-delight. Second, in § 25 of the *Doctrine of Virtue*, Kant speaks of the 'pleasure in the perfection of *others*' which also seems to leave little leeway. Third, in *EXII*, where Kant lists the four moral predispositions, no. 3 is 'love of one's neighbor', and no. 4 is "respect for oneself (self-esteem)" (TL 6:399.7). So it appears that there is bifurcation between the *love of others* on the one hand and *self-respect* on the other which might suggest that there is no room for love of *oneself.* – However, not only does Kant speak of a division of *self-love* into *amor complacentiae* and *benevolentiae* (cf. RGV 6:45).[34] There is also a reasonable argument to assume that there is, after all, such a thing as *amor complacentiae* caused by oneself and directed to oneself. For if *amor complacentiae* is directed towards the idea of the human being as such that is capable of natural and moral perfection, then *I*, who I am as such a human being myself as well, must also be the object of *amor complacentiae*. And the same could be true if *amor complacentiae* is directed toward actual striving for perfection.

---

34 As mentioned above, however, the usage of "amor complacentiae" and "amor benevolentiae" in the *Religionsschrift* is different from the *Tugendlehre* because there these loves are considered as rational and elements of maxims.

In any event, a definition of what *amor complacentiae* is in the context of *Menschenliebe*[35] could be as follows:

(AC)* *Amor complacentiae* is the pleasure joined immediately to the representation of the natural and moral perfection – understood as an ideal or as actual striving – of other human beings or of oneself.

To conclude, let us address a final objection. *Amor complacentiae*, it could be argued, cannot be the *Menschenliebe* as a moral predisposition because this disposition is supposed to make us receptive to moral duties and possibly receptive to the moral duties of love which are subsumed under the general duty of benevolence – and how could the pleasure in the perfections of others make us receptive to the duty of benevolence resp. beneficence? But here, too, a look at the literature of Kant's time turns out to be helpful. Schmidt (1772), for instance, refers to the way theologians use these terms and then claims that *amor complacentiae* and *amor benevolentiae* bear upon each other: "denn wir sind so beschaffen, daß wir einem Gegenstande, welcher uns wegen seiner eigenen Vollkommenheiten gefällt, ergötzet, und den wir lieben, alles Gute wünschen und auch nach Vermögen beschaffen" ('for we are so constituted that we delight in an object which pleases us on account of its own perfections, and which we love, wish well and also procure to the best of our ability', Schmidt 1772, 331); *amor complacentiae* is, he argues, "die Quelle der Liebe des Wohlwollens" ('the source of love of benevolence', Schmidt 1772, 331). But if this is correct, then indeed amor complacentiea as a moral predisposition is the aesthetic 'ground' for benevolence.

References

Arroyo, Christopher, 2016, "Kant on the Emotion of Love", *European Journal of Philosophy*, 24/3, 580–606.

Baron, Marcia, 2014, "Kantian Moral Maturity and the Cultivation of Character", in: Alix Cohen (ed.), *Kant on Emotion and Value*, Basingstoke: Palgrave MacMillan, 69–87.

Baxley, Anne M., 2010, *Kant's Theory of Virtue. The Value of Autocracy*, Cambridge: Cambridge University Press.

Cohen, Alix, 2014, *Kant on Emotion and Value*, Basingstoke: Palgrave MacMillan.

Deimling, Wiebke, 2014, "Kant's Pragmatic Concept of Emotions", in: Alix Cohen (ed.), *Kant on Emotion and Value*, Basingstoke: Palgrave MacMillan, 108–125.

Fahmy, Melissa, 2010, "Kantian Practical Love", *Pacific Philosophical Quarterly*, 91, 313–331.

---

35 Rinne (2018, 13) is quite right that *amor complacentiae* is a "broader notion" than I acknowledged it in Schönecker (2010).

Failla, Mariannina/Madrid, Nuria Sánchez (eds.), 2021, *Kant on Emotions: Critical Essays in the Contemporary Context*, Berlin/Boston: de Gruyter.

Filippaki, Eleni, 2012, "Kant on Love, Respect and Friendship", *Kant Yearbook*, 4, 23–48.

Geiger, Ido, 2011, "Rational Feelings and Moral Agency", *Kantian Review*, 16/2, 283–308.

Goy, Ina, 2013, "Virtue and Sensibility (TL 6:399–409)", in: Andreas Trampota, Oliver Sensen, and Jens Timmermann (eds.), *Kant's "Doctrine of Virtue". A Comprehensive Commentary*, Berlin/Boston: de Gruyter, 183–206.

Grenberg, Jeanine, 2014, "All You Need Is love?", in: Alix Cohen (ed.), *Kant on Emotion and Value*, Basingstoke: Palgrave MacMillan, 210–223.

Guyer, Paul, 2017, "Kant on Moral Feelings. From the Lectures to the Metaphysics of Morals", in: Paul Guyer, *Virtues of Freedom. Selected Essays on Kant*, Oxford: Oxford University Press, 235–259.

Korsgaard, Christine M., 2014, "From Duty and for the Sake of the Noble: Kant and Aristotle on Morally Good Action", in: Alix Cohen (ed.), *Kant on Emotion and Value*, Basingstoke: Palgrave MacMillan, 33–68.

Muchnik, Pablo, 2014, "The Heart as Locus of Moral Struggle in The Religion", in: Alix Cohen (ed.), *Kant on Emotion and Value*, Basingstoke: Palgrave MacMillan, 224–244.

Rambach, Johann J., 1744: *Dogmatische Theologie oder Christliche Glaubenslehre*, Frankfurt/Leipzig

Rinne, Pärttyli, 2018, *Kant on Love*, Berlin/Boston: de Gruyter.

Römer, Inga, 2018, *Das Begehren der reinen praktischen Vernunft. Kants Ethik in phänomenologischer Sicht*, Hamburg: Meiner.

Sherman, Nancy, 2014, "The Place of Emotions in Kantian Morality", in: Alix Cohen (ed.), *Kant on Emotion and Value*, Basingstoke: Palgrave MacMillan, 11–32.

Schmidt, Michael I., 1772, *Der Katechist nach seinen eigenen Eigenschaften und Pflichten, oder die rechte Weise die ersten Gründe der Religion zu lehren*, Bamberg/Würzburg: Göbhard.

Schönecker, Dieter, 2010, "Kant über Menschenliebe als moralische Gemütsanlage", *Archiv für Geschichte der Philosophie*, 92/2, 133–175.

Schönecker, Dieter, 2013a, "Das gefühlte Faktum der Vernunft. Skizze einer Interpretation und Verteidigung", *Deutsche Zeitschrift für Philosophie*, 61/1, 2013, 91–107.

Schönecker, Dieter, 2013b, "Kant's Moral Intuitionism. The Fact of Reason and Moral Predispositions", *Kant Studies Online*, Feb. 2013, 1–38.

Schönecker, Dieter, 2022, "Kant's Argument from Moral Feelings: Why Practical Reason Cannot be Artificial", in: Hyeongjoo Kim and Dieter Schönecker (eds.), *Kant and Artificial Intelligence*, Berlin/Boston: de Gruyter, 169–188.

Stattler, Benedict, 1789, *Vollständige christliche Sittenlehre für den gesammten christlichen Haus- oder Familienstand*, Augsburg/München.

Walch, Johann G., [4]1775, *Johann Georg Walchs philosophisches Lexikon*, Leipzig.

Walschots, Michael, 2017, "Hutcheson and Kant: Moral Sense and Moral Feeling", in: Elizabeth Robinson and Chris W. Surprenant (eds.), *Kant and the Scottish Enlightenment*, London: Routledge, 36–54.

Wolff, Christian, 1754, *Grundsätze des Natur- und Völckerrechts*, Halle: Regner.

Pärttyli Rinne

From Self-Preservation to Cosmopolitan Friendship: Kant and the Conceptual Structure of Love[1]

Abstract: This article provides a concise overview of some of the main features of the conceptual structure of love in Kant's major writings. I have previously argued (Rinne 2018) that by analysing Kant's notion of love in the contexts of his discussions of self-love, sexual love, love of God, love of neighbour and love in friendship, we can detect an 'ascent of love' from the strongest impulses of human nature to the highest ethical ideals of cosmopolitan friendship. Here I supplement my previous 'ascent model' of love in Kant with a different model, which I call the 'expanding circle model'. This model builds on the Stoic metaphor of expanding spheres of subjective concern and affection, and highlights the *continuity* between Kant's different notions of love. The two models are not mutually exclusive and rather complement each other. In conclusion, I problematise the practical import and the actual universality of Kant's cosmopolitan notions of love.

1 Introduction

The main aim of this article is to provide a concise overview of some of the main features of the conceptual structure of love in Kant's philosophy. In recent years, scholars working on Kant's ethics have begun to recognise the significance of love for Kant's ethical project. The ethical life is not merely about respect for the moral law, but includes our emotions and emotive dispositions, and the cultivation of our emotive capacities in social relationships. While there is growing consensus in the literature that love is important for Kant, the concept of love in Kant is itself still in need of clarification.[2]

I have previously argued (Rinne 2018) that by analysing Kant's notion of love in the contexts of his discussions of self-love, sexual love, love of God, love of neighbour and love in friendship, we can detect an *ascent of love* from the strongest impulses of human nature to the highest ethical ideals of cosmopolitan friendship.

---

1 I wish to thank Martin Brecher for his helpful comments on a draft version of the paper.
2 For some recent discussions, see e. g. Moors 2007; Horn 2008; Fahmy 2010; Schönecker 2010; Arroyo 2016; Hanley 2017; cf. Rinne 2018, 2022.

https://doi.org/10.1515/9783111291130-008

Love begins with animal nature, and Kant uses the terminology of love to describe the rudimentary impulses of crude animality. He identifies the impulse of self-preservation as *love of life* and the sexual drive or sexual inclination as *sexual love* (e.g. MS 6:424; Anth 7:276; Anth-Mrongovius 25:1359–1361). To be sure, Kant also problematises the status of the fundamental, arational natural forms of love *as love:* the mere natural impulses cannot be called "true love" (see AA 8:337) or "genuine love" (Anth-Mrongovius 25:1361), which require reason, respect, and benevolence. I have also argued that with respect to imperfectly rational human beings (who represent something more, or something different than mere animal nature) Kant divides his notion of love generally into love of benevolence [*Liebe des Wohlwollens*] and love of delight [*Liebe des Wohlgefallens*]. In his ethics, he allows the paradigmatic form of self-love (i. e. benevolence toward oneself) only on the condition that one is benevolent towards all others as well, which resultant love he then calls "universal love of human beings" [*allgemeine Menschenliebe*] (MS 6:451). In the framework of Kant's moral philosophy, the Christian commandment of neighbourly love receives a secular, rationalistic reinterpretation in terms of an imperfect duty of *practical love.* In general, Kant calls on duty bound agents to strive for an ethical community, the pursuit of which is linked not only to his political philosophy and philosophy of history, but importantly to his philosophy of religion and his ethics. Understanding the Kantian path towards the ethical community requires (or so I argue) being attentive to notions of love and cosmopolitan friendship as important aspects of the ethical doctrine. In religious terms, God's love of benevolence is the ground of creation (MS 6:488–490; cf. MS-Vigilantius 27:720 f.) and his love of moral delight is the final end that human beings may hope for if they sincerely strive to become moral (RGV 6:145 f.) (see Rinne 2018, 95–105).

There is a hierarchy of loves in Kant's philosophy with respect to their rational and moral qualification, such that the animal impulses of love are arational and amoral[3], whereas, for instance, practical love for other human beings is rational and moral. It is hence possible to conceptualise love in Kant in terms of ascending levels of rationality, such that arational animal impulses of love represent a 'lower' level in contrast to 'higher', ethical notions of love. Kant's ethics and philosophy of religion include a demand for progress towards the highest good not only in terms of respect but also in terms of love, both on subjective (or individual) and communal levels. The overall textual evidence thus warrants the use of the metaphor of an *ascent* in the context of Kant's discussions of love. The Kantian 'ascent of love'

---

3 I.e. the animal impulses are neither moral nor immoral.

involves a 'journey'[4] of moral progress towards a perfected state of happiness proportionate to virtue, which ideal state would in its perfection concern all human beings. This perfection is something that can only be hoped for in an afterlife or through an infinite, intergenerational process of species-level approximation.

However, it remains unclear how exactly the 'lower' natural loves are related to the 'higher' moral or religious loves. Do the different aspects of love in Kant's philosophy somehow share a common core, and how much continuity is there between his different notions of love? What is the possible unity that the general division of love into love of benevolence and love of delight introduces to Kant's overall conception of love? Are the various notions of love tied together merely nominally, or through some kind of loose 'family resemblance'? To which extent is it possible to speak of *one love* in the philosophy of Kant?

In this article, I supplement my previous notion of an 'ascent of love' in Kant with a different model, which I call the 'expanding circle model'. While the notion of an ascent of love in Kant is a heuristic metaphor based loosely on Diotima's (or Plato's) account of love in the *Symposium*,[5] the idea of the 'expanding circle' is historically derived from the Stoic school. I now believe that the metaphor of an expanding circle may also be required to capture Kant's overall conception of love (alongside the notion of an ascent). True, Kant associates certain notions of love with the 'lowest' natural aspects of desire, and he speaks of love often as related to our pursuit of the highest good, and in this sense the Platonic *eros* can be said to loom in the background of Kant's conceptualisations of love. However, many of Kant's specific discussions of love can be made better sense of by highlighting their resemblance to the Stoic notion of expanding circles. Besides Stoicism, Kant's philosophy of love must also be understood with reference to the Christian religion. The overall structure of Kant's concept of love comes to light when it is analysed as an original reworking of Stoic and Christian influences, keeping in mind the conceptual heritage of the Platonic *eros*. This is not to deny the influence that Kant's more immediate predecessors like Rousseau or Hutcheson had on his conceptions of love (see e. g. Hanley 2017), nor is it to undermine the historical interconnections between Platonism, Stoicism, and Christianity (see e. g. Thorsteinsson 2010; Long 2003; Long 2013), but merely to sketch out a broad historical environment which provides a certain amount of consistency to notions of love (in Kant) which otherwise might seem hopelessly disparate.

In Kant, love begins with oneself and gradually expands (or ought to expand) to the rest of humanity. In general, love denotes spheres of affection, concern, and

---

4 I thank Rae Langton for suggesting the word 'journey' to me in this context.
5 For a brief comparison between Plato's and Kant's accounts of love, see Rinne 2018, 10 f.

desire. There are surprising continuities between different aspects of love in Kant, which the metaphor of the expanding circle brings to the fore. It is this *continuity in love* that interests me, and how *reason* supports, modifies, or perhaps undercuts the interrelations between the various aspects of love in Kant. I will show that there is more continuity in Kant's conceptions of love than one might easily think. I will also argue that it may even be possible to speak of *one love* in the philosophy of Kant, by which I mean that in Kant, the 'higher' aspects of love proceed from the 'lower' ones as their rational modifications, and that the ultimate purpose of love (conditioned by respect) is the establishment of a *cosmopolitan community of love and respect*, a peaceful, friendly union of all human beings. By showing this, I hope to improve our understanding of love in Kant, and our understanding of the conceptual structure of love more generally.

The article is divided roughly into three main parts. In the first part, I explicate the motivation for the expanding circle model of love in Kant by briefly relating Kant's account of the natural impulses of love with the Stoic metaphor of concentric circles, expressed through the notion of *oikeiosis*, an affective perception and appropriation of objects (the first object being oneself) (see e. g. Long & Sedley 1987, 351; Ramelli 2009, xxx–xlvii). In the second part, I discuss the relationship between natural love and rational love. I articulate the continuity between Kant's accounts of natural love and the duty of love by looking at how the general division of love functions as a mediator between self-love and love of others. Drawing from a recent discussion by Hanley (2017), I show how for Kant, the Christian commandment of love occasions a secular ethical argument, through which the natural love of benevolence for oneself is rationally extended to concern all human beings. In the last part I discuss love as a communal, cosmopolitan notion. I show the relevance of concepts of love and friendship to Kant's understanding of the human pursuit of the global ethical and divine communities. Connecting notions of love to the idea of an expanding circle, I illuminate Kant's cosmopolitanism from a novel perspective. In Kant's philosophy, the concept of love appears as indispensible for understanding human nature and promoting ethical progress (cf. Arroyo 2016).

2 On the Narrowest Circles of Love

Kant's interest in Stoic ethics is well-known, and there has a been a fair amount of discussion documenting and problematising Kant's debt to Stoicism with respect to his moral and legal philosophy, and his philosophy of history.[6] One notion that has rarely come up in these discussions, however, is that of love, and even when love is mentioned in the context of Kant's cosmopolitanism or his relationship with Stoicism (e. g. Kleingeld 2012, 165–169; 2016, 15), the role of love is not assessed in detail (cf. Cavallar 2015, 127, 131), or it is glossed over (Nussbaum 1997, 20–22).[7]

For the Stoics, ethical doctrine begins with the animal impulse of self-preservation (Long and Sedley 1987, 350; see also Annas 1993, 262). The animal is immediately aware of, or familiar with itself, and this affective self-appropriation or *oikeiosis* motivates it to look after itself. With respect to human beings endowed with reason, Stoic ethics includes an expansion of one's sphere of concern from oneself toward others further and further removed from oneself, beyond one's blood relationships and local affectionate ties.[8] The Stoic disposition of cosmopolitanism includes an acknowledgment of a universally shared rational human nature. Kant was of course well-aware of these fundamentals of Stoic ethics, especially through Cicero and Seneca (see Heath and Schneewind 1997, 471 f.).[9] Cicero, for instance, holds the following:

> From the beginning nature has assigned to every type of creature the tendency to preserve itself [...]. Common also to all animals is the impulse to unite for the purpose of procreation, and a certain care for those that are born. [...] (Cicero 1991, 6; I.11–12) The most widespread

---

6 See e. g. Reich 1939a and 1939b; Annas 1993, 162–175, 266; cf. Schneewind 2010, 277–295; Oksenberg Rorty & Schmidt 2009. Discussions of Kant's cosmopolitanism often make links to the Stoic school in terms of 'world citizenship' (however the concept is interpreted) or an inclusive 'circle of all human beings' (Nussbaum 1997; Kleingeld 2012, 2; Cavallar 2015, esp. 99, 126 f., 160; Kleingeld 2016, 15).

7 Kleingeld (2012, 166–168) helpfully notes a link between Kant's views on love and his moral cosmopolitanism, and mentions (2016, 15) that in Kant's *Religion* the "idea of a cosmopolitan [moral] community is to inspire a 'moral disposition of brotherly love' (Rel 6:200)" but she doesn't take her analyses further in terms of love. Cavallar offers an interesting link between between the notion of the concentric circles and the Kantian duty of benevolence (Cavallar 2015, 127) and notes the role of judgment in Kant's account of love for all human beings (Cavallar 2015, 131), whereas Nussbaum complains that in contrast with Stoic "love of humanity", Kant's "pessimistic view" can only define social enlightenment "in terms of the suppression of evil forces in human beings, rather than of their education" (Nussbaum 1997, 20 f.). Nussbaum does not engage with any of the passages where Kant discusses 'love of humanity' or *Menschenliebe*, nor does she consider Kant's philosophy of education. For an account of cosmopolitan education in Kant, see Cavallar (2015).

8 See e. g. Annas (1993, 267); cf. Nussbaum (1997, 9); Ramelli (2009, lxxxi); cf. Cicero (1991, I.58–59; see also I.50–51). It is not essential for my argument to have an exact understanding of the demandingness of Stoic ethics with respect to the scope of duties in terms of extension or 'weight', and I will refrain from attempting such an interpretation.

9 Klaus Reich (1939) has demonstrated Kant's intimate acquaintance with Cicero's *On Duties* [*De Officiis*] (see also Nussbaum 1997, 5; cf. Irwin 1998, 97n.18).

fellowship existing among men is that of all with all others. [...] the bonding of blood holds men together by goodwill [*benivolentia*] and by love [*caritas*] (Cicero 1991, 22 f.; I.51–54).[10]

What I find fascinating is that if we map Kant's notions of human natural impulses and his communal ethical ideals onto something like the above picture, we find that the 'degrees of fellowship' laid out originally by the Stoic school are always delineated by Kant in terms of *love* – all the way from the 'narrowest' to the 'widest' circle. I will now draw up these Kantian circles of love.

In the *Religion* Kant states that there is an "original predisposition [*Anlage*] to good in human nature" (RGV 6:26). This predisposition is threefold, and divided with respect to Kant's overall conception of human rationality. The two lower degrees of the predisposition to good represent "self-love", such that the lowest level (of animality) consists of mere animal impulses, whereas the second level (of humanity) includes reason as subservient to natural inclinations. The third level (of personality) consists of the moral-rational capacity to feel respect for the moral law. Arational animal self-love is itself divided into three aspects: "*first*, for self-preservation; *second*, for the propagation of the species, through the sexual drive, and for the preservation of the offspring thereby begotten through breeding; *third*, for community with other human beings, i.e. the social drive." (RGV 6:26)[11]

Kant's second, prudentially rational aspect of self-love involves comparative judgments in social contexts, according to which the human being judges herself happy or unhappy. This comparative tendency of the 'self-love of humanity' gives rise to a competitive drive to strive for equal or superior social worth (or rank) in comparison with others. Because of the corruptive tendency of this self-love, or the "unsocial sociability"[12] associated with it, it has been common for

---

10 The one Stoic who most clearly uses the *geometric metaphor* of the concentric circles is the late Stoic Hierocles (see Ramelli 2009). Hierocles's doctrine of *oikeiosis* clearly relies on the earlier Stoic accounts of the spheres of concern, and it has become commonplace in scholarship to associate the circle metaphor with Stoic doctrine more generally, even with respect to authors like Cicero who don't actually use the geometric metaphor (e.g. Den Boer 1979, 78 f.; Nussbaum 1997, 9; Heater 2002, 47; see Cavallar 2015, e.g. 84 f., 99, 126 f.). Derek Heater traces the cosmopolitan interpretation of "degrees of kinship and friendship" back to the Peripatetic Theophrastus (Heater 1996, 13), and associates Theophrastus with the origin of the "concentric circles" (while making the point that the geometric metaphor is as such not found in Theophrastus) (Heater 2002, 45; cf. Cavallar 2015, 160).
11 Of all the commentators who have discussed this passage, to my knowledge only Schneewind (2009, 107) has noted the similarity between Kant's view and Stoic doctrine.
12 Arroyo (2016) argues that pathological or emotive love is generally an expression of unsocial sociability. According to Arroyo, Kant holds that actions based on the emotion of love for others always have a competitive nature where each person tries to put herself in a superior position in relation to the other. While it is true that actions based on the pathological emotion of love

scholars to emphasise Kant's debt to Rousseau in his understanding of self-love (e. g. DiCenso 2012, 48; Pasternack 2014, 94; Wood 2009, 127 f.; see Rinne 2018, 22). Rousseau himself was also influenced by the Stoics (e. g. Brooke 2006, esp. 112 f.; Cavallar 2015, 84–86), and I think we should see Kant's conception of the social aspects of self-love as equally indebted to the Stoics and Rousseau. Of course, Kant's story of how we move on from mere self-love to loving others is distinctly his own.

In this respect, the question of what exactly it means for something to be a "predisposition to the good" is key. Some scholars, like Stephen Palmquist, assume that 'animal mechanical self-love' is good simply in biological terms, because it "enhances the likelyhood of our survival" (Palmquist 2016, 66, cf. xxiv). However, Kant states that the predispositions "further" [*befördern*] compliance with the moral law (RGV 6:28). It is not clear how an adaptive survival function would "further compliance with the moral law", and Kant, I take it, would never say that natural impulses of survival are morally good. What he could say is that biological adaptations, manifested through natural inclinations, are good in the sense of not being in themselves reprehensible (RGV 6:58), but this doesn't solve the problem of how they function as predispositions to the moral good. What I wish to propose here is that in terms of love, Kant's real target is *selfishness* or *egoism*.[13]

The natural predisposition of (self-)love furthers compliance with the moral law to the extent that it shifts the focus of one's actions from oneself to others, and gradually serves to mitigate egoism and promote other-regardingness. As every student of Kant's ethics knows, in morally relevant decision-making scenarios it is self-love which has to yield to respect for the moral law, and in these cases self-love is often, though not always, represented by selfish inclinations (such as the inclination to make a lying promise for one's own benefit). But even though all inclination based activity in Kant gets technically subsumed under the umbrella

---

for others are technically subsumed under "self-love", Arroyo's reading assumes that "self-love" is always coupled with competitive "self-interest" (Arroyo 2016, 595 f.). This, however, is not the case, and Kant holds both in his lectures and his published works that it is possible to love others pathologically without having one's own interest [*Eigennutz*] in view (MS-Vigilantius 27:670; GMS 4:398.9–11; see also Mo-Collins 27:414). To my knowledge, Kant's only statement on the relationship between (emotive) love for others and unsocial sociability explicitly dissociates "mutual love" [*Wechselliebe*] from unsocial sociability. According to Kant, in an early social condition defined by "concord, contentment" and pre-moral "mutual love", unsocial sociability would not arise (AA 8:21; see also Anth-Friedländer 25:585). For a detailed critique of Arroyo's position, see Rinne (2022).

13 My proposal draws inspiration not only from the Stoics, but also from a recent reading of Kant's conception of *practical love* by Ryan Patrick Hanley (2017), who argues generally that enlightment philosophies of love are very much directed to the mitigation of the socially harmful aspects of self-love, or to the extension of self-love to others.

term "self-love", such activity is not necessarily self-directed or concerned merely with oneself. In terms which may sound paradoxical to a non-Kantian reader, there can be other-regarding aspects involved in what will in the final analysis still be called "self-love", and even some selfish actions (such as seeking sexual pleasure) may nevertheless include something which is beneficial beyond the agent's concern for herself. I argue that this other-regarding or community-regarding tendency of even the rudimentary natural forms of sexuality (or sexual love) and parenting (or parental love) is the first point of contact between the narrowest and the wider circles of love. This does not imply that the agents involved in these animal behaviours should be intentionally, consciously, or even actually other-regarding in the sense of *overriding* any selfish concerns for the good of others. Rather, for those impulses to be predisposed to the moral good, and to the highest communal moral good more specifically, it is enough that they do in fact somehow promote a sphere of existence or concern beyond oneself.

We can make this point clearer by looking at Kant's discussions of these animal impulses and their relation to the notion of community in Kant's anthropology lectures and his lectures on ethics. Even within 'animal self-love', we will see gradations and an expansion of love from the self towards community. Love of life is merely the impulse to preserve oneself, and as the first affectionate relation (to oneself), it is the natural foundation for all other kinds of concern. Kant appreciates natural sexual love more than love of life precisely because the sphere of concern in sexual love is broader. In the Mrongovius lectures on anthropology we find the following:

> Sexual love brings the human being a certain measure of honor, whereas too much love of life is cowardice and brings disgrace. The latter is self-seeking in that it aims merely at self-preservation. But sexual love is already connected to a concern for others in that it has the propagation of the species as its basis. Sexual love is love that shares itself with others. But love of life [is] private love; hence sexual love is nobler. (Anth-Mrongovius 25:1361; see also MS 6:425; Anth-Friedländer 25:615)

It appears that because of being at least minimally other-oriented, the other-oriented drives have a "nobler" appearance, and they therefore bear a closer resemblance to morality than mere self-seeking drives.

Parental love springs from sexual love (Anth-Friedländer 25:613–615; see 25:584). As connected to the social instinct, parental love forges *the family*, which for Kant is the earliest natural foundation of society: "Human beings have an inclination to be in society, hence they form families, and like to have social relations, from which larger societies later arise, and upon which we can base the inclination to form nations." (Anth-Friedländer 25:585) We can now see how Kant sketches the basic trajectory from the natural instincts of love to the formation of society, and as Kant's comprehensive conception of the highest good involves an ethico-religious community, it is thus possible to understand the instincts of animal mechanical self-love as predisposed to the good: the trajectory begins with love of life, and sexual love, parental love, and the social drive express expanding extension of concern for others. As such, these aspects of love are the natural predispositions on which human societies are based. But it is still highly unclear how the foundational natural loves are connected to the 'higher', rationally other-regarding loves, such as (practical) love for one's neighbour or love in being universally a "friend of human beings". Can we even speak of continuity between the instincts of love and the types of love for which reason is required? To answer this question, it is necessary to analyse the way in which natural and rational elements of love are brought together in Kant's discussions of the general division of love into *love of benevolence* and *love of delight*.

3 Expanding the Circles of Love

As already mentioned above, in the *Religion* Kant describes the "natural predispositions to humanity" in terms of a self-love, which involves reason (RGV 6:27), and which is hence cognitively 'higher' than mere animal mechanical self-love. Further on he explains, that the self-love which "must be rational"[14] can be divided into love of benevolence [*Liebe des Wohlwollens*] and love of delight [*Liebe des Wohlgefallens*], and that this division also holds for the concept of love more generally. At bottom, love of benevolence for oneself means desiring that things go well for oneself, and love of delight for oneself means taking pleasure in the satisfaction of those maxims which have one's own happiness as their end.[15] Together with reason, the 'higher' kind of self-love necessarily involves imagination, projected end states of various courses of action, and a more or less vague, idealised temporal structure, which groups one's maxims of self-love together in terms of *prudence*. Kant's moral philosophical writings confirm in rich detail that he does use the general division of love beyond the context of mere self-love. Most prominently, he uses the general division in the context of love for other human beings (including one's friends), and often in conjunction with the Christian commandment to love one's neighbour as oneself (see e.g. PP-Herder 27:53; Mo-Collins 27:417–421; MS-Vigilantius 27:673–680; MS 6:399–402; 6:450 ff.). Both love of benevolence and love of

---

14 For a discussion of how exactly this phrase should be understood, see Rinne (2018, 7 f., 43–45).
15 There is also a moral love of delight in oneself, which is self-contentment in one's being conscious of one's ability to override selfish maxims through one's respect for the moral law (RGV 6:45 n.). See Rinne (2018, ch. 1) for a full exposition of the conceptual structure of self-love.

delight for other human beings appear also in emotive terms; such that in Kant's earlier lectures on ethics, both the desire for the happiness of others (or the desire to benefit others), i. e. love of benevolence, and the delight taken in the physical or moral perfections of others, i. e. love of delight, are grounded in inclination. (See Rinne 2018, ch. 4) As Dieter Schönecker points out (in this volume; see also Schönecker 2010), in Kant's mature, published moral philosophy love of delight is a subjective predisposition necessary for one's receptivity to duty. What I wish to focus on here is the way in which instincts of love are connected to moral practical love, and I will show this connection by making two small textual points. To point out the continuity of love from its instinctual basis to moral practical love, it has to be shown that 1) instincts of love are connected to inclination based love of benevolence, and that 2) inclination based love of benevolence (and delight) remain connected to moral practical love. This is to show that when pure practical reason induces the duty of practical love, the grounding motivational incentive of action is indeed subverted (the foundational incentive becomes respect for the law rather than inclination), and love becomes a rational maxim, but inclination-based benevolent love, and the (at least minimal) capacity to take delight in others remain subjectively in place, and inform the actual activity of the imperfectly moral agent in a non-ideal world. Pure practical reason does not annihiliate the feeling of love (*pace* Streich 1924, 29, 39), which also shows that the circles of love are indeed concentric. This is of course not to say that there wouldn't be crucial differences between different aspects of love.

It appears that a continuum between instinctual love and practical love can be established through the notion of self-benevolence.[16] In the Friedländer notes on anthropology we find an interesting passage which connects the instinct of self-preservation with the notion of one's own happiness. It may not be surprising

---

16 Apparently, the impulse of sexuality remains qualitatively distinct from the cognitive or psychological aspects of practical love. In *The Metaphysics of Morals* Kant says that sexual love (in the narrow sense of sexual impulse or inclination) cannot be counted as either love of benevolence or love of delight, and that even though sexual inclination can unite with moral love, it is a unique kind of pleasure [*Lust*] which "has nothing in common with moral love properly speaking" (MS 6:426.30; cf. Mo-Collins 27:417, where Kant classifies the sexual inclination as sensuous *Liebe des Wohlgefallens*). While the sexual instinct is predisposed to the good because of its other-directedness, in Kant's mature moral philosophy, sexual inclination is different in kind from the loves at issue in love's general division. Kant may have changed his mind about the nature of sexual inclination between the Collins lectures and the publication of *The Metaphysics of Morals*. It is also possible that his later refusal to classify sexual inclination as love of delight is due to the new functions that 'delight' receives in the critical philosophy, first as love of beauty in the third *Critique* (see KU 5:298–301), and then as the moral predisposition of love of human beings in the 'Doctrine of Virtue'.

that such a link might be found, but to document it is important for drawing up the continuity[17] in Kant's concept of love: "Love of life and of happiness is no special inclination, but the general condition of the satisfaction of all inclinations." (Anth-Friedländer 25:584) In Friedländer, love of life and the desire for happiness do not seem to be clearly distinct from each other, as they are in the *Religion*. Remember that in the *Religion* the notion of happiness is restricted to rational creatures and comparative judgments, but in Friedländer it seems that love of life and love of happiness are equivalent, or together constitute the general condition where the agent (or the human animal) seeks to satisfy her inclinations. On this basis, it would appear that the impulse of self-preservation is the instinctual foundation of the desire to be happy, which in Kant's mature moral philosophy is nothing but love of benevolence for oneself. This reading provides a powerful continuum between love of life and love of benevolence for oneself. The interpretation can be corroborated with a well-known passage from *Groundwork* I, where Kant explains that the true function of reason is to establish a morally good will, and not to provide the imperfectly rational creature with inclination-based happiness: "Now in a being that has reason and will, if the actual end of Nature were its *preservation*, its *prosperity*, in a word its *happiness*, then she would have made very bad arrangements for this in appointing the creature's Reason as the accomplisher of this purpose." (GMS 4:395) According to Kant, instinct is the straightforward guide to inclination-based happiness, and in the above passage Kant views *preservation* and prosperity as the basic constituents of happiness (even though, as in the *Religion*, natural happiness also requires reason, but only as subordinate to inclinations; cf. Anth-Mrongovius 25:1361). As the impulse of self-preservation is precisely love of life, and love of benevolence for oneself is the subjective principle of happiness, the continuity between the instinct of love of life and the instrumentally rational inclination to be happy (i. e. love of benevolence for oneself) seems beyond doubt. But what does *this* continuity have to do with the *moral love for others?*

As is well-known, Kant distinguishes between pathological[18] and practical love for others, such that pathological love for others cannot be commanded, whereas practical love for others, in harmony with Jesus' second commandment, is a duty. In the *Groundwork*, practical love "lies in the will and not in the propensity of sen-

---

17 In this context, I mean by 'continuity', that even in a case where there appears to be a category difference between a) an aspect of love for which reason is not required or b) an aspect of love the extension of which is narrow (closer to 'self'), and an aspect of love for which reason is required or that is broader in scope (extending further beyond the 'self'), some quality, attribute etc. of the first kind of love (a or b) is preserved in the latter kind of love (or can even be viewed as somehow grounding the latter kind).

18 I.e. inclination-based, not sick or perverted.

sation [*Empfindung*]" (GMS 4:399), whereas in the second *Critique* practical love means striving to practice all one's duties towards one's neighbours "gladly" [*gern*] (KpV 5:83). As doing something *gladly* implies inclination, the second *Critique* account of practical love contains a reference to the emotive framework of the agent, which reference is not visible in the *Groundwork* account of practical love. However, for Kant's rational justification of the duty of love, we have to look to the 'Doctrine of Virtue' of the *Metaphysics of Morals* where we see that practical love for others actually comes in degrees that refer to emotive or affectionate proximity in the agent-recipient relation, and that the duty of love is justified as involving an explicit connection to love of benevolence for oneself.[19] In *The Metaphysics of Morals* Kant explicitly states that feelings of love and respect accompany [*begleiten*] the performance of duties of virtue to others (MS 6:448; see Schönecker 2013). The duty of love itself, however, is not a feeling [*Gefühl*], but the rational necessitation to adopt a maxim of benevolence for others, such that the maxim yields practical, beneficent results (MS 6:449): "In accordance with the ethical law of perfection 'love your neighbor as yourself', the maxim of benevolence (practical love of human beings) is a duty of all human beings toward one another, whether or not one finds them worthy of love." (MS 6:450) The justification that Kant gives for this duty amounts to the notion that for the maxim of my own happiness to be universalisable, this maxim has to be conditioned with the happiness of others: "I want everyone else to be benevolent toward me (*benevolentiam*); hence I ought also to be benevolent toward everyone else." (MS 6:451; see 6:393)[20] Love of benevolence for oneself is the inclination to be happy and to be loved (benevolently) by others, and love of benevolence for others is "the inclination or will to promote the ends of others." (MS-Vigilantius 27:620). As we see in Kant's condensed argument above, the *phenomenal quality* (i.e. the empirical will and possibly inclination) related to the duty based love for others is derived from self-love as self-benevolence; i.e. the fact that there exists a duty to love others, and what this duty amounts to, can only be understood in the universalisation procedure through an intimate acquaintance with what self-love is like. The duty of

---

19 I am indebted here to Hanley, who has recently argued that "practical love is best understood as proper self-love (*Eigenliebe*) extended by reason to others in a way that can meet the universalising test of the categorical imperative." (Hanley 2017, 151; cf. Fahmy 2010)

20 Kant assumes that everyone in need wishes to be helped by others. Someone who was known to be unwilling to assist others would in turn be denied help, and therefore that person's maxim of self-interest would contradict itself (see MS 6:453; GMS 4:423; MS-Vigilantius 27:497–498). Note that Kant's argument would not apply against the kind of egoist who would, in the case of need, rather die than be helped by others. Maybe such a person does not exist, and Kant doesn't seem to entertain the possibility of the existence of this kind of person.

love subordinates the maxim of benevolence to the moral law. As the psychological recognition of benevolence is based on self-love, however, it seems that at least the apparent quality of benevolence as the desire to promote someone's ends remains unaltered in the universalisation process, and this quality is founded on self-benevolence. (See Hanley 2017, 151–157) Kant himself seems to put this point across even more bluntly: "The love of benevolence towards others does not differ from that towards oneself" (MS-Vigilantius 27:675).

From the perspective of pure practical reason, the scope of the maxim of love of benevolence ought to be universal, such that the maxim includes oneself and all others as objects of benevolence. Kant calls this love "universal love of human beings" [*allgemeine Menschenliebe*] (MS 6:451). Contrary to what one might think however, universal love of human beings does not imply a demand for impartiality in terms of *practical love.* Kant thinks that agents cannot demand love from others as a matter of *right* (see MS 6:383) and regarding love the categorical imperative only concerns the general maxim of benevolence (MS 6:389 f.). Universal love is merely well-wishing toward everyone, "greatest in its *extent*, but the smallest in its *degree*" (MS 6:451), amounting to a mere delight taken in the happiness of all others (MS 6:452). In practice one is permitted to be partial based on affective proximity (in so far as no strict duty is at stake), i. e. one has the "permission to limit one's maxim of duty by another (e. g. love of one's neighbor in general by love of one's parents)" (MS 6:390). In other words, "in wishing I can be equally benevolent to everyone, whereas in acting I can, without violating the universality of the maxim, vary the degree greatly in accordance with the different objects of my love (one of whom concerns me more closely than another)." (MS 6:452)

We see now on the one hand, how reason imposes constraint conditions on the manifestation of aspects of natural love, and on the other, how it creates obligations to extend the scope of love. This way reason modifies the intensity and social extension of love, whereas the natural, qualitative core of the benevolent feelings of love remains in place through the process of expanding spheres of concern. All of this, I believe, shows clearly a continuity in Kant's conception of love. In harmony with the Stoic metaphor, there is a conceptual and emotive-cognitive continuum from the instinct of self-preservation (love of life) to the rational (even if weak), universal love of all human beings. My last task will be to connect this continuum to Kant's idealised notions of the ethico-divine community, in order to complete my expanding circle view of love in Kant.

4 A Cosmopolitan Community of Love and Respect?

Discussions of Kant's cosmopolitanism often focus on the legal and political dimensions of the notion (see e. g. Bohman & Lutz-Bachmann 1997, Kleingeld 2016, Sanahuja 2017), and Kant's debt to Stoicism in terms of cosmopolitan right has been fairly well documented (e. g. Nussbaum 1997). Kant's ethical cosmopolitanism has received less attention, and even those authors, who very helpfully point out that the comprehensive highest good in Kant's philosophy must ultimately be understood as a communal notion combining ethical and religious perspectives (Cavallar 2015, Guyer 2017), have not had that much to say about love and friendship in this context (cf. Kleingeld 2012, 165–172).

In his discussion on friendship in the 'Doctrine of Virtue' Kant writes not only about friendship as an intimate union of love and respect between two people, but also about a universal disposition of being a friend of human beings in general:

> A *friend of human beings* [*Menschenfreund*] as such (i. e., of the whole race) is one who takes an affective interest in the well-being of all human beings (rejoices with them) and will never disturb it without heartfelt regret. Yet the expression 'a *friend* of human beings' [*Freund der Menschen*] is somewhat narrower in its meaning than 'one who merely loves human beings' (a *philanthropist*). For the former includes, as well, thought and consideration for the *equality* among them, and hence the idea that in putting others under obligation by his beneficence he is himself under obligation, as if all were brothers under one *father* who wills the happiness of all. (MS 6:472 f.)

Much of Kant's doctrine of ethico-theological cosmopolitanism (of love) can be plausibly viewed as packed into the above passage. The first thing to note is the subtle distinction that Kant makes between the terms *Menschenfreund* and *Freund der Menschen*, which both translate in English as "friend of human beings".[21] The former is one who merely harbors affectionate benevolence towards the whole human race, i. e. a philanthropist who possesses the weak universal love of human beings I discussed in the previous section (see MS 6:450; see also MS-Vigilantius 27:676). The latter friend, however, is one who humbles herself through respect, and an acknowledgment that all human beings are fundamentally equal. In the above passage, the acknowledgment of equality connects to the religious perspective, where a divine father is seen as the supreme lawgiver of morality. There are thus two interwoven strands of thought simultaneously at play here. The first deals with the expansion of the ethical sphere of concern in terms of love and

---

21 I thank Dieter Schönecker for making me aware of this distinction.

friendship, and the second connects this expansion with a representation of the global ethical community in religious terms. Concerning the first perspective, Kant asks in the earlier Collins lectures on ethics: "To what extent are men the better for engaging in friendship? People do not favour everyone with their benevolence, but would sooner confine themselves, in that respect, to a small circle." (Mo-Collins 27:427) As already noted, early societies arise from the family or through sects, and the problem with these kinds of relationships is that they "close the heart" towards outsiders and "impair [...] goodness" (Mo-Collins 27:428). Particular friendships based on a moral outlook are generally of aid in overcoming mistrust and opening up one's heart to others (*ibid.*). Good hearted, well-disposed people who can establish friendships with anyone are *world citizens* [Weltbürger] (Mo-Collins 27:430). In Vigilantius, the general love of humanity is explicitly connected to the common descent of humankind: "there is a general love for every other person as such, for certain kinds of persons, and for the entire human race. Patriotism, the love of the fatherland, also belongs here, as does cosmopolitanism: in both, the determination to love of others rests upon common descent" (MS-Vigilantius 27:673).[22] Being everyone's friend does not mean making friends with everyone, but is equivalent to possessing universal benevolence (MS-Vigilantius 27:676).[23] These passages show clearly how the universal love for others, harbored in the cosmopolitan outlook of being a friend of human beings [*Freund der Menschen*], is directly continuous with Kant's notion of (moral) love of benevolence for others, which, as I have shown, is naturally rooted (even though morally modi-

---

22 For discussions of Kant's notorious racial theory, see e.g. Louden (2000, 93–100). According to Kant, all human beings belong to the same species and share a common descent (e.g. AA 25:1187), while different racial characteristics are based on innate predispositions or germs which are activated on the basis of climate (Louden 2000, 96 f.). Kant's remarks on race reveal an obvious racial hierarchy, such that other races are inferior to the white race. However, given Kant's moral universalism all human beings should be capable of development, even if Kant appears to think that the white race has a head start. (Cf. Louden 2000, 99–106) Kleingeld (2007; 2012) argues that Kant "radically changed his mind" on race in his later philosophy.

23 In Vigilantius, Kant worries that cosmopolitan love may be too general, so as to make one lose sight of individual friendships, even though he retains that "the great value of love of human beings rests in the universal love of human beings as such." (MS-Vigilantius 27:673) In Vigilantius, one might interpret Kant to be advocating a position according to which "love of the fatherland" serves as a fulcrum between the narrower and wider circles of love (see also Kleingeld 2012, 26–34), somewhat similary to a recent position in contemporary political philosophy advocated by Nussbaum (2013). However, the doubt against universal love expressed in Vigilantius cannot be found in the *Religion* and *The Metaphysics of Morals*. In his mature philosophy, Kant obviously adopted a significantly more positive stance towards the notion of universal love compared to his early pre-critical thought (compare the 'Doctrine of Virtue' with Kant's 'Remarks in the Observations on the Feeling of the Beautiful and Sublime'; e.g. MS 6:450–452; cf. AA 20:25).

fied) in the love of benevolence for oneself, which in turn rests ultimately on the instinct of self-preservation, i.e. love of life. There is thus an expanding circle of love in Kant's philosophy.

From the perspective of philosophy of religion, it is important to see the extent to which Kant discusses the attributes of (the practically postulated existence of) God in terms of love. As is well known, Kant holds that one's (rational) hope for the highest good is dependent on the practical postulation of the existence of God, such that the inevitable imperfection of the embodied human being may eventually be remediated by God, on the condition that the human being views all moral laws as divine commands and strives to become moral. In *The Metaphysics of Morals* Kant thinks that the divine end of God's plan can only be seen "as proceeding from *love*, that is, as the *happiness* of human beings." (MS 6:488) The intention of the world's author "can have only love for its basis." (MS 6:491). This love, through which (from a religious perspective) God gives the human race the moral laws, is also love of benevolence: "God's love for us (also expressed by the words: *God is love*) is thus the divine benevolence and kindness toward us, which constitutes the foundation of the potestas legislatoria divina." (MS-Vigilantius 27:721; cf. RGV 6:141) If we think of the rational procedure through which the concept of God is established in Kant's writings, i.e. that the concept of God is derived from moral reason as connected to the end of happiness, we can see that insofar as the concept of God rests on the ideal union between moral reason and happiness, any notion of God's love of benevolence will be grounded in human love of benevolence. In other words, it appears that the only way to say anything (from a practical perspective) about divine love of benevolence, is by first being acquainted with what human love of benevolence is like. In the *Religion*, Kant discusses the idea that "God is love" in terms of *love of moral delight*, which God (hopefully) comes to have for human beings, on the condition that human beings strive to love God by means of morally good life conduct (RGV 6:145 f.; see KpV 5:83 f.; MS-Vigilantius 27:720; RGV 6:120). Textual evidence thus shows that from a *religious perspective*, God's love 'surrounds' the human moral endeavour, both as the ground and (hoped for) end of that endeavour.[24]

The long passage quoted at the beginning of this section ends by connecting the notion of the friend of human beings [*Freund der Menschen*] to the idea of universal "brotherhood" under one "father". This connection can be understood in the light of the *Religion*, where Kant asserts that the global "ethical commonwealth", which can be gradually built on juridico-civil societies, is only possible under

---

24 For a more comprehensive account of the structure of love of God in Kant's philosophy, see Rinne (2018, ch. 3)

the practical supposition of an almighty ethical law-giver (RGV 6:98 f.).[25] In the *Religion*, striving for the highest good in terms of an ethico-religious community becomes an explicitly communal endeavour: "this highest moral good will not be brought about solely through the striving of one individual person for his own moral perfection but requires rather a union of such persons into a whole toward that very end, i. e. a system of well-disposed human beings" (RGV 6:97 f.; see also AA 8:279 f. n.). According to Kant, this project, which is essentially moral, will require the establishment of a universal church, which emphasises morality (rather than ecclesiastical faith), and which can be historically founded only on the Christian religion, because of the [alleged] moral purity of Christianity in comparison with other religious belief-systems (such as Judaism or Islam) (RGV 6:124–132; 6:193; AA 7:50 ff.; see Louden 2000, 130–132; cf. Tampio 2014, 184 f.). Kant describes the ideal end-state of this global project (which cannot be externally forced) in terms of a *family*, where the ethical community and the universal, "true" church seem to become equivalent (RGV 6:101): "It [a church representing an ethical community] could best of all be likened to a household (a family) under a common though invisible moral father, whose holy son [...] stands in blood relation with all the members of the family [...] a free, universal, and enduring union of hearts." (RGV 6:102)

When Kant's cosmopolitanism is analysed from the perspective of ethics and philosophy of religion,[26] notions of love and friendship come to the fore. The ethico-religious community is necessarily at least a community of love and respect (see MS 6:488), and cannot be understood from a religious point of view without accounting for the comprehensive notion of *love of God:* Insofar as the "father" wills the happiness of his children (the "holy son" and the "brothers"), his relationship to the community is one of love of benevolence (conditioned by his justice). The children love the father by gladly doing what he commands (KpV 5:83), and insofar as they have sincerely cultivated universal love of benevolence for each other (while taking to heart the notion of respect), the father loves them with his love of moral delight. The ideal family is a happy family. From the perspective of mere ethics, a similar idea (i. e. that a community of love and respect ought to be

---

25 Kant argues that an ethical community requires public legislation, but because a community of human beings can only issue external public laws (not internal moral laws), a transcendent law-giver is required for communal ethical legislation. For a well founded criticism of Kant's argument, see Guyer (2017, 296 f.).

26 In harmony with Cavallar (2015); cf. Pasternack (2014, 177), who associates the notion of "cosmopolitanism" with external conduct (2014, 177). For Pasternack, apparently, the ethical community would not be "cosmopolitan", even if the community would consist of all human beings (cf. MS-Vigilantius 27:673, where '*Kosmopolitismus*' is explicitly connected with universal love).

brought about) is expressed by Kant in terms of friendship (cf. Wood 1999, 316;[27] Rinne 2018, 162–166), and through the metaphor of being a "citizen of the world" [*Weltbürger*]. As the moral life is not a solitary endeavour, and our virtue depends in part on others (as e.g. Moran 2012; Pasternack 2014, 178; and Bhardwaj (in this volume) have fruitfully acknowledged), friendships are indispensable sites for both pleasure and moral progress (see also Formosa 2010). Private friendships cultivate the disposition to open one's heart to others, and the universal disposition of friendship, i.e. of being a friend of human beings or metaphorically a *Weltbürger*, is one of cosmopolitan love and respect:

> It is a duty to oneself as well as to others not to *isolate* oneself [...] but to use one's moral perfections in social intercourse [...]. While making oneself a fixed centre of one's principles, one ought to regard this circle drawn around one as also forming part of an all-inclusive circle of those who, in their disposition, are citizens of the world – not exactly to promote as the end what is best for the world but only to cultivate what leads indirectly to this end: to cultivate a disposition of reciprocity – agreeableness, tolerance, mutual love and respect (affability and propriety, *humanitas aesthetica et decorum*) and so to associate the graces with virtue. (MS 6:473)

Kant's discussion of the "duty not to isolate oneself" appears in the 'Doctrine of Virtue' immediately after his account of what it is to be a *Menschenfreund* and a *Freund der Menschen*. As we know from the Collins lectures on ethics that Kant identifies a *Menschenfreund* (someone who has a universal disposition for friendship) with being a citizen of the world [*Weltbürger*] (Mo-Collins 27:430), it is safe to say that the citizens of the world in the passage quoted above are at least *Menschenfreunde*, and that they ought to become *Freunde der Menschen*. It is interesting that Kant characterises the friend of human beings in affective (or sensory-aesthetic) terms: the friend of human beings (in both senses) necessarily has love of benevolence for others (be it from inclination or from duty), but in this context Kant seems to emphasise the emotive terms of "satisfaction" [*Vergnügen*] (MS 6:450; GMS 4:398) and "rejoicing" [*Mitfreude*] (MS 6:472; see also GMS 4:398) in

---

27 Wood contrasts the model of family with that of friendship, and argues that even though Kant uses the metaphor of family to describe the ethical community, the ethical community would be better understood in terms of friendship (Wood 1999, 316). The expanding circle model of love in Kant represents the notions of family and friendship as connected in terms of love. Both are naturally grounded in natural love, and can incorporate moral reason and be modified with that reason ("moral friendship" is dependent on moral dispositions from the start). From a natural-historical perspective, the aspects of love related to the family are the earliest ones, and these loves ground early society. With respect to the ideal ethico-religious community, the notion of the family reappears as a religious, patriarchal metaphor of that community. From a strictly ethical perspective, Kant emphasises notions of friendship as vehicles toward the ethical community.

the well-being of others (cf. Mo-Collins 27:430; MS-Vigilantius 27:676). Apparently, striving to become a *Freund der Menschen*, while cultivating private friendships, can indirectly serve as a bridge between narrower and wider circles of affective concern, such that the quasi-moral notions of "affability and propriety" ('graces') can be associated with the moral notions of love and respect regarding humanity as a whole ('virtue') (see MS 6:488.16–19). For Kant, the widest, ideal circle of love is a circle of love and respect of all human beings towards all other human beings. In religious terms, this circle is a patriarchal family of brothers who are friends under God, the divine, loving father.[28]

5 Conclusion

Hanley has recently argued that whereas the "traditional conception of love" consisted of a "triangle" of self-love, love for others, and divine love, the "enlightenment conception of love" (Kant's theory of love included) "reduced this triangle to a line", "a flat continuum defined by the two poles of love of self and love of others." (Hanley 2017, 17) We can now appreciate that the historical shift in the geometrical metaphors of love as proposed by Hanley is actually not applicable to Kant. Kant continues to relate the concept of love to that of the highest good, and he holds on to notions of divine love from an ethico-religious perspective (true, he rejects theological foundations for normative justifications of love). An investigation of the complicated relationship between self-love and love of others in Kant's philosophy reveals, that the metaphor of an expanding circle captures Kant's position more accurately than the metaphor of a flat line. If we combine the metaphors of an 'ascent of love' and an 'expanding circle of love', we end up with a surprising result. The geometric metaphor best suited to capture the overall conceptual structure of love in Kant appears to be that of an *inverted cone*, such that the cone's lowest point (the inverted tip) represents love of life (individual self-preservation), and the wide, circular base (now at the highest point) represents the ideal ethico-religious community of friends of human beings, the global ethico-divine "family". Within the inverted cone, love can be seen to flow dynamically upwards from natural instincts to widening circles of moral love. In Kant's philosophy, to expand the circle of love is a moral demand, and the process of expanding love (conditioned by respect) is ideally both a subjective and a communal, species-level endeavour. In this process, the natural impulses and feelings of love (together with sympathy) serve as the emotive basis for acknowledging

---

28 Cf. Rinne 2018, 164–166.

and comprehending the rationally commanded duties of other-regarding love. Because of the processual nature of love, and because the instincts of love continue to exist as the phenomenal roots of moral love (even though morality subordinates feelings of love to respect for the moral law as an incentive to action), it is possible to speak of 'one love' in the philosophy of Kant, even if only in a qualified sense. As the Stoics knew well, in the flow of life love changes, and yet the basic nature of loving affection remains largely the same.

I wish to end with a word of warning. The picture of love in Kant I have painted in this article has been a relatively happy one. We are animals capable of morality; driven by natural instincts, and if we just sincerely strive to become more moral, we can eventually all love and respect each other, and live together peacefully on planet Earth. Even though something like this is indeed Kant's considered view of human moral progress, it is not exactly clear who is meant by 'we' in the above picture. Certainly, Kant's view of the widest, ideal circle of love includes at least white, heterosexual men. In honesty, Kant was a racist, sexist, and a homophobe, and it is at least somewhat ambiguous whether he meant to include people of colour, women, or sexual minorities as fully-fledged members in his universal (Christian, patriarchal) ethico-religious community. Fair enough, he may have changed his mind on some (racial) issues, and his mature moral theory should indeed not discriminate, but I think it is telling in itself, that dedicated Kantian scholars of our time are forced to take great pains in various contexts to show that 'it is not as bad as it looks'. In this essay, I cannot investigate in detail the points of contact between Kant's moral theory, his anthropology, and his cosmopolitanism. I can only caution generally, that instead of adopting an attitude of elevated enthusiasm, we should remain alert and critical about questions of inclusion and equality in any discourse that claims to advocate the normative ideal of universal love. My aim here has been merely to clarify the conceptual structure of love in Kant, using the Stoic metaphor of an expanding circle. Irrespective of the details of Kant's anthropology, I believe to have shown that there are intricate continuities in Kant's conceptions of love, and that these continuities show that the trajectory from crude self-preservation to cosmopolitan friendship cannot be understood without accounting for the operation of the concept of love. To see how notions of love are intertwined in a complex network of concepts in Kant's philosophy, may also help us to understand love more generally. The metaphor of an expanding circle of love, as connected to the question concerning love's conceptual structure, may have applications beyond the study of Kant.

References

Annas, Julia, 1993, *The Morality of Happiness*, New York: Oxford University Press.

Den Boer, W., 1979, *Private Morality in Greece and Rome: Some Historical Aspects*, Leiden: Brill.

DiCenso, John, 2012, *Kant's Religion within the Boundaries of mere Reason. A Commentary*, Cambridge: Cambridge University Press.

Bohman, James/Lutz-Bachmann, Matthias (eds.), 1997, *Perpetual Peace. Essays on Kant's Cosmopolitan Ideal*, Cambridge, MA: MIT Press.

Brooke, C., 2006, "Rousseau's Political Philosophy. Stoic and Augustinian Origins", in: Patrick Riley (ed.), *The Cambridge Companion to Rousseau*, Cambridge: Cambridge University Press, 94–123.

Cavallar, Georg, 2015, *Kant's Embedded Cosmopolitanism. History, Philosophy, and Education for World Citizens*, Berlin/Boston: de Gruyter.

Cicero, 1991, *On Duties*, edited by M. T. Griffin and E. M. Atkins, Cambridge: Cambridge University Press.

Fahmy, Melissa S., 2010, "Kantian Practical Love", *Pacific Philosophical Quarterly*, 91, 313–331.

Formosa, Paul, 2010, "Kant on the Highest Moral-Physical Good. The Social Aspect of Kant's Moral Philosophy", *Kantian Review*, 15, 1–36.

Guyer, Paul, 2017, "Kantian Communities. The Realm of Ends, the Ethical Community, and the Highest Good", in: Paul Guyer, *Virtues of Freedom. Selected Essays on Kant*, Oxford: Oxford University Press.

Hanley, Ryan Patrick, 2017, *Love's Enlightenment. Rethinking Charity in Modernity*, New York: Cambridge University Press.

Heater, Derek, 1996, *World Citizenship and Government. Cosmopolitan Ideas in the History of Western Political Thought*, Basingstoke: Palgrave Macmillan.

Heater, Derek, 2002, *World Citizenship. Cosmopolitan Thinking and its Opponents*, London: Continuum.

Heath, Peter/Schneewind, Jerome B., 1997, "Explanations of Names", in: Peter Heath and Jerome B. Schneewind (eds.), Immanuel Kant, *Lectures on Ethics*, Cambridge: Cambridge University Press, 455–474.

Irwin, T. H., 1998, "Kant's Criticisms of Eudaimonism", in: Stephen Engstrom and Jennifer Whiting (eds.), *Aristotle, Kant, and the Stoics. Rethinking Happiness and Duty*, Cambridge: Cambridge University Press, 63–101.

Kleingeld, Pauline, 2007, "Kant's Second Thoughts on Race", *The Philosophical Quarterly*, 57/229, 573–592.

Kleingeld, Pauline, 2012, *Kant and Cosmopolitanism*, Cambridge: Cambridge University Press.

Kleingeld, Pauline, 2016, "Kant's Moral and Political Cosmopolitanism", *Philosophy Compass*, 11/1, 14–23.

Lloyd, Genevieve, 2009, "Providence as Progress. Kant's Variations on a Tale of Origins", in: Amélie Oksenberg Rorty and James Schmidt (eds.), *Kant's Idea for A Universal History with a Cosmopolitan Aim. A Critical Guide*, Cambridge: Cambridge University Press, 200–215.

Long, A. A., 2003, "Stoicism in the Philosophical Tradition. Spinoza, Lipsius, Butler", in Brad Inwood (ed.), *The Cambridge Companion to Stoicism*, Cambridge: Cambridge University Press, 365–392.

Long, A. A./Sedley, David N., 1987, *The Hellenistic Philosophers. Vol. 1. Translation of Principal Sources with Philosophical Commentary*, Cambridge: Cambridge University Press.

Long, A. G. (ed.), 2013, *Plato and the Stoics*, Cambridge: Cambridge University Press.

Louden, Robert B., 2000, *Kant's Impure Ethics. From Rational Beings to Human Beings*, New York: Oxford University Press.

Nussbaum, Martha C., 1997, "Kant and Stoic Cosmopolitanism", *The Journal of Political Philosophy*, 5/1, 1–25.

Nussbaum, Martha C., 2013, *Political Emotions. Why Love Matters for Justice*, Cambridge, MA: Harvard University Press.

Oksenberg Rorty, Amélie/Schmidt, James (eds.), 2009, *Kant's Idea for A Universal History with a Cosmopolitan Aim. A Critical* Guide, Cambridge: Cambridge University Press.

Palmquist, Stephen R., 2016, *Comprehensive Commentary on Kant's Religion within the Bounds of Bare Reason*, Chichester: Wiley-Blackwell.

Pasternack, Lawrence R., 2014, *Kant on Religion within the Boundaries of Mere Reason*, London/New York: Routledge.

Ramelli, Ilaria, 2009, *Hierocles the Stoic: Elements of Ethics, Fragments and Excerpts*, translated by David Konstan, Atlanta: Society of Biblical Literature.

Reich, Klaus, 1939a, "Kant and Greek Ethics I", *Mind*, 48/191, 338–354.

Reich, Klaus, 1939b, "Kant and Greek Ethics II", *Mind*, 48/192, 446–463.

Rinne, Pärttyli, 2018, *Kant on Love*, Berlin/Boston: de Gruyter.

Rinne, Pärttyli, 2022, "Kant and Love of Human Beings: A Response to Arroyo and Hanley", in: *Studi Kantiani*, XXXIV, 189–208.

Sanahuja, Lorena C., 2017, *Toward Kantian Cosmopolitanism*, Cham: Palgrave Macmillan.

Schneewind, Jerome B., 2009, "Good out of Evil: Kant and the Idea of Unsocial Sociability', in: Amélie Oksenberg Rorty and James Schmidt (eds.), *Kant's Idea for A Universal History with a Cosmopolitan Aim. A Critical Guide*, Cambridge: Cambridge University Press, 94–111.

Schneewind Jerome B., 2010, *Essays on the History of Moral Philosophy*, Oxford: Oxford University Press.

Schönecker, Dieter, 2010, "Kant über Menschenliebe als moralische Gemütsanlage", *Archiv für Geschichte der Philosophie*, 92/2, 133–175.

Schönecker, Dieter, 2013, "Duties to Others From Love (TL 6:448–461)", in: Andreas Trampota, Oliver Sensen, and Jens Timmermann (eds.), *Kant's "Tugendlehre"*, Berlin/Boston: de Gruyter, 309–341.

Streich, Detlev, 1924, *Der Begriff der Liebe bei Kant*, Doctoral Dissertation, Greifswald: Ernst Moritz Arndt Universität. [Note: only available copy in the archives of the Berlin Staatsbibliothek.]

Tampio, Nicholas, 2014, "Pluralism in the Ethical Community", in: George E. Michalson (ed.), *Kant's Religion within the Boundaries of Mere Reason. A Critical Guide*, Cambridge: Cambridge University Press, 175–192.

Thorsteinsson, Runar M., 2010, *Roman Christianity and Roman Stoicism. A Comparative Study of Ancient Morality*, Oxford: Oxford University Press.

Wood, Allen, 1999, *Kant's Ethical Thought*, Cambridge: Cambridge University Press.

Kate Moran
Kant on Friendship and Misanthropy

Abstract: In the course of his discussion of moral friendship, Kant includes a warning against revealing too much of ourselves to our friends – this can include saying too much about our moral struggles, or even suggesting that we need our friend's help. As many scholars have observed, these are puzzling claims, since we might have thought Kantian friendship to be immune to the dangers of comparison that threaten other types of association. In this essay, I suggest that a clue to Kant's warnings might be found in his discussion of misanthropy. Crucially, the kind of misanthropy Kant appears to be most concerned about is a kind of disappointment in humanity that affects our ability to like others and thus be motivated to will well toward them. The essay offers an analysis of this disappointment informed by Adrienne Martin's recent discussion of so-called 'normative hope.' Ultimately, I argue, friendship is particularly susceptible to disappointed normative hope – and thus misanthropy – precisely because of the closeness and openness that characterize the relationship. This helps to explain Kant's words of caution regarding friendship.

I Some Puzzles About Friendship and Beneficence

Readers of Kant's discussions of friendship in the *Doctrine of Virtue* and various lectures on ethics are sometimes struck by what would appear to be a kind of pessimism on Kant's part.[1] Friendship – specifically the type of friendship that he calls 'moral friendship' – is an ideal toward which agents have a duty to strive (MS 6:469). It is a relationship of "equal mutual love and respect" between two sensible agents who struggle to be virtuous (*ibid.*). Ideally, participants in a moral friendship struggle toward virtue together in a relationship of perfect equality, within which they can discuss their moral challenges without fear of undue judgment or public embarrassment. As Kant describes it, "*Moral friendship* (as distinguished from friendship based on feeling) is the complete confidence of two persons in revealing their secret judgments and feelings to each other, so far as such disclosures are consistent with mutual respect." (MS 6:471) And yet, because the participants in a moral friendship are sensible agents, danger looms. Friendship offers a kind of

---

1 See, for example, Baron (2002), Biss (2019), Denis (2001), Stohr (2014), Vilhauer (2021).

https://doi.org/10.1515/9783111291130-009

intimacy that can be helpful with regard to the moral end of improved self-knowledge and self-scrutiny, but it is precisely this sort of intimacy that can pose a threat in the context of a tendency toward intrapersonal comparison and rivalry.[2] Indeed, one gets the sense from reading Kant's remarks on *non*-moral friendship that a friendship not shaped or restricted by principles of respect, equality, and restraint is always on the brink of destruction. Kant remarks that, "friendship is so delicate [...] that it is never safe for a moment from interruptions if it is allowed to rest on feelings, and if this mutual sympathy and self-surrender are not subjected to principles or rules preventing excessive familiarity and limiting mutual love by requirements of respect" (MS 6:471).

In the face of these dangers, Kant argues that a certain level of reserve is required so that a moral friendship may sustain itself. Sometimes Kant appears to recommend reserve regarding things that seem understandable enough – moral friendship requires disclosing one's innermost thoughts and moral struggles with another, but there would seem to be no requirement to disclose every last detail, however private, about these moral struggles. Thus, moral friendship, which requires that we maintain a balance of love and respect, requires that we be able to share our innermost thoughts with another person, but not in such a way or to such an extent that it damages the respect that the person has for us. Kant reportedly argues in the Kaehler/Collins lectures, for example:

> The question arises, whether, in such friendship, there is still a need for reserve? Yes, but not so much for one's own sake, as for that of the other; for everyone has his weaknesses, and these must be kept hidden even from our friends. Intimacy relates only to dispositions and sentiment, not to decorum; that must be observed, indeed, and one's weaknesses in that respect concealed, so that humanity should not be offended thereby. Even to our best friend, we must not discover ourselves as we naturally are and know ourselves to be, for that would be a nasty business. (Mo-Collins, 27:427)

Much later, in the Vigilantius lectures on moral philosophy, Kant similarly argues that

> Intimacy in the mutual disclosure of thoughts calls for *caution*, i. e., that we open our mind to the other only so far that we do not run the risk of thereby forfeiting his respect, by the standards of his judgment and the degree of his practical prudence. (MS-Vigilantius, 27:684 f.)

This advice might seem sound enough, as far as it goes, but we might wonder about the premises on which it is based – in particular, the notion that there is something potentially damaging about complete openness, especially when it comes to the re-

---

2 For further detail on Kant's notion of moral friendship, see Biss (2019) and Moran (2012).

spect that our friend has for us. The claim would appear reasonable when it comes to colleagues and mere acquaintances: we want to put our best foot forward in these cases. So, too, when we are first getting to know someone; here, again, it may seem prudent not to reveal too much too early. Still, we might legitimately wonder why such openness threatens to harm feelings of respect within a *moral* friendship. As already noted, that type of relationship is premised on a shared understanding of moral failure and moral striving. Why should candor threaten respect in a relationship centered around overcoming our moral short-comings? If we can't open ourselves up within a moral friendship, where can we do this?[3]

What is more, there appear to be moments in which Kant recommends something beyond mere caution regarding how much detail one provides in describing one's moral shortcomings to a friend. In other passages, Kant recommends a kind of *withholding* of information about one's needs that might seem to verge on misrepresenting oneself to one's friend. So, for example, in the Kaehler/Collins lecture, he remarks that, "It is therefore not good to have a friend whom we burden with appeals for help in distress; we are thereby a trouble to him for he thinks at once that he will often be called upon in this fashion. We do better to endure hardships alone, rather than burden others." (Mo-Collins, 27:419 f.) And in a longer passage in the *Doctrine of Virtue*, Kant argues,

> But still it is also a heavy burden to feel chained to another's fate and encumbered with his needs. – Hence friendship cannot be a union aimed at mutual advantage but must rather be a purely moral one, and the help that each may count on from the other in case of need must not be regarded as the end and determining ground of friendship – for in that case one would lose the other's respect – but only as the outward manifestation of an inner heartfelt benevolence, which should not be put to the test since this is always dangerous; each is generously concerned with sparing the other his burden and bearing it all by himself, even concealing it altogether from his friend, while yet he can always flatter himself that in case of need he could confidently count on the other's help. (MS, 6:470 f.)

Even if Kant is not exactly recommending that we *lie* to our friends, it is striking that he would suggest that we withhold what would seem to be fairly important information from them. After all, isn't it precisely when we feel that we need help that a friend can be a comfort – even if she doesn't provide any material as-

---

3 Stohr offers several hypotheses, for example, that reserve in friendship protects the dignity and equality of its participants (Stohr 2014, 5 f.). The view she ultimately develops – that reserve is an important element in maintaining the so-called 'moral front region' bears some similarity to the argument later in this essay regarding misanthropy and normative hope.

sistance?[4] Indeed, we might think that Kant is equivocating in the passage above: it might make sense to say that a friendship that is *based* on what each party can do for the other is obviously susceptible to dangers of comparison and 'score keeping'. But why suppose that simply sharing one's needs with another person in a friendship otherwise grounded in mutual love and respect would pose the same risk? Nevertheless, it seems clearly to be Kant's view that acts of service or beneficence within a friendship are potentially harmful to the relationship. In addition to the above advice for the friend who might find herself in need, he also offers advice for the friend who might be tempted to help her friend. He reportedly argues that "the only way [...] to confer a benefit without injuring the sense of honour, is to so wrap it up that it would seem a duty of friendship if the other were to accept it, so that only a duty is being met" (MS-Vigilantius, 27:697).

Of course, Kant's recommendations about how to perform beneficent actions within friendship – if one must – have an analogue in his moral philosophy, where one *does* have an obligation to help others. Kant's concerns regarding beneficence generally are not dissimilar to his concerns about acts of assistance within the context of friendship. In particular, Kant worries about the danger that beneficent actions pose with respect to the delicate balance of equality between benefactor and recipient. This worry arises, in first instance, because he thinks that acts of beneficence create obligations. This, as far as Kant sees it, is an analytic claim: duties of love just are those duties whose successful performance puts others under obligation. (MS, 6:448) But beyond this, there are further concerns about how each of the parties (benefactor and recipient) will think about and respond to this fact of obligation. In the face of these concerns, Kant's view is that the best option by far is to perform these actions anonymously. Where that option is not open to a benefactor, Kant again suggests that one ought to dress the act of beneficence up as if it were actually owed:

> He must also carefully avoid any appearance of intending to bind the other by [the act of beneficence]; for if he showed that he wanted to put the other under an obligation (which always humbles the other in his own eyes), it would not be a true benefit that he rendered him. Instead, he must show that he is himself put under obligation by the other's acceptance or honored by it, hence that the duty is merely something that he owes, unless (as is better) he can practice his beneficence in complete secrecy. (MS, 6:453)

In sum, we have an obligation to adopt the ends of others as our own, but Kant displays a striking realism about human psychology where one is either benefactor or recipient, both within the narrower context of friendship, and more generally.

---

4 For further critical discussion of this point see Baron (2002).

Still Kant's suggestions regarding friendship and beneficence are not simply meant to operate as guards against negative or unpleasant feelings – for example, of inferiority, neediness, or indebtedness. Rather, I take it that Kant's view is that these scenarios pose a broader problem within a moral community. I want to suggest in the remainder of this essay that we can find a clue to understanding Kant's concerns in his discussion of misanthropy. In what follows, I offer a sketch of Kantian misanthropy and argue that misanthropy is a response to a kind of moral disappointment. Such disappointment is in many respects similar to what Adrienne Martin has described as a disappointment with regard to normative hope (Martin 2013). Since, as I will argue, the disappointment of normative hope has serious consequences when it comes to a particular species of moral motivation, I think we can understand some of Kant's concerns and suggestions above as focused on avoiding this kind of normative disappointment in an effort to preserve an attitude toward humanity that is important – if not strictly speaking necessary – from the standpoint of moral motivation.

II Misanthropy as Dislike and Disappointment

It is important at the outset to make a distinction between what Kant calls the 'misanthrope from dislike' and the 'misanthrope from ill will'. The former ('misanthropy from dislike') is what Kant calls *anthropophobia* and is what I will refer to as 'misanthropy' in the discussion that follows, unless otherwise noted. Kant makes the distinction between the two types of misanthropy most clearly in the Kaehler/Collins lectures:

> Misanthropy is hatred of mankind, and takes two forms: aversion from men, and enmity towards them. In the first case we are afraid of men, regarding them as our enemies; but the second is when a man is himself an enemy to others. The aversive man shrinks from men out of temperament, he sees himself as no good to others, and thinks he is too unimportant for them; and since, for all that, he has a certain love of honour, he hides and runs away from people. The enemy of mankind shuns his fellows on principle, thinking himself too good for them. Misanthropy arises, partly from dislike, and partly from ill-will. The misanthrope from dislike thinks all men are bad; he fails to find in them what he was seeking; he does not hate them, and wishes some good to all, but simply does not like them. Such people are melancholy folk, who can form no conception of the human race. But the misanthrope from ill-will is he who does good to nobody, and pursues their harm instead. (Mo-Collins, 27:431 f.)

The misanthrope from ill-will actively dislikes others and pursues their harm. The misanthrope from dislike, on the other hand, does not harbor any ill-will toward others: his is a tendency to turn away from them. He has the

> tendency to withdraw from society, the fantastic wish for an isolated country seat, or even (in young people) the dream of happiness in being able to pass their life on an island unknown to the rest of the world with a small family, which the novelists or poets who write Robinsonades know so well how to exploit (KU, 5:275 f.).

Crucially, he does not think himself *better* than others: the disappointment with humanity that causes him to retreat includes even himself.

It may, in this vein, be helpful to think about misanthropy (*anthropophobia*) in terms of the distinction that Kant makes among the concepts of *Wohlgefallen*, *Wohlwollen*, and *Wohlthun*. Kant uses these terms, especially in his discussion of duties to others in the *Doctrine of Virtue* to describe the types of other-regarding attitudes and maxims that play a part in the successful performance of duties of love.[5]

The first of these, *Wohlgefallen* (or well-liking) belongs – as its name would suggest – to the faculty of feeling. As such, liking another person is not something that is under an agent's immediate control, though, of course, there are things a person can do in order to encourage or foster a feeling of well-liking. Kant observes, for example, that helping others can bring about a feeling of love for them (*MS*, 6:403). Though an agent cannot be under any obligation to like or love another person, it is clear that *Wohlgefallen* is nevertheless a great aid in performing our duties of beneficence toward others. After all, it is easier to help people when we like them.

Clearly, the misanthrope from dislike suffers from a kind of deficiency in well-liking or *Wohlgefallen*. Indeed, in the *Doctrine of Virtue*, Kant straightforwardly describes this type of misanthrope as "[s]omeone who avoids other human beings because he can find no *delight* (*Wohlgefallen*) in them, though he indeed wishes all of them well" (MS, 6:450, author's emphasis). Again, it is important to note that the misanthrope does not harbor any hatred toward others. Kant's descriptions of the misanthrope evince a kind of disappointment and weariness – the misanthrope cannot bring himself to see anything worth liking in humanity. The result of all of this, as we have seen, is that the misanthrope tends to withdraw from others and isolate himself, either literally or at least in his own thinking.

In many of the passages in which he discusses aversive misanthropy, Kant makes it clear that the misanthrope's disappointment does not fundamentally interfere with his ability to wish others well. So, in the passage from the *Doctrine of Virtue* quoted above, Kant describes the misanthrope as a person who finds no delight in others "though indeed he *wishes* all of them well" (MS, 6:450, author's emphasis). And in the third *Critique*, Kant notes that the aversive misanthrope is "cer-

---

5 See Rinne (2018) for detailed discussion.

tainly philanthropic enough as far as their *benevolence* (*Wohlwollen*) is concerned" (KU, 5:275, author's emphasis). This brings us to Kant's notion of *Wohlwollen*, and it is here that Kant's picture of the misanthrope truly begins to take shape. Literally, '*Wohlwollen*' means 'well-willing', though Mary Gregor translates it as 'benevolence'. The term is interestingly ambiguous, however, since it appears to operate on both sides of the important Kantian distinction between wishing and willing. Kant sometimes uses it to refer to a kind of inefficacious wish that things go well for others. So, for example, Kant notes that there is a sense in which we can wish everyone well, but that this does not mean that we can formulate and pursue maxims that bring about everyone's happiness: as he puts it, "the benevolence present in love for all human beings is greatest in its extent, but the smallest in its degree" (MS, 6:451). In other passages, however, *Wohlwollen* appears to refer to nothing less than a sincere and detailed benevolent maxim. To be benevolent – that is, to exhibit *Wohlwollen* – is to have a plan to adopt another's ends that one intends to carry out. In that sense of the term, the only thing that stands between *Wohlwollen* and a beneficent act is the carrying out of the maxim. So, for example, a few lines later in the discussion of duties of love in the *Doctrine of Virtue*, Kant argues that "it is quite obvious that what is meant here is not merely benevolence in *wishes* [...]; what is meant is rather active, practical benevolence (beneficence), making the well-being and happiness of others my *end*" (MS, 451 f.).

Where, precisely, does the misanthrope stand with respect to *Wohlwollen*? Although Kant claims that the misanthrope is "certainly philanthropic enough as far as [...] benevolence (*Wohlwollen*) is concerned" (MS, 6:450), I take him to be making a point largely about benevolent *wishing*, rather than benevolent *willing*, or benevolent maxim formation. The misanthrope, in other words, wishes most people well, but does not typically form maxims of beneficence on which she intends to act. In the Vigilantius lecture notes, for example, Kant remarks that,

> We may aptly call the negative misanthrope *anthropophobus*, i.e., one who withdraws himself from everyone, because he is unable to love them. It is impossible for him to find anything pleasing in other people, because he has made it a principle that in his regard everyone is oblivious to all the respect due to himself; he wishes them well, indeed, per se, but *cannot prevail upon himself to contribute thereto.* (MS-Vigilantius, 27:672, my emphasis)

Note that one important result of the misanthrope's sense of despondency or resignation is that it is imperfect duties (especially toward others) whose performance will be most endangered. The misanthrope from dislike will certainly be capable of abiding by perfect duty. However, it is with respect to forming and acting on maxims of beneficence, in particular, that the misanthrope's sense of disappointment and resignation serves as a hindrance. Here, the misanthrope's sense of disappointment and resignation is an important clue to understanding this phenomenon. And to better understand this sense of resignation, it is helpful to consider Kant's account of how misanthropy comes about and develops in the individual.

III The Sources of Anthropophobia

A Personal Slights

Some of Kant's discussions of misanthropy hint toward its being brought about by a kind of personal slight, or series of personal slights. In the Vigilantius lectures, for example, Kant reportedly remarks that the misanthrope "has experiences nothing but ingratitude for services rendered, disloyalty, misuse of integrity, love spurned, etc. and therefore sees all men as false, and so on" (MS-Vigilantius, 27:672). Kant concludes in the same passage that misanthropy thus "has its ground in *displicentia*" (*ibid.*). One should, of course, always be careful not to rely too heavily on individual words in Kant's recorded lectures. Still, the list of experiences that he reportedly selects here as potential initiators of misanthropy is telling. Ingratitude, disloyalty, and the like would all seem to describe cases in which the misanthrope has offered something – an act of beneficence, an offer of trust – and been disappointed by the response from another agent. It is interesting, in other words, that Kant doesn't include more straightforward violations of *perfect* duty on this particular list. Here, at least, the misanthrope is described as the agent who goes out on a limb for others, only to be met with ingratitude.

Other passages provide support to the idea that misanthropy often has its sources in an illicit generalization from a few bad cases. In the *Anthropology*, Kant remarks that "It is true and prudent that I never again trust someone who has once cheated me, for he is corrupt in his principles. *But to trust no other human being because one has cheated me is misanthropy.*" (Anth, 7:205, author's emphasis) Here, we do seem to have an example of misanthropy that emerges at least in part because of violated perfect duty. Still, it is perhaps telling that the description of the case is that of a personal slight that occurs after one person extends trust to another.

This point about the personal nature of many misanthropy-inducing episodes is nicely illustrated by Kant's discussions of beneficence and gratitude. Kant observes that an extreme form of ingratitude, according to which a recipient comes to hate his benefactor, would be the

"devilish degree of the vice, since it is utterly repugnant to human nature, to hate and per-
secute those who have done one a kindness, and *since it would also cause untold harm, if
all men were thereby deterred from well-doing, and so became misanthropes, on seeing that
they would be ill-used for their benevolence*" (Mo-Collins, 27:439 f., author's emphasis).

Later, in the *Doctrine of Virtue*, Kant will come to call this form of ingratitude
'qualified ingratitude' (MS, 6:459), contrasted with mere unappreciativeness. In
many of his discussions of ingratitude, one of Kant's central concerns is the chilling effect that instances of ingratitude have on moral motivation generally. An element of this chilling effect appears to be the tendency for isolated instances of
ingratitude to foster or encourage a more widespread disappointment in other
people.

B Disappointed Expectations

Despite Kant's description of the personal slight whose offense becomes general-
ized into misanthropy, these sorts of scenarios do not appear to be by any
means necessary for misanthropy to come about. Indeed, cases of ingratitude or
misplaced trust may simply be instances of a larger phenomenon involving the disappointment of our moral expectations of others. So, again, in the Kaehler/Collins
notes, Kant reportedly remarks that "the misanthrope from dislike thinks all men
are bad; *he fails to find in them what he was seeking*; he does not hate them, and
wishes some good to all, but simply does not like them" (Mo-Collins, 27:431).

A more detailed description of the phenomenon appears in the *Critique of the
Power of Judgment:*

> Falsehood, ingratitude, injustice, the childishness in ends that we ourselves hold to be impor-
> tant and great, in the pursuit of which people do every conceivable evil to each other, so con-
> tradict the idea of what they could be if they wanted to, and are so opposed to the lively wish
> to take a better view of them that, in order not to hate them, since one cannot love them,
> doing without all social joys seems to be only a small sacrifice. (KU, 5:275 f.)

The passage offers a helpful account of the vices, hopes, and psychological mech-
anisms of the misanthrope's tendency to withdraw from society. It begins with a
litany of moral failure and viciousness – here Kant includes more central cases
of the violation of perfect duty (falsehood, injustice) in addition to the recurring
example of ingratitude. But, as the story goes, misanthropy doesn't simply come
about because we observe cases of moral failure. Rather, the real source of misanthropy seems to be a kind of disappointed hope regarding what other agents are

capable of morally. A reflection on misanthropy and misology makes the point rather poignantly:

> If one expects more of reason and the heart than the two can accomplish, this will foster a hatred of reason and a hatred of human beings. Misology and misanthropy. Only experienced people encounter this. (Refl. 2570, AA 16:424)

Misanthropy thus seems to get a foothold when we notice a gap between what we know or hope other agents are capable of morally, and what they in fact do. To take a contrasting case, though we might sometimes be frustrated by the behavior of small children, their actions presumably cannot inspire feelings of misanthropy, precisely because we do not have the expectations of them that we do of developed moral agents.

Note, however, that misanthropy is not simply the result of having our moral expectations disappointed. Something else happens simultaneously at the level of *Wohlgefallen*, or well-liking. As Kant tells the story in the passage from the third *Critique*, above, we *want* to like other people. But when their moral failure makes itself apparent to us, we are caught in a bind. We cannot 'love' them as we had wanted to, yet we also cannot be brought to hate them. The stopgap measure we take, Kant argues, is to withdraw from them in order to escape this untenable choice between the love that we had hoped to have and hatred of them. This account of things also makes sense of the personal nature of some of the above examples, and the fact that many of the examples concern an agent who extends charity, trust or love to another person, only to be hated, cheated, or spurned. Those cases, I would argue, exemplify just that series of events described by Kant in passage above. The agent offers something to another person on the hope or assumption that they will react kindly or virtuously, but that hope or assumption is then thwarted by the other person's response. On this account, then, it is not so much the slight itself – the ingratitude or disloyalty, etc. – that serves to encourage a misanthropic retreat from society. Rather, it is the disappointed hope for moral cooperation and reciprocity, and the related inability to like the other as one had hoped, that is the proximate cause of misanthropy.

IV Normative Hope and Disappointment

In her book, *How We Hope* (2013), Adrienne Martin develops a theory of what she calls 'normative hope' that is useful in understanding Kant's special concern with misanthropy. To be clear, Martin is not offering Kantian exegesis in her text – she introduces the notion of normative hope by way of clarifying certain reactive attitudes, especially disappointment and gratitude. Nevertheless, her description of normative hope seems to me entirely compatible with the Kantian account described here. Further, I shall argue that once we understand the dangers that Kant appears to associate with the repeated disappointment of normative hope, we can better understand the suggestions that Kant makes in the context of friendship and beneficence. In particular, I argue, these suggestions constitute a kind of indirect duty to avoid certain behavior likely to induce normative disappointment, which in turn has a tendency to foster feelings of misanthropy and the tendency to withdraw from one's moral community.

For the purposes of this discussion, it will be useful to examine normative hope alongside normative expectation. The notion of normative expectation is already familiar, especially in the context of contemporary discussions of reactive attitudes like anger and resentment. When we feel angry with another agent, so the story goes, our anger is a reaction to that agent's failure to live up to normative expectations. The precise nature of these expectations will naturally vary according to the details of the normative theory at hand, to say nothing of any attendant theory of freedom and responsibility. Strawson famously introduces the idea of reactive attitudes in an effort to discuss moral responsibility without needing to settle metaphysical questions about the freedom of the will.[6] But reactive attitudes function just as well against the backdrop of a fully-fledged account of moral autonomy. Thus, a kind of moral indignation is, on the Kantian view, an appropriate and altogether expected response to an agent who fails to live up to normative expectations.

Martin's observation, however, is that we can also locate an attitude distinct from normative expectation. This is what she calls normative hope. It may be easiest to understand Martin's notion of normative hope by considering cases in which we don't yet have normative expectations of others, but nevertheless have normative hopes regarding their actions and choices. Martin's example for this kind of case is that of the not fully morally-developed teenager. When, to take Martin's example, the teenager lies to her parents, her parent may be able to dismiss feelings of anger by reminding herself that the teenager is not fully developed morally, and perhaps still has some way to go before she is fully responsible. It nevertheless makes sense for the parent to be disappointed, because she had *hoped* that her daughter would be able to live up to this moral standard. (Martin 2013, 138) On Martin's account, normative disappointment is a response to the disappointment of normative hope, whereas anger and resentment are responses to the disappointment of normative expectation.

---

6 Strawson (1962).

Having isolated the attitudes of normative hope and disappointment, the next important step is to observe that, while these attitudes are conceptually and psychologically distinct from normative expectation and anger, they can nevertheless *coexist* in cases of fully-developed moral agents. As she explains,

> [N]ormative hope and normative expectation are not necessarily in either conceptual or psychological tension with each other. It is possible to simultaneously see a person's status or situation as a reasoner in both hopeful and expectant ways: thus one stands ready to justify feeling both disappointed and resentful if the person in question fails to meet one's hope and expectation [...] (Martin 2013, 136).

Martin offers a vignette in a grocery store parking lot as an example. Suppose I am struggling with bulky shopping bags in a grocery store parking lot and drop the keys to my car. Another shopper with free hands sees me but does not stop to offer to pick the keys up. Martin thinks that the feeling this scenario induces is normative disappointment. I might not have grounds to *expect* that my fellow shopper would pick up the keys, but I nevertheless *hope* that she will. I am thus disappointed when she doesn't.

This sort of example might encourage a Kantian interpretation of normative hope according to which the distinction between normative expectation and normative hope tracks the distinction between perfect and imperfect duty. The latter duties are, by definition, not *owed* to us, so we cannot have any *expectation* that they will be performed. Still, we might *hope* that they will be. This may be part of the story, but I think we can have normative hope in cases of perfect duty as well. Take, for example, cases in which there is great temptation to violate one's duty, or in which fulfilling one's duty requires an agent to make a great effort. Here normative expectation and normative hope might co-exist. I may, for example, have certain normative expectations grounded in the fact that a friend has promised to help me coach a children's sports game. If the weather is cold and windy on the day of the event, I may simultaneously hope that she will overcome the temptation to stay inside where it is warm. While we recognize that the agent ought to perform her duty – and thus recognize that she can – we can also adopt a hopeful attitude toward her making the choice she ought to make.

It is this last point, about the conceptual and psychological compatibility of normative hope and normative expectation, that I take to be friendly to the Kantian account of morality and obligation. As rational agents, we can expect – of ourselves and others – that we can and will live up to the commands of duty. Simultaneously, however, we recognize that we are sensible agents, always subject to inclination and self-interest, so there is always a question about whether we will, in fact, live up to these normative expectations. The first observation about our rational nature is associated with a kind of Kantian normative expectation.

The second observation about our sensible nature and continuous moral struggle is associated with the hope that we will live up to moral ideals. Kantian anger or indignation would then be the response to moral failure, understood as a failure to live up to expectations. Disappointment would be the response to the sensible agent's failure to live up to the hope that she be able to overcome inclination and desire.

We can now return to the discussion of misanthropy. Given the description of misanthropy and its sources outlined in the previous section, I think it is most accurate to say that misanthropy is a response to disappointed moral *hope*, as opposed to moral *expectation*. To see this point, recall the way in which many instances of misanthropy, on Kant's account, seem to have their origin in a moment in which an agent hopefully extends a kind of moral benefit of the doubt to another – by offering beneficence, or trusting another person, for example. On one level, we clearly have reason to *expect* that the other agent will be appropriately grateful, or not betray our trust. But on another level, these actions display a kind of moral hope that the agent in question will rise to the occasion and not disappoint us by placing self-interest above duty. Misanthropy arises when this hope is disappointed.

The link between disappointment and misanthropy then follows the pattern sketched above in section three. While moral disappointment does not necessarily undermine our ability to respect the moral law or adopt the ends of others as our own, it does appear to have a marked negative effect on our ability to *like* people. And, as Kant notes in the passage from the third *Critique* cited above, this damage to our liking of others generates what we nowadays might call a kind of cognitive dissonance, since we also *want* to like others and have a good opinion of them as agents. It is this dissonance that we attempt to solve by retreating to isolation and avoiding others.

Unfortunately, the misanthrope's defense against normative disappointment is itself dangerous from the point of view of morality for several reasons. First, an agent who withdraws from others and cannot bring herself to like them is far less likely to be beneficent than the agent who participates readily in a moral community. The misanthrope, as we have seen, *wishes* others well enough. Nevertheless, *liking* others is undeniably helpful when it comes to enacting our duties to help others. Kant notes, for example, that "bitter merit, which comes from promoting the true well-being of others even when they fail to recognize it as such" produces no feeling of enjoyment in the benefactor (MS, 6:391). Second, the misanthrope's tendency to withdraw from others seems obviously to have a deleterious effect on our ability to participate sympathetically with others, both because it is difficult to participate sympathetically with a person whom one dislikes, and also because it is difficult, if not impossible, to participate sympathetically when one has withdrawn from community with others.

V Conclusion: Friendship and Etiquette

Let us now return to Kant's recommendations regarding conduct in friendship. On the face of things, we might think that any association with misanthropy is misplaced. After all, a friend who reveals too much of herself to me, or who asks for help when she is in need, is not thereby being ungrateful or disloyal. Still, I think, there is something of a clue in Kant's description of moral friendship as a rare type of relationship, characterized by maximal openness and love – though, of course, always tempered with respect. Specifically, moral friendship would seem to be uniquely vulnerable to misanthropy, because its participants do – to use a phrase – go out on a limb for each other, morally speaking. In the first instance, of course, this means that there will be an expectation that confidences will not be shared with third parties or otherwise exploited. Further, however, we can also presume that participants in a moral friendship genuinely *want to like each other.* However, such well-liking is particularly vulnerable to disappointed hope, especially when we have already invited our friend to share their moral struggles with us. Maintaining a proper reserve, and not disclosing too much of ourselves, might thus be a way of ensuring that friends can maintain well-liking, even when they are intimately familiar with their friend's moral hurdles and moral failures. Moral friendship between two imperfect agents, in other words, opens the door to the possibility of disappointed normative hope. Maintaining reserve ensures that candor does not result in disappointment.

The phenomenon is particularly apparent within friendship, but the point generalizes to some extent. Take, for example, Kant's remarks in section 48 of the *Doctrine of Virtue* ("On the Virtues of Social Intercourse"):

> It is a duty to oneself as well as to others not to isolate oneself (*seperatistam agere*) but to use one's moral perfections in social intercourse (*officium commercii, sociabilitas*). While making oneself a fixed center of one's principles, one ought to regard this circle drawn around one as also forming part of an all-inclusive circle of those who, in their dispositions, are citizens of the world – not exactly to promote as the end what is best for the world but only to cultivate what leads indirectly to this end: to cultivate a disposition of reciprocity – agreeableness, tolerance, mutual love and respect (affability and propriety, *humanitas aesthetica et decorum*) and so to associate the graces with virtue. To bring this about is itself a duty of virtue. (MS, 6:473)

As the passage demonstrates, it is not only in the context of friendship that an indirect duty to cultivate certain dispositions obtains. The preceding remarks about normative hope and misanthropy also help to explain why mere "tokens" (as Kant calls them) like *"affability, sociability, courtesy, hospitality,* and *gentleness"* could be counted as duties of virtue. As Kant explains, these tendencies "promote the feeling of virtue itself by a striving to bring this illusion as near as possible to the truth" and they "promote a virtuous disposition by at least making virtue fashionable (*beliebt)*" (MS, 6:473 f.). Kant's claims regarding what we might call etiquette might appear on their face at odds with his moral theory. After all, these 'tokens' can certainly not take the place of respect for the moral law, or for others. A person who displays affability while cheating another only adds another layer of deception to the first. And, to be sure, it is possible to fulfill one's perfect duties, and some of one's imperfect duties at least, while being curt or curmudgeonly. But Kant's remarks on etiquette are not claims about first-order duties, so to speak, but about the kind of social atmosphere in which morality thrives. Even if etiquette is merely a sort of show or illusion, it is nevertheless a show we put on in order to make it easier to live in community with others, and to help stave off moral disappointment.

References

Baron, Marcia, 2002, "Love and Respect in the *Doctrine of Virtue*", in: Mark Timmons (ed.), *Kant's Metaphysics of Morals: Interpretive Essays*, New York: Oxford University Press, 391–407.

Denis, Lara, 2001, "From Friendship to Marriage: Revising Kant", *Philosophy and Phenomenological Research*, 63/1, 1–28.

Biss, Mavis, 2019, "Friendship, Trust, and Moral Self-Perfection", *Philosophers' Imprint*, 19/50.

Martin, Adrienne, 2013, *How We Hope*, Princeton: Princeton University Press.

Moran, Kate, 2012, *Community and Progress in Kant's Moral Philosophy*, Washington, DC: Catholic University of America Press.

Rinne, Pärttyli, 2018, *Kant on Love*, Berlin/Boston: de Gruyter.

Stohr, Karen, 2014, "Keeping the Shutters Closed: The Moral Value of Reserve", *Philosophers' Imprint*, 14/23.

Strawson, Peter, 1962, "Freedom and Resentment", in: Gary Watson (ed.), *Proceedings of the British Academy*, 48, 1–25.

Vilhauer, Benjamin, 2021, "Sages, Sympathy, and Suffering in Kant's Theory of Friendship", *Canadian Journal of Philosophy*, 51, 452–467.

Kiran Bhardwaj
Friendship as a Scaffolding Duty to the Highest Good

Abstract: This essay begins with a brief introduction to what Kant says about the ideal of friendship, as well as his other categories of friendship. Then it examines an account of Kantian friendship that argues that we must engage in moral friendships, as they are a necessary means to develop virtue. This essay will suggest that that account needs two extensions. First, moral friendship is in the service of both of our imperfect duties: of self-perfection, and also of helping others. Second, the best human friendships can help us see, in microcosm, what a kingdom of ends where we bring about our own perfection and the happiness of others could be like. As such, moral friendship, which may actually be achieved 'here and there', helps to secure our hopes for what is possible as a result of our moral activity.

There have been many concerns raised against Kantian ethics because it doesn't seem to make the right kind of room for intimate attachments. One line of this familiar criticism is that Kantian ethics has an overly-strong requirement of impartiality. This requirement of impartiality would mean that either those using the theory are inappropriately blind to those we love when we impartially decide what to do, *or* risk having 'one thought too many' when we decide that this is an occasion in which we can prioritize assisting a loved one (Williams 1981, 2).[1] Similarly, other critics suggest it would be inconsistent for Kantian ethics to make room for permissible partiality towards our friends, given its focus on treating all moral agents in the relevantly same way.[2]

Another challenge has come from feminist critics of Kant, who say that the kinds of things that we associate with intimate relationships – choices guided by emotion, for instance – are left out of the Kantian ethical picture. Carol Gilligan's

---

[1] Another version of this criticism can be illustrated by Michael Stocker's famous case of a person who goes to the hospital to visit a friend, and in response to the friend's gratitude, explains that he is "only doing his duty" (Stocker 1976, 462).

[2] For example, Robert C. Solomon writes, "On the Kantian model, the particularity of love would seem to be a form of irrationality – comparable to our tendency to make 'exceptions' of ourselves, in this case, making exceptions of persons close to us" (Solomon 1998, 18). See Velleman (1999, 340) for further discussion, as there are options for Kantians to respond about why it may be possible to argue for differential treatment of different persons.

https://doi.org/10.1515/9783111291130-010

In a Different Voice draws out the ways in which the moral reasoning of men and boys differs from the moral reasoning of women and girls, and validated the latter. Some readers of the Gilligan study took it to be evidence against Kantian ethics: Annette Baier wrote, for example, that "the emphasis in Kantian theories on rational control of emotions, rather than on cultivating desirable forms of emotion, is challenged by Gilligan" (Baier 1994, 30).[3]

However, Kant's discussion of friendship is deeply interesting, and perhaps not as flawed as some of its critics contend. This essay will do a few things: it will introduce what Kant says[4] about the ideal of friendship and three other categories of friendship. Then it will examine Kate Moran's take on the duty of friendship. Moran argues that Kantian agents *must* engage in friendships of a certain kind (Moran 2012, 170). The final two sections of the chapter will partially agree with her view.

However, I will argue that Moran's view needs two extensions. She argues that moral friendship is a duty because it allows us to bring about our moral self-perfection (Moran 2012, 199 f.). I argue in Section 3 that it does more than that: moral friendship is in the service of *both* of our imperfect duties: of self-perfection, *and also* of bringing about the permissible happiness of others. If my interpretation is correct, then friendship is, in microcosm, a social system where we both bring about our own perfection *and* the happiness of others (something like the kingdom of ends). This view will be explored in Section 4. As such, moral friendship – which may, importantly, actually be achieved 'here and there' – does an incredible amount to secure our hopes for what is possible as a result of our moral activity.

---

3 These two sets of interlocutors are also discussed in Moran (2012, 169) and Velleman (1999, 339 n. 3).

4 There are three passages in the corpus where Kant extensively discusses friendship. The first is a section at the end of the Doctrine of Virtue where Kant talks about the ideal of friendship (MS 6:469–473). The second source is the Collins lectures on ethics, in which Kant is described to be giving a description of three kinds of friendship: the friendship of need, the friendship of taste, and moral friendship (Mo-Collins 27:422–450, see especially 27:423–427). Finally, he discusses friendship in the Vigilantius lectures (MS-Vigilantius 27:675–686). ("Observations on the beautiful and the sublime" also has some passing discussion of the topic of friendship, as connected to the experience of the sublime.)

As for the chronology of these passages: the *Lectures on Ethics* are understood to be from before the publication of the *Metaphysics of Morals* (1797) (Sullivan 1996, vii). The earlier Collins lectures probably reflect what Kant taught in his ethics courses from 1775–1780 or so (Schneewind 1997, xvi). They come close to some of Kant's mature views without presenting Kant's characteristic views (like the Categorical Imperative) (Schneewind 1997, xvi). The later Vigilantius lectures reflect a course that Kant gave in 1793–94, a period much closer to the publication of the *Metaphysics of Morals* in 1797 (Schneewind 1997, xviii).

1 Kant on Friendship

1.1 Love and Respect in Friendship

Let us begin by reviewing some claims that Kant makes about friendship. In the *Metaphysics of Morals*, Kant describes the moral ideal[5] of friendship as "the union of two persons through equal mutual love and respect" (MS 6:469). The first part of this description – a union of two persons – is obvious. The second part – equal love and respect – requires a bit more unpacking. The passage reads as follows:

> how can [a human being] be sure that if the *love* of one [friend] is stronger, he may not, just because of this, forfeit something of the other's *respect*, so that it will be difficult for both to bring love and respect subjectively into that equal balance required for friendship? – For love can be regarded as attraction and respect as repulsion, and if the principle of love bids friends to draw closer, the principle of respect requires them to stay at a proper distance from each other. (MS 6:470, my brackets).

It is intuitive that love is a central part of friendship, even if there remain interpretive questions about Kant's conception of love (see Rinne 2018 for a fuller analysis, including Chapter 5 on love in friendship). Love provides for the intimate nature of friendship. In such love, goodwill is directed to the well-being of the friend and one *takes action* in order to bring it about (MS 6:469 and 6:448 f., following Kant's immediately prior explanation of love). To successfully act requires knowledge of the right kind: I must know enough about my friend to be able to accurately understand what would be good for them, as well as consistent with their moral obligations. So, intimacy is an important part for the love of friendship to be effective.

The intimacy of such friendship must be balanced with something else. This something, for Kant, is respect: that is, I recognize the dignity of my friend as a

---

5 In the *Critique of Pure Reason*, Kant describes the difference between an idea and an ideal. Each ideal corresponds to some idea. The idea is a concept that is universal. An ideal is the instantiation of the idea that has empirical qualities: exemplary version of a particular object related to a particular idea. (Also see description in Mo-Mrongovius II 29:604 f.). So, for example, we can apply the *idea* of moral perfection to a particular object: the person. The *ideal* of the virtuous person is the individual who possesses everything that we need to be good: "goodness of soul, or purity, or fortitude, or serenity, etc." (KU 5:235). Such a person cannot exist, but poses a standard for our action (KrV A 568 f./B596 f.). As Kant describes it, "As the idea gives the *rule*, so the ideal in such a case serves as the *archetype*" (KrV A 569/B 597).

person (MS 6:462). And even though it is unattractively described as 'repulsion' in the passage, we might think of it in its more explanatory version as a kind of limiting condition on how intimate we choose to be with a given person at a given time or in which actions we take on their behalf.[6,7] The end state of such a friendship is one where the two friends can reveal their inner lives to each other, *on the condition* that "such disclosures are consistent with mutual respect" (MS 6:471). Kant suggests, for example, that friends might choose not to disclose all of their needs to each other in order to ensure that their relationship is *not* based merely on mutual advantage (and is not liable to fall into being so) (MS 6:470 f.). We could imagine some versions of this danger: the friend, intentionally or not, might take advantage of their friend or take them for granted (which would be troubling even if done mutually by both parties). We do best in friendship when we think about how to frame our mutual revelations to each other, using the right kinds of tact or reserve in order to continue to treat my friend with the respect they are owed as a person.

We should not assume that Kant thinks that this ideal for friendship is easy to approximate. He mentions two difficulties in particular: (a) it is difficult to ensure that the friends have equal and reciprocal degrees of love and respect for each other, and (b) that it is equally difficult to ensure that each friend's love and respect for their friend are each in appropriate balance with the other (MS 6:469 f.).

First, it is essential that the friends consider each other to be equals, and that their love for each other and their respect for each other are reciprocal. However, achieving parity is difficult. Due to the difficulty in knowing the truth about others' motivations (and sometimes the truth about our own motivations) we have an epistemic barrier in ensuring that our intentions regarding our friends are equal. We might, if we're not careful, find ourselves in an ill-balanced friendship, where one

---

6 The Collins lectures speak of friendship very differently than the later Vigilantius lectures and the *Metaphysics of Morals* – as a "maximum of mutual love". In these early lectures, friendship is framed around love for others and happiness (Mo-Collins 27:423). We might find it interesting that there is no discussion of respect in that early text. In contrast, the later Vigilantius lectures do contain this emphasis on both love and respect (MS-Vigilantius 27:682), and are much more closely aligned with the description from the *Metaphysics of Morals*.

7 Respect is described as a maxim, one in which we "[limit] our self-esteem by the dignity of humanity in another person" (MS 6:449). I might, for example, avoid expressing the parts of my inner life that tend towards the usual human vices – arrogance, or defamation, or ridicule – that would not be morally beneficial to both my friend and myself. We might refrain from gossiping when we know we're not a good check for each other. (In contrast, I might be willing to expose my judgmental side so if I know my friend will steer me straight). I might not express a pleasure in being able to do something well when I know my friend struggles with it. Similar cases might require similar actions.

friend discloses far more than the other, or where one friend has more goodwill to their friend than their friend has for them.

Second, ensuring equality of our love and our respect for the friend also seems difficult, if not impossible (MS 6:469 f.). Kant points out that we are the kind of creatures who are inclined to compare ourselves to others and to seek superiority to others – even our friends (Moran 2012, 176 f., referring to RGV 6:27). In becoming close to a person, we become particularly vulnerable to vicious tendencies toward comparison and competition because we know more about that person (Moran 2012, 177). Kant seems especially worried about the following scenario. One part of friendship is to help our friend by pointing out their faults. Ideally, the friend will not take offense because he understands that this is a duty of friendship (Baron 2013, 376). Yet given our susceptibility to wanting to compare ourselves with others, it is likely that things may *not* go so well and the friend will fear that they have lost their friend's respect. Moreover, the fault-finding friend is susceptible to the tendency to compete, which may cause them to feel *pride* in themselves and contempt for their friend. Thus, reflecting on our friend's faults may actually lead us to lose respect for them (Baron 2013, 373).

1.2 Perfect Friendship and Moral Friendship

It certainly would be difficult to achieve the ideal of friendship Kant discusses, above. Is it impossible to achieve? Kant writes that striving to develop such friendships is a duty, but such friendships are unattainable in practice (MS 6:469).[8] Yet in other places, he also writes that moral friendship "actually exists here and there in its perfection" (MS 6:472). How to resolve this apparent inconsistency?

Our best interpretive move may be to read Kant as referring to two kinds of friendship in this set of passages: 'perfect friendship', and 'moral friendship'. The ideal of 'perfect friendship' is unattainable, but 'moral friendship' actually exists here and there.[9] 'Moral friendship' – which involves reciprocal frank conver-

---

8 This is in line with his other writings on ideals (which include virtue, the highest good, the kingdom of ends). The only ideal that suggested has been attained is the ideal of moral perfection in the Son of God – a clear reference to Christ or a Christ-figure (RGV 6:61).

9 Kant compares moral friendships to 'black swans'. After Europeans discovered in the 1600s that black swans *did* exist, the meaning of the metaphor shifted to indicate that our discovery that something *does* exist proves the wrongness of making such wide-ranging assumptions in the first place.. If so, we might think that the surprise of finding out that moral friendships *can* exist here and there – despite of all our shortcomings – should lead us to hope that we can have some kind of community (at least a two-person one) that is in line with what duty requires.

sation and the sharing of sentiments – is as good as it gets for humanity, and although rare is not non-existent (Baron 2013, 374; Korsgaard 1999, 199). 'Perfect friendship', in contrast, is characterized by feelings of equal mutual love and respect (Korsgaard 1999, 199) and is an unrealizable ideal.[10]

If the perfect friendship is the ideal of friendship, and is as such unachievable, we can understand moral friendship as an approximation of that ideal.[11] However, it is not just any approximation: it is one in which the friends are committed (as well as they can be) to the end of morality, not just a close association based upon feelings, common interests, or necessity. That difference is what makes moral friendship significant and distinct from other kinds of imperfect friendships.

1.3 Other Kinds of Friendships

Kant more clearly sets out other categories of friendships in his ethical writings.[12] In the *Metaphysics of Morals*, Kant distinguishes moral friendship – as discussed above – from what he calls a friendship based on feeling (or 'pragmatic friendship'), in which we take on the ends of others from *feelings* of love, rather than love as a moral engagement with another person (MS 6:471, MS 6:450).[13]

---

10 Baron takes this distinction to explain why Kant referred to moral friendship as "merely" moral friendship (Baron 2013, 374, referring to MS 6:472). I find this explanation to be less persuasive, as earlier in the Metaphysics of Morals Kant had an entire section dedicated to duties to ourselves "merely as a moral being" (MS 6:428). I do not think it is wise, then, to take the word 'mere' as a signifier of a lack of importance or standing in the theory.

11 The distinction between perfect friendship and moral friendship seems to line up nicely to how Kant distinguishes between the ideal as an archetype (*prototypon*) and their imperfect copies *(ectypa)*, all of which fall short of the archetype. Thanks to Martin Brecher for this point. We can understand the perfect friendship as the archetype, of which there are imperfect approximations in existence – the best of these that exist are moral friendships.

12 Putting an exact count to the kinds of friendships that Kant categorizes is difficult. We would need to decide whether we want to treat the three notions of friendship in the Collins lectures as canonical, and if so, whether the 'pragmatic friendship' lines up with a friendship or taste, or need, or both (as I will assume).

In contrast to the view in this essay, Lara Denis counts four notions of friendship: first, friendships of taste, need, and disposition (the same as moral friendship) (see Mo-Collins 27:425 f.). These three kinds of friendship are realizable (Denis 2001, 3). The fourth kind of friendship, perfect friendship, is not realizable (Denis 2001, 3). It incorporates elements of the other kinds, particularly the characteristics of moral friendship (Denis 2001, 3). My rendering will be very similar to Denis's view.

13 Kant also mentions 'the friend of humanity' distinct from his discussion of moral or perfect friendship (MS 6:472). This friend of humanity takes an 'affective' interest in the well-being of oth-

Kant also gives a different tripartite division of friendships in the earlier Collins *Lectures on Ethics* (Mo-Collins 27:424–427). Kant is described as distinguishing between three types of friendships: the friendship of need, friendship of taste, and the friendship of disposition.[14] What are these kinds of friendship, and how are they related to his later distinction between 'moral' and 'pragmatic' friendships (as well as our interpretive category of 'perfect' friendships)?

A *friendship of need* is a special relationship out of self-interest where "participants may entrust each other with a reciprocal concern in regards to their needs in life" (Mo-Collins 27:424 f.). These sound very much the pragmatic 'unions aiming at mutual advantage' Kant contrasted the moral friendship against in the *Metaphysics of Morals* (MS 6:470). Hobbesian actors in a state of nature could form these kinds of friendships, in minimalistic ways. Or for example, two people with similar backgrounds in a new and unfamiliar place may spend time with each other so they won't be alone. We should think of these friendships as based on reciprocal mutual aid. Thus, friendships of need clearly seem to be one kind of pragmatic friendship.

A *friendship of taste* is where friends take pleasure in mutual association (Mo-Collins 27:426). Moran writes that what makes this type of relationship valuable to us is that each party can learn from the other – such friendships broaden our horizons (Moran 2012, 182). I might appreciate a friend because of their excellent music taste, another friend because of their witty conversation, another friend because they know a lot about the cinema. On Kant's view, the reason I find these friends so valuable is because they have some skill that I do not possess. It seems likely that we should think of this kind of friendship as another kind of "pragmatic friendship": this time where each friend remedies a want of *expertise* for the other. Unlike the other two categories Kant delineates in the Collins lecture, Kant describe the friendship of taste as an "analogue of friendship" (Mo-Collins 27:426). The friends take pleasure in their mutual association, but do not seem to be concerned with each other's happiness.

---

ers (MS 6:472) – and as such, is a person who practices benevolence. Nonetheless, the 'friend of humanity' is benevolent with extreme care and humility, given that they are concerned with the equality between persons (MS 6:472 f.).

14 As Lara Denis notes, these three categories of friendship are taken from Aristotle (*Nicomachean Ethics*, Book 8, Chs. 3–6) (Denis 2001, 3). She does not explain this point further, but we might think the friendship of need sounds very much like Aristotle's description of friendships based on the sake of utility; the friendship of taste similar to Aristotle's description of friendships that are based only on pleasure. Both of these friendships are contingent. Aristotle's perfect friendship, in contrast, is the friendship of virtuous persons who are alike in virtue – which may well sound like Kant's moral friendships (*Nichomachean Ethics*, Book 8, Ch. 3).

What Kant calls 'a friendship of disposition' in the Collins lectures, in contrast to the first two kinds of friendship, best matches up to the moral friendship from the *Metaphysics of Morals*. The similarities are as follows. Kant describes both as 'rare' (though not impossible, like the perfect friendship), and founded on the friends both being concerned with the same moral commitments (Mo-Collins 27:429, MS 6:469). Moreover, such a friendship is motivated by how we want to be engaged with one another, yet are fearful of what may come if our friends abuse our trust (Mo-Collins 27:426 f., MS 6:471 f.). Such a friendship is the way in which we can securely allow confidences with each other (MS 6:471).

In short, we now have – across a span of texts – four categories of friendship: (a) perfect friendship, the ideal; (b) moral friendship, the best humanly-achievable friendship, and two kinds of pragmatic friendship, (c) a friendship of taste, and (d) a friendship of need.

2 Moran on the Duty of Friendship

Many Kantians have responded to the critics, described in the introduction, who think that Kant's ethical theory has no room or inappropriate room for intimate attachments (Moran 2012, 168).[15] While Kate Moran agrees with other defenders of Kant[16] that friendship does have a role in the theory, she disagrees with their strategy. It's possible to argue that friendship is one way to engage with our imperfect duties – our duties to set the happiness of others and perfecting ourselves as ends, which we promote in ways that are to our discretion (Moran 2012, 169 f.). Yet Moran points out if we argue in that manner, it does not appear that a Kantian agent has any kind of *obligation* to seek out relationships like friendship (Moran 2012, 170). If friendships are one way of acting on our imperfect duties, well and good – but it seems like friendship is perhaps optional. I could perform other actions that help me to work towards fulfilling my imperfect duties and not have done anything wrong (Moran 2012, 170).

---

15 Certainly Kant did not intend to suggest radical individuality: he writes that "The human being is a being meant for society [...] and in cultivating the social state he feels strongly the need to *reveal* himself to others" (MS 6:471). He follows the section on friendship with one in which he says "It is a duty to oneself as well as to others not to *isolate* oneself" (MS 6:473).
16 She seems to be thinking particularly of Marcia Baron's 1984 defense of Kant in "The Alleged Repugnance of Acting from Duty".

In contrast to those accounts, Moran thinks that moral friendship plays a unique role in human lives to develop a moral character (2012, 171).[17] As such, we have a duty to participate (or to try to participate) in moral friendships (Moran 2012, 170).[18] Moral friendship, as we know, "is a kind of friendship that exists between two parties who are less than perfectly moral, yet who strive to become moral" (Moran 2012, 184). Thanks to their trust and comfort with each other, friends can share their feelings and thoughts with each other (Moran 2012, 184 f.). This trust and comfort will allow, Moran thinks, for us to help to morally perfect ourselves.

An important duty in Kantian ethics is the duty to know ourselves (Moran 2012, 186, referring to MS 6:441). Unfortunately, we also have a tendency toward self-deception (Moran 2012, 188). We can do some things on our own to try to mitigate this tendency. We can engage, for instance, in thought experiments of "imagining how one's actions might affect others, or how one's actions might come into a conflict with the ends of others" (Moran 2012, 193, referring to KU 5:293–295). While we are tasked with knowing ourselves, sometimes even the most earnestly self-scrutinizing person may not recognize what they may be doing wrong. We also can fail to act with the appropriate kinds of self-scrutiny in the first place.

We will not be able to secure the kind of objectivity needed for moral self-examination on our own. We have to share our thoughts with others to secure ourselves against errors (Moran 2012, 186, 88; referring to Mo-Collins 27:427, MS-Vigilantius 27:616, 27:683, and MS 6:469). However, it is very difficult to trust others enough to do so. One reason that we mistrust others is because we fear their judg-

---

17 Kant never makes a claim that friendship is a necessary condition for us to be able to achieve self-perfection, even though he does claim that friendship is a duty (MS 6:469). I read Moran's claim to depend upon on human features as agents – that given the kinds of creatures that we are, who are not fully transparent to ourselves and who are prone to self-deception – we would find a deeply difficult task to be even more intransigent if we did not have the aid that moral friendship can provide (both epistemically and otherwise). As such, she links the reason that we have a duty to pursue moral friendships *to* the reason we have a duty to pursue self-perfection. Those who do not have access to others they could work to develop moral friendships with might still find it possible to strive towards self-perfection, but progress would be difficult and even more unreliable. Thank you to Martin Brecher for pushing me to clarify.

18 Kant explicitly calls friendship a 'duty' (MS 6:469). In the *Metaphysics of Morals* passage, he writes that friendship does not *secure* happiness for us, but does make us *deserving* of happiness (MS 6:469). We know what it takes to be worthy of happiness: it is to be virtuous (GMS 4:393). That makes our question the following: how does friendship make us virtuous? Virtue is where an agent has a will that is not only good but is also strong. She is able to resist motivations (e. g., self-interest) that tempt her to override her motivation to do what the moral law demands of her (MS 6:380, 405; Mo-Mrongovius II 29:627). Engaging in friendships then, must help us develop a *good* will, a *strong* good will, or both.

ment (MS 6:471 f.). We are, of course, imperfect people – revealing truths about ourselves that are less admirable may lead an observer to think less of us. A second kind of reason that we mistrust others is that the more they know about us, the more they could harm us.[19] Betrayal, for instance, is more potent when it is done from a position of information – knowing what the betrayed person most values (Baron 2013, 368, 371). As a result of these kinds of concerns, we might be tempted to posture in front of others, or obscure our actual behaviors or intentions.

Friendship is an "aid in overcoming the constraint that we harbor, from mistrust, towards those we associate with, and in opening up to them without reserve" (Mo-Collins 27:428). With regards to our *friends* we feel secure in our trust. Our friend, then, can provide a needed buttress against self-deception (Moran 2012, 192).[20] Friends who have known us for a longer period are especially attuned to the idiosyncratic mistakes that we make about ourselves (Moran 2012, 191). We know that we have certain moral bad habits – they come with the territory of being human. We tend towards arrogance in some instances, self-contempt in others (Moran 2012, 189). Both are ways in which we can deceive ourselves about our moral worth (MS 6:441). Our friends can help us identify where we have gone wrong in our reasoning or in our actions – developing virtue, for creatures like us, cannot be a one-person exercise.

If Moran is right – and I believe she is – we can develop both a good and strong will not only because friendships help us avert our natural mistrust of others, but also because friendships are the best available strategy we have for our self-examination to be successful.

Thus, Moran argues, we can understand what Kant means when he says that we have a duty to participate (or try to participate) in moral friendships (Moran 2012, 170). She contends that this duty to pursue character-improving friendships stems from our duty to work toward the highest good. The highest good is the good that we, as human agents, necessarily set as an end for ourselves: in which we attain moral perfection, and receive proportionally deserved happiness (KpV 5:129, RGV 6:4 f., 6 f. n.). We have a duty to perfect our own virtue (part of working toward the highest good) and so we have a duty to take part in activities that improve our moral character, including friendship with some person (Moran 2012,

---

19 Moran will add a third reason to this list: our tendency to compare ourselves to others and to seek superiority (Moran 2012, 177). This will be explored slightly later in this section.
20 Nonetheless, Kant thinks that each of us must be careful about how we counsel our friends if we see them tending toward one or the other vice: we don't want to point out the moral failings of our friend in a way that compromises their self-respect. Tact is required (MS-Vigilantius 27:685, MS 6:470).

178). As Kant points out in the *Groundwork,* to will an end means also to will the means to that end (Moran 2012, 200). Moral friendship is, according to Moran, an essential means to the end of moral self-perfection. Thus, we must engage in moral friendships with others.

Moral friendships help us to perfect ourselves morally. In contrast, Moran suggests that the other two kinds of friendships (of need and of taste) offer possibilities in which Kantian agents can practice their imperfect duties to others (Moran 2012, 171).[21] The friendship of need is, on Moran's reading, an opportunity to practice our imperfect duty of beneficence (Moran 2012, 179). I promote my friend's happiness because I am engaged in mutually aiding her. The friendship of taste, where we take pleasure in the company of others who we can learn from, is a way to fulfill our duty to perfect our talents. Moran argues that this is because we are poised to learn from other people who are dissimilar to us (Moran 2012, 183).[22] I might become a wittier conversationalist by speaking with a clever friend, or develop a better taste in music by listening along with my music-loving friend. Thus, the other two kinds of friendship are opportunities to practice our remaining imperfect duties. The moral friendship is solely directed toward our moral self-perfection (Moran 2012, 199).

We should agree with Moran that friendships are an essential means to perfecting ourselves, as one part of our duty of bringing about the highest good. Her arguments about the friendship of need and the friendship of taste are deeply interesting.

However, there are two things that striving towards perfect friendship serves to do that are missed by Moran's account: *first,* doing so promotes the duty to bring about the happiness of others *as well as* the perfection of each. *Second,* Kant says

---

21 Of course, friendships of need nor taste do not necessarily focus on an imperfect duty at all, even if one performs the same actions – such relationships *could* be merely focused on self-interest or interest in the other (Moran 2012, 178). However, Moran's point is that both kinds of friendships can take on morally-grounded forms. In the modern world, resources do not necessarily need to be used for survival but instead can be rededicated in ways that allow a more universal outlook (Moran 2012, 179, referring to Mo-Collins 27:425, 428). Moran is not referring to *any* friendship of need, but a more sophisticated and morally-grounded version, one that better resembles a moral ideal (Moran 2012, 179). Likewise, a more sophisticated version of the friendship of taste could also extend our horizons and, in so doing, allow us to better perfect our talents (Moran 2012, 182 f.).

22 Both of these kinds of friendship have their dangers, according to Moran. Our disposition to seek superiority over others unfortunately might lead us to destroy our friendships of need. So we must practice this duty without "a sense of pride, resentment, or vanity" (Moran 2012: 181). The friendships of taste are also dangerous: where we become jealous of our friends' talents or take too much pride in our own accomplishments (Moran 2012, 183).

that moral friendships are rare but achievable. As such, these friendships can illustrate to us what might be possible as a result of our moral actions. In the following, I will set out arguments for each of these views.

3 Moral Friendship and the Imperfect Duties

3.1 Moral Friendship and Beneficence

We should agree with Moran's argument: friends are incredibly good at helping each other identify what is true about themselves, and in doing so, can assist their friend's pursuit of moral perfection (MS 6:470). Yet I disagree with Moran's view that we should take moral friendship as *primarily* concerned with self-perfection (Moran 2012, 199). I think we have reason to think that moral friendship is not merely aimed at perfecting our characters, but also is in the service of mutually assisting each other – and as such, is directed toward our duty of beneficence.

In order to understand why this is a better reading, let us return to how Kant describes the ideal of friendship. Kant writes that it is:

> an ideal of each participating and sharing sympathetically in the other's well-being through the morally good will that unites them, and even though it does not produce the complete happiness of life, the adoption of this ideal in their disposition toward each other makes them deserving of happiness (MS 6:469).

This description should indicate to us that both of our imperfect duties are in play.[23] Not only do we do what makes us "deserving of happiness" – to develop and act with a good will – we 'participate and share' in the other's well-being. It may be the case that our activities do not, ultimately, produce happiness – after all, Kant considers happiness to be a fickle concept.[24] Nonetheless, it is reasonable to suppose that in addition to promoting self-perfection, friendship also promotes happiness.

---

23 Perhaps beneficence is not the only duty in play. In the *Metaphysics of Morals*, Kant lists three duties of love (of benevolence): beneficence, gratitude, and sympathy (MS 6:452 ff.). It may also be true that (as indicated by the quoted text from MS 6:469) that sympathetic sharing is also an important part of friendship. Thanks to Pärttyli Rinne for this suggestion.

24 As Kant writes in the *Groundwork*, "the concept of perfect happiness is such a vague concept that although everyone wants it, they can never say definitively and self-consistently what it really is that they wish and will" (GMS 4:418).

This seems in line with what we ordinarily take to be true about friendship: we should promote each other's well-being in a variety of ways. Moral friendship is more than sharing our inner judgments and feelings, but is a matter of reciprocal concern for the other person's permissible wants and needs. The *Lectures on Ethics* support this claim. In the Collins lectures, Kant describes friendship as important because it is concerned with reciprocity in cultivating happiness (Mo-Collins 27:422 f.). Likewise, the Vigilantius lectures indicate that each friend ought to promote the other's well-being (MS-Vigilantius 27:676, 682).

Our friends should not be the exclusive beneficiaries of our work to assist others, but we might think that we can assist them in special kinds of ways, given our intimate knowledge of their projects. A friend who knows our secret anxieties about an upcoming talk might offer to listen to a practice run, and a friend who has been entrusted with truths about our identity or our lives (e.g., that we are gay, or adopted, or are struggling with addiction) can help us navigate a world that can often be unjust or unkind. We can assist our friend in promoting their permissible ends, according to their own conception, in a way that is not accessible for those who do not know them as well.

We also can help our friend refine their conception of happiness. We have many desires that would not lead to our overall well-being. We also have desires that could lead to our happiness, but are mutually inconsistent or jointly unrealizable. Kant thinks that we must bring our inclinations and desires into some kind of tolerable system that is subordinated to, and consistent with, what the moral law requires (KpV 5:73). If our friend is placing too much emphasis on the importance of being thought well of (at the expense of what they authentically care about), we can point that out – which might assist them, in turn, to refine their conception of what they truly value. Or if they are behaving in ways that are selfish, we too can point that out to them.[25]

If this is a promising reading of moral friendship, then we have reason to believe that moral friendships afford us special opportunities to both perfect ourselves morally and non-morally as well as to bring about the permissible happiness of others.

---

25 I have focused on the ways in which beneficence might be part of moral friendship. We might also be able to imagine how moral friendships could be able to support our development of non-moral talents, however, instead of solely our moral self-perfection. – Moran, for example, thinks of the friendship of taste as an opportunity to perfect our talents: "By associating with different types of people, we naturally cultivate our ability to think from other perspectives and to imagine how our actions might be consistent – or inconsistent – with their ends" (Moran 2012: 193).

3.2 An Objection

We should ask if there is good reason to think that moral friendship is only direct-ed towards morally perfecting ourselves and not aimed at beneficence, as Moran seemed to suggest. One reason might be because Kant warns us of dangers of help-ing our friend in the context of a moral friendship. There is a passage of the *Meta-physics of Morals* in which Kant suggests that assisting a friend in securing their advantage might result in a loss of respect for the friend (MS 6:470 f.). I want my friend to be better off than she is, so I help her. But if I do this, he suggests, I may lose my respect for her, because I see that she is unable to help herself (MS 6:470). As a result, Kant says that in a moral friendship, your friend is someone who you can always rely on, but you never *do* rely on – if you have a burden, you even should conceal that burden from your friend (MS 6:471). So there is textual reason to think that perhaps Kant thought that moral friendship was much more about moral self-perfection than it was about beneficence.

Nonetheless, Kant's worry does not undermine the claim that beneficence is a proper part of moral friendship. We should instead take his concern as a call for *due care*, especially with regard to certain kinds of beneficence. For example, Mar-cia Baron's interpretation of that passage of Kant is that he is speaking of *financial* burdens, not emotional or other kinds of burdens (Baron 2013, 377). As he says in the Vigilantius lectures, asking for financial assistance from a friend might lead to the weakening of the friendship (MS-Vigilantius 27:684). However, there are many non-financial opportunities to promote my friend's well-being. I can come to his art show, or spend time enjoying a walk with him (something that promotes both of our well-being!) These kinds of activities do not seem to lead me to lessen my respect for my friend.

Moreover, there is an important difference between soliciting our friend for help in a particular direction, and the friend choosing freely to assist us in a cer-tain way that they know will promote our happiness. Kant only says that the assis-tance that we can expect from the friend should not be the "end and determining ground of friendship" (MS 6:470). However, it may so happen that I choose to fulfil my duty of beneficence (among other ways) to assist her on some occasions, when I judge that it is consistent with what the moral law requires.

We want our friend to be happy, because happiness is a conditional good pre-dicated on their being virtuous. And part of being engaged in a moral friendship is to assist each other in their pursuit of becoming more virtuous. Nonetheless, we should not take moral friendships to involve sitting on our hands with regard to our friend's happiness. We should just be careful that we do not fall away from the primary concern of maintaining both love *and* respect for our friend in equal shares.

3.3 On Moran's Account of Friendships of Need & Taste

I also suggest that we should also re-think Moran's view on the other two kinds of friendships (that is, friendships of need and friendships of taste). Moran suggests that the other kinds of friendship afford opportunities to practice beneficence and perfecting our talents.

The distinction between actions in accordance with duty and actions *from* duty may be helpful in seeing why revision may be necessary. If a person would like to cheat someone but decides not to in case they are found out, we know that they are acting in line with duty ('not cheating') but not *from* duty (their motivations are due to their anxieties about what would happen *if* they cheated). Similarly, a person might aid someone solely because they happen to like how it makes them feel when they help someone. Such actions are 'in accordance' with what duty requires of us, but in these particular cases they are not motivated by the moral law. In contrast, an agent who acts in certain ways because they know it is what the moral law requires (or constrains their behavior purposefully based upon what the moral law requires) would be acting *from* duty. A person might be motivated both by affection for another person and duty. In that case, their maxim for action would still need to be following what the moral law requires – any feelings they might have for that person would need to be subordinated to their motivation to act morally.

I suggest that the friendships of need and taste are ways in which we can engage in practices that are often in accordance with duty (toward beneficence and perfecting ourselves). However, our motivations in these pragmatic friendships are not necessarily tied to duty. They are instead tied to mutual advantage of some variety (e. g., that seeing my friend happy makes me happy, or that their happiness allows them to be in a position to be a friend to me). Again, friends could be acting in accordance with duty, but not *from* duty, when they practice beneficence or cultivate their talents. And since their motivations are not dutiful ones, their nonmoral motivations might distort their actions. I might end up prioritizing my friend (a person I love) over other people who might be able to use my assistance. I might begin to *use* my friend who has talents very different from mine as a mere means to perfecting myself. I might try to promote my friend's happiness, but impose my conception of happiness on her instead of being sensitive to the choices she has made.

This means that while I can work on becoming better in friendships of need and friendships of taste – being attentive to what would make my friend happy, or ways in which I have a capacity that needs to be cultivated – the motives are untethered to the moral law unless we engage in moral friendship. *Moral* friendship is where we unite what we may have learned from our friendships of need and friendships of taste, yet are not susceptible to the same kinds of potentially non-moral behavior. And given that moral friendships are based on equal and reciprocal love and respect for each other, their resulting beneficent or self-cultivating actions are motivated by duty (although perhaps also motivated from love for our friend[26] or self-respect). My beneficence to my friend is limited by my respect for her; my friend can provide me with insight into how to develop my talents in a way that fundamentally is in line with her respect for me.

In short, moral friendship is based upon respect and moral love for the friend as a rational agent in a way that the friendship of need and the friendship of taste are not. Friendships of need and friendships of taste are based on conditional kinds of reciprocity – that I have been beneficent to my friend, and my friend has been beneficent to me; or that my friend has talents that I do not, and vice versa. Such friendships can easily unravel. In contrast, in moral friendship we unconditionally respect our friend as a moral agent. The imperfect duties also are practiced in moral friendship – but in a very different way than in the other two kinds of friendship.

4 The Ideal of Moral Friendship as a Bridge to the Highest Good

4.1 The Highest Good, Virtue, and Happiness

So far, we should accept Moran's interpretation that moral friendship is an important means to self-perfection. We also should accept that moral friendship is also a way of working to fulfill our duty to bring about the permissible happiness of a person that we have a special kind of knowledge about. In short, perfect friendship is a relationship between persons focused both on the virtue of the friends, as well as (secondarily) their happiness.

This description of moral friendship – where we are tasked both with developing our virtue and promoting our friend's happiness – might start to remind us

---

26 I here follow Kant's discussion about moral motivation, insofar as we can be motivated to act both because of moral law and empirical incentives, so long as those empirical incentives are 'subordinated' to the moral law (RGV 6:36). So my loving desire that my friend be happy no matter what, must be subordinated to the direction of the moral law about the permissibility of her desires, and her pursuit of her own perfection.

very closely of the highest good.[27] As Stephen Engstrom explains, the concept of the highest good is "the idea of a state or condition in which happiness is proportioned to virtue" (Engstrom 1992, 747).

One kind of frustration Kant realizes that we might have with the ideal of the highest good is that Kant both says that it is unrealizable *and* that we must work to attain it and must believe that we can attain it (RGV 6:66 f., KpV 5:113).[28] The unrealizability of the ideal, and how human actors might give up on such an unrealizable ideal, leads Kant to commitments like needing to posit the existence of God and our immortal souls. He suggests that we need some way to avoid despair when faced with an impossible task (KpV 5:121 f., 126 f.).[29]

However, we might be able to think that moral friendships are (very occasionally) realizable, even if perfect friendships are not. If so, this means that even if we know that most persons in this world may not be virtuous, and that conditions in this world are often apt to not promote happiness (much less happiness that is perfectly proportioned to virtue). We also may know that even moral friendships are not the ideal of friendship – but they are *possible,* even if rare. In what follows, I

---

27 Other Kantians have argued that friendship is in the direction of the kingdom of ends. Allen Wood argues that friendship is the clearest model in human life for the kingdom of ends (Wood 1999, 279). Christine Korsgaard argues that "Friendships are human moral achievements that are lovely in themselves and testify to the virtue of those who sustain them. To become friends is to create a neighborhood where the Kingdom of Ends is real" (Korsgaard 1999, 194).

28 Kant is very clear about the importance of our being able to hope that we can become morally perfect, and proportionally happy. As Kant writes, a person "must be able to *hope* that, by the exertion of *his own* power, he will attain to the road that leads in that direction, as indicated to him by a fundamentally improved disposition" (RGV 6:51, 6:48). We have made mistakes in the past (RGV 6:116), and will face similar temptations in the future against which we can't be sure we will be able to act morally. A 'reasonable hope' would be grounded in that we ordinarily can see steady improvement in our dispositions and one's improved strength of will (RGV 6:68). It is not certainty (RGV 6:76).

Secondly, we must hope that we will become happy to the degree that is proportional to our desert (MS 6:377). Kant is sensitive to our needs as empirical creatures. If our hope was merely directed toward becoming morally perfect, it would be overly demanding for creatures with needs and wants. However, our hope is directed toward deserving happiness (and receiving it) as well as being virtuous.

The moral ideals give us a way of hoping that we can successfully meet our duties, because we can imagine what it would be like if these ideals were to come to pass (thanks to successful execution of our duties). Hope makes us feel capable of taking on sometimes burdensome tasks, and ensures that we feel like there is a possibility of appropriate reward that will follow.

29 With the length of time afforded by an immortal soul, we could continue to perfect ourselves; with God's assistance, we would be granted the amount of happiness that we deserve. If we are not inclined to make those metaphysical commitments, we may despair that the highest good could ever come about.

will explore how we might be able to think of moral friendships as a kind of way in which we can scaffold toward the highest good, by focusing our attention on what just two people can achieve together.[30] In this way, the existence of moral friendships might be able to make us feel like striving towards the ideal of the highest good is not as purposeless as we might fear, when we reflect on our limitations.

4.2 The Relationship between the Kingdom of Ends and the Highest Good

The highest good and the kingdom of ends are closely related but not identical concepts. To follow a distinction from Barbara Herman, we might want to articulate a difference between a kingdom of good wills and the highest good (which involves good wills as well as happiness) (Herman 2007, 64). The reason that this difference is important is because the highest good requires happiness to be *proportional* to virtue, and that such proportionality is necessary, not coincidental (Engstrom 1992, 750).

A community of virtuous human agents could not ensure on their own that the happiness of each person is necessarily and rightly in proportion to their virtue. At best we might be able to promote each other's happiness to the best of our ability. We can do various kinds of work in social cooperation to try to achieve something very like the highest good (see Engstrom's remarks on this topic, 1992, 778 f.). For these reasons, we might think of the kingdom of ends as the humanly-achievable portion of the highest good. We may not be able to ensure the necessary proportionality of happiness to each person's virtue, but we *can* work to promote our own virtue and each other's happiness. (For anything more, we would need the metaphysical postulates of Kant's moral religion.) This means that the kingdom of ends has quite an important role for us – it sets a goal for what we can achieve cooperatively together.

---

30 Compare, for example, what Allen Wood says about how people must work toward a moral community (Wood 1970, 189 f.). We can work towards building such a community, but building one seems incredibly out of reach, especially when we consider what is in the scope of our control as an ordinary individual.

4.3 The Imaginative Ideal of Friendship and the Kingdom of Ends

However, we know we only have limited control over what we can do – and even the goal of what moral agents could achieve together might seem intractable, and we might again become susceptible to despair.

I suggest that working to achieve moral friendship might help to address our concerns about the seeming impossibility of even the kingdom of ends. Each of us can aim to be a deliberator who consults the moral law, and sets following the moral law as an end. In so doing, we would act in ways that (were we all to do so) would bring about the kingdom of ends.

The ideal of moral friendship is a two-person version of the kingdom of ends, wherein each person is works to become virtuous and acts to bring about the happiness of their friend (although they would not have sufficient control to make that happiness necessarily proportionate). We can imagine what it would be like for each of us to be in a friendship *like that* – it would have all the features of the best friendships.

Second, we can imagine how those nascent moral friendships serve to scaffold to the kingdom of ends. We can imagine a community of persons engaging in moral friendships, and moral friendships between multiple persons. A community formed of such relationships would add links on the chain so it wasn't just a community of two, but a community of many. Such a community would be a kingdom of ends on earth. Moral friendships can help us find it plausible why we ought not despair that the highest good could not come to pass.

If this argument is right, then the ways in which we engage in friendships – trust in others, and reciprocity that's not based upon contingent features of our world, but respect for the other person as a moral agent – can help guide how I work to engage with other members of my community, to the degree I feel that I can.[31] We should also take our deliberations with our friends to form a model for our work engaging with other members of our community – and should seek to engage with more persons in ways that are relevantly like moral friendships.

---

[31] In the *Metaphysics of Morals*, Kant discusses a "friend of human beings" who gives "thought and consideration for the *equality*" of persons (MS 6:473). Marcia Baron, in her explanation of that passage of the *Metaphysics of Morals*, says that Kant takes friendship to have two proper forms: (1) the union of two persons through equal mutual love and respect, and (2) being a "friend of human beings as such" (Baron 2013: 366; MS 6:469, 472). Perhaps in Kant's discussion of the second type of friendship, we can see how the highest good can result from the friendship between two people turning each into more of a "friend of human beings as such".

Conclusion

In this paper, I argued that Moran's argument for how friendship is a best practice for persons to become virtuous needs two supplements: *first,* that we should conceive of the ideal of friendship as also incorporating our duty to bring about each other's happiness, and *second* to recognize that moral friendships can help us imaginatively bridge to what the kingdom of ends (which is the humanly-achievable portion of the highest good) might be like. Friendship is deeply important for us, as a way to respond to our mistrust of others and develop ways in which we can trust others.

With regard to friendships, we might think that their bridging function helps respond to worries we might have about *partiality.* Because friendships are partial, they explain the special knowledge we have about our friends and concern we have for them. They are also grounded on mutual respect. Yet unlike other conceptions of friendship, when we engage in friendship we must ensure that we do not close our hearts towards others (Mo-Collins 27:428). We can love our friends, but not at the expense of concern for others who are not our friends – and should seek to develop moral friendships with others, where is possible.

References

Aristotle, *Nicomachean Ethics*, translated by Terence Irwin, Hackett Publishing 1999.

Baier, Annette, 1994, *Moral Prejudices*, Cambridge, MA: Harvard University Press.

Baron, Marcia, 1984, "The Alleged Moral Repugnance of Acting from Duty", *The Journal of Philosophy*, 81/4, 197–220.

Baron, Marcia, 2013, "Friendship, Duties Regarding Specific Conditions of Persons, and the Virtues of Social Intercourse", in: Andreas Trampota, Oliver Sensen, and Jens Timmermann (eds.), *Kant's "Tugendlehre"*, Berlin/Boston: de Gruyter, 366–382.

Denis, Lara, 2001, "From Friendship to Marriage: Revising Kant", *Philosophy and Phenomenological Research*, 63/1, 1–28.

Engstrom, Stephen, 1992, "The Concept of the Highest Good in Kant's Moral Theory", *Philosophy and Phenomenological Research*, 52/4, 747–780.

Gilligan, Carol, 1982, *In a Different Voice*, Cambridge, MA: Harvard University Press.

Herman, Barbara, 2007, "A Cosmopolitan Kingdom of Ends", in: Barbara Herman, *Moral Literacy*, Cambridge, MA: Harvard University Press, 51–78.

Kant, Immanuel, *Critique of Practical Reason*, translated by Lewis White Beck, New York: Macmillan 1956.

Kant, Immanuel, *Critique of the Power of Judgment*, edited by Paul Guyer, translated by Paul Guyer and Eric Matthews, New York: Cambridge University Press 2000.

Kant, Immanuel, *Groundwork for the Metaphysics of Morals*, translated by Arnulf Zweig, edited by Thomas E. Hill Jr. and Arnulf Zweig, New York: Oxford University Press 2002.

Kant, Immanuel, *Lectures on Ethics*, edited by Peter Heath and J.B. Schneewind, translated by Peter Heath, New York: Cambridge University Press 1997.

Kant, Immanuel, *Metaphysics of Morals*, translated by Mary Gregor, New York: Cambridge University Press 1996.

Kant, Immanuel, "Observations on the feeling of the beautiful and sublime", translated by Paul Guyer, in: Immanuel Kant, *Anthropology, History, and Education*, edited by Günter Zöller and Robert B. Louden, New York: Cambridge University Press 2007.

Kant, Immanuel, *Religion within the Boundaries of Mere Reason*, edited by Allen Wood and George di Giovanni, New York: Cambridge University Press 1998.

Korsgaard, Christine M., 1999, *Creating the Kingdom of Ends*, New York: Cambridge University Press.

Moran, Kate, 2012, "Friendship and Moral Improvement", in: Kate Moran, *Community and Progress in Kant's Moral Philosophy*, Washington, DC: The Catholic University of America Press, 168–203.

Rinne, Pärttyli, 2018, *Kant on Love*, Berlin/Boston: de Gruyter.

Schneewind, Jerome B., 1997, "Introduction", in: Immanuel Kant, *Lectures on Ethics*, translated by Peter Heath, New York: Cambridge University Press, xiii–xvii.

Solomon, Robert C., 1988, "The Virtue of (Erotic) Love", *Midwest Studies in Philosophy*, 13, 12–31.

Stocker, Michael, 1976, "The Schizophrenia of Modern Ethical Theories", *The Journal of Philosophy*, 73/14, 453–466.

Sullivan, Roger J., 1996, "Introduction", in: Immanuel Kant, *Metaphysics of Morals*, edited by Mary Gregor, 2nd edition, New York: Cambridge University Press, vii–xxvi.

Velleman, J. David, 1999. "Love as a Moral Emotion", *Ethics*, 109/2, 338–374.

Williams, Bernard, 1981, "Persons, character, and morality", in: Bernard Williams, *Moral Luck*, New York: Cambridge University Press, 1–19.

Wood, Allen W., 1970, *Kant's Moral Religion*, Ithaca, NY: Cornell University Press.

Wood, Allen W., 1999, *Kant's Ethical Thought*, New York: Cambridge University Press.

Index of Persons

https://doi.org/10.1515/9783111291130-011

Index of Subjects

aesthetic   42, 107–109, 114, 117, 119, 121, 123–125, 144
– misanthropy (see also misanthropy)   123 f.
affects   12, 85, 87–90, 95–99, 101–105, 115, 149
amor benevolentiae (see also love of benevolence)   107, 117, 119 f., 122, 124 f.
amor complacentiae (see also love of delight)   107 f., 110, 114, 117–125
anger   159–161
animality   12, 35, 37, 46, 48, 50, 56, 64, 128, 132
animals   17, 20 f., 30, 45–47, 91, 131, 146
anthropological (see also anthropology)   8, 35, 37, 47, 53, 57
anthropology (see also anthropological)   2, 10, 18, 42, 47, 56–58, 88, 134, 136, 146, 156
anthropophobia   123, 153 f., 156
attentiveness   12, 85, 95–97, 101, 103–105
autocracy   12, 85–87, 89, 95
autonomy   35, 73, 86, 90, 92, 123, 159

beneficence   4, 6, 13, 76 f., 80, 96 f., 117 f., 120 f., 125, 140, 149, 152–156, 159, 161, 175–180
benevolence   6, 8, 10, 13, 46, 91, 107, 117 f., 120, 123, 125, 128, 140–142, 151, 155, 157, 171

Christianity   129, 143
community   46, 128, 130–132, 134 f., 139–141, 143–146, 153, 159, 161–163, 169, 182 f.
– cosmopolitan   130, 140–145
– ethical (see also community, moral)   128, 141, 143 f.
– ethico-religious   135, 143–146
– moral (see also community, ethical)   131, 153, 159, 161, 182
composure   88, 92 f., 95–97, 101–103, 105
consent   12, 38–40, 63, 66–76, 78, 80–83
– informed   66 f., 74–76, 78, 81–83
– valid   63, 66, 69–72, 74–76, 81, 83

cosmopolitanism (see also community, cosmopolitan; friendship, cosmopolitan; love, cosmopolitan)   130 f., 140 f., 143, 146
crimina carnis
– contra naturam   50, 52
– secundum naturam   50

desire (see also inclination; sexual desire)   6, 30, 35, 37, 42–48, 51–53, 55–58, 71, 73, 79–81, 86, 89 f., 92 f., 118, 129 f., 136 f., 139, 161, 177, 180
dexterity of the inclination to beneficence in general   107, 117–120
dignity   8, 12, 36, 39, 44 f., 49, 54–57, 151, 167 f.
disappointment   5, 14, 79, 149, 153–155, 157–163
displeasure   121, 123 f.
duty, duties
– imperfect   128, 155, 160, 163, 165 f., 172, 175 f., 180
– inner   39 f., 50
– of love   10, 12, 14, 77, 85 f., 90 f., 102, 116, 120 f., 125, 130, 138, 152, 154 f., 176
– of right   39 f., 50
– of virtue   66, 90, 95, 138, 162 f.
– perfect   39, 60, 155–157, 160, 163
– positive   53, 77

egoism   133
emotion   1 f., 12 f., 101, 118, 127, 132, 165 f.
end
– in itself   23 f., 68, 76
– of nature (see also natural end; *Naturzweck*; *Zweck der Natur*)   52–54, 57, 137
ends
– in themselves   23, 66–69, 76, 121
– obligatory   65 f., 76 f.
– of others   10, 76, 93, 96, 138, 152, 161, 170, 173
enjoyment   20, 41–47, 49, 53, 56–58, 161
equality (see also humanity, equal)   7, 140, 146, 149–152, 169, 171, 183

https://doi.org/10.1515/9783111291130-012